The Saint of the Prisons

©**TRIADA**
For present edition - 2019

For orders:
E-mail: orders@triada.be
+32476505884

ISBN 978-2-931030-00-4
The Saint of the Prisons

The Saint of the Prisons

*Notes on the life of Valeriu Gafencu,
collected and annotated by
the monk Moise*

With foreword and afterword by
Father Ciprian Grădinaru, Belgium

Translated by
Monk Sava – Oaşa Monastery

Table of Contents

« Read and spread »[1]

---

[1] Phrase used at the end of all communist manifests, during the period when Communism was illegal.

For your Understanding

To be adequately understood, world history must be theologically judged.

Alongside all the social, political or military conflicts that history has recorded in chronicles and archives, ever since man's creation, there is another war taking place (much more important, yet invisible to the human eye): the devil's war against God. The battlefield of this war is man's heart. As a result of man's choice, recorded history emerges.

The history of the Church is a history of oppression, of martyrdom for Christ. The oppression, initiated in the first century after Christ by the Roman Empire, continued afterwards by the barbarians and then by the Ottoman Empire. However, the twentieth century remains beyond doubt the most atrocious period in the history of Christianity, due to the bloodiest persecution that it had to endure: the communist oppression.

From an ideological standpoint, Communism aimed to build a world without social classes or private property by claiming that the wealth of the country belongs to everyone equally. The communist ideal was an egalitarian society, led by a single political party. Communists deceptively asserted that state power belonged to the workers. In reality, power, just like all other resources of the country, was concentrated in the hands of a small group of party leaders.

Many things have been said and written about Communism. Regardless of the arguments in favor of or against Communism as an ideology, its implementation will remain in history as the incarnation of Satan's presence in and among people. Indeed, Satan created and used Communism as a means to conquer as many souls as rapidly and permanently as possible.

Communism found itself clearly as an antichristic materialization in history; its metaphysical character is more than obvious. Murder, as a political weapon, and as the basis of all communist "achievements," puts an end to life: "the murderer", as Jesus Christ calls him (John 8: 44), wants to take revenge on the Giver of Life. The violence and terror[2] which Communism imposed on people are opposite to the love and kindness preached by the Gospel.

The general feelings of distrust, [3] fear—of constantly induced by Communism in the whole society—are in opposition to the faith that God, and anyone who wants to resemble Him, has in man. Christ came to set us free, whilst Communism is characterized by an unprecedented restriction of human freedom. Christ is the Truth and He wants us to know Him; in Communism, deception is the daily bread for the sons of "the Father of lies" (John 8: 44). Besides the deep hatred for anyone and anything resembling Christ, Communism's highest ideal—the creation of the "new man" (an idea of Christian origin, but perverted by the devil)—was proven by history to be exactly the opposite of the new man reborn and healed in the Church. The new man of the Church is the one who gains the highest form of freedom: freedom in Christ, which cannot be restrained by the barriers of time or space.

Last but not least, all communist forerunners, ideologists and leaders (Marx, Engels, Bauer, Feuerbach, Tkacev, Neceaev, Bakunin, Lenin, Stalin) were under an

---

[2] Karl Marx (1964), *The Class Struggle in France 1848-1850*, New York: International Publishers.

[3] One of Stalin's slogans was "vigilance and distrust."

obvious satanic influence, some even declaring themselves inspired by the "prince of the dark," while others demonstrated this state of mind and soul and through their behavior.[4]

The undeniable genius who used Communism to enslave over a third of the world population so rapidly, the genius whose "generous" and "humanitarian" ideas appealed and continue to appeal to many recent or contemporary "intellectuals,"[5] cannot belong to a man or an interest group. It belongs to Antichrist himself, who, according to all prophecies, will initially be a gentleman, an "enlightened being" serving the peoples of the world.

The devil laid the foundation of Communism, suggesting once again to man that he could build Heaven on earth through mankind's joined power, excluding God (Adam's eternal trap — the temptation of the proud man: to achieve divinization without the presence of God). Essentially, this heresy (named chiliasm or millennialism) appears at several points in time throughout Christian history. It is typical of the man who rejects Christ's message, of he who refuses the Mystery of the Cross. This was truly the ultimate dream of Marx, Engels, and their disciples. As they stated, at the end of the total Revolution aimed at destroying the "Old World", the communists dreamed to bring on earth the Kingdom of Heaven — the

---

[4] Alain Besancon (2007) *Originile intelectuale ale leninismului (Intellectual Origins of communism)*, Bucuresti: Humanitas or Nikolai Berdiaev (1997) *Marele inchizitor(The Great Inqusitor). Dostoievski – lecture teologice (Theological Reading)*, Polirom.

[5] Unfortunately, even nowadays many people in the Western world continue to believe that Communism is a wonderful ideology, that has just been poorly implemented in the former communist countries.

place where the new man (perfect and re-educated) could live eternal and complete happiness.

Therefore, all those who chose to reach Heaven by following Jesus Christ's path (by turning away from sins and fighting the devil), became obstacles in the achievement of the "mighty goal" and, consequently, had to be eliminated. Their mere existence became a mirror that reflected the madness of the Marxist ideology.[6]

Hence, for the majority of those who suffered under Communism, the fight was carried out at the personal and the spiritual level. This fight did not occur primarily in prisons, mountains, or against Communism as system or ideology, but against the Evil present inside the people themselves (as passions or as disbeliefs), or the personified evil of Satan — who acted through those who fell prey to him.

The Communist regime in Romania and its aim

On 23 August 1944, Romania was occupied by the Soviet forces. As a result, a political and economic regime subservient to the Soviet Union was established in Romania. This was possible with the tacit agreement of Western powers and through a secret agreement between Churchill and Stalin concerning the division of spheres of influence. Indeed, the trajectory of the country was one contrary to Romania's national interests.

One of the first things done by the Soviets was to help the communists take over the political leadership of the country by falsifying the 1946 elections and by imposing foreign leaders. Furthermore, they disbanded

---

[6] "The fool hath said in his heart, there is no God" (Psalms 52: 1)

all political parties and arrested their leaders. Afterwards, in December 1947, they forced the king Mihai I (Michael I) to resign and established the Popular Republic, opening the way towards a totalitarian state, based on a single party.

As of 1947, the Communist terror had been imposed on the whole country. In 1948, the security service called *Securitate* was established. This was the equivalent of the Soviet NKVD/KGB. Its main mission was to establish absolute control so as to utterly destroy those opposing the regime. The *Securitate* used all possible means to fulfill its objectives.

From the onset, according to the model already implemented in the USSR, Romanian communists chiefly followed a number of objectives that, according to their line of thought, would have allowed them to create the "new man," re-educated:

- to destroy the traditional social order, fundamental to Christian values, in order to separate people from their past and to remove their roots. It is known that a man with no roots is a man without identity and thus easy to manipulate. Only by employing this strategy could the Communists have hoped to replace traditional society with A. Huxley's "Brave New World" and to establish a new religion – atheism.

- to modify the content of the notion of morality (Lenin argued in one of his speeches that the true morality of the new man — the Communist — is not the traditional morality which is rooted in Christianity, but one according to which "good" is defined by the ideals of the Communist Revolution. Therefore, according to the Communist ideology, if a man or an idea serves those ideals, she/he/it is good, and if not, she/he/it is evil.

- to introduce a feeling of distrust and insecurity in all strata of society by promoting generalized lying, corruption and treason. The *Securitate* imposed its collaborators everywhere. These were people convinced — voluntarily or by force — to continuously monitor their relatives and friends and to write reports about the alleged anti-system activities of those observed. If somebody dared to speak against the regime, that person would be arrested, charged, and imprisoned.

- to alter knowledge and to limit the thought horizons by manipulating and confiscating the language. "Of all the monopolies enjoyed by the Soviet State, none would be so crucial as its monopoly on the definition of words. The ultimate weapon of political control would be the dictionary"[7]. It is interesting to note the out-of-the-ordinary intensive activity to write and re-write dictionaries taking place in the USSR after 1950.

Indeed, on a deeper level, namely on a spiritual level (the unseen war between good and evil), the main objective was to remove Christianity from society and to dehumanize people.

I am convinced that only by reading this book through a spiritual and historical lens (presented concisely until now) will emphasize its importance. Otherwise, it will only be standard literature, and the person we will discuss next — the new martyr Valeriu Gafencu — will remain just one of the many venerable figures of our Church history.

But only those who study and know history, only those who strive to understand it in a spiritual light, and

---

[7] Robert C. Tucker (1956) "Stalin and the Uses of Psychology" in *World Politics* 8: 4 July, 477.

not in that of the rulers of the world, may understand the present. It is the only way to hope to survive as a Christian in these present days, characterized by the spirit of antichrist who becomes more and more powerful, whose cold tentacles reach out silently and greedily towards everybody's hearts.

Following the example of the martyrs across two thousand years of Church history, the martyrs of the prisons also preferred renouncing this perishable life, together with all it may seem to offer, rather than renouncing Christ by collaborating with the Communist regime and becoming traitors to the credo of their brothers.

Rady Gyr, one of the most well-known among the poets persecuted by the Communists, said something extraordinary: "in prisons, I learned in my own flesh what it truly means to be a Christian." It is within this paradigm, between "in my own flesh" and "truly" that the drama of the life and of the death of those imprisoned consumed itself. And in truth, it is within this fine distinction that the salvation is worked out for us, Christians; the path from the moral sphere to the spiritual one.

We think about the rich man (Matthew 19:16-30) who accomplished everything according to the Law, that is, the exterior, moral deeds, but could not renounce a life that found peace in the self-sufficient, legalistic accomplishment of the Lord's commandments. He suspected he had shortcomings, but he could not admit to them by following Christ and thus letting Him heal them. And this young person, tempted as he was to refuse the truth about himself, afraid of the daily perspective of assuming his own cross and following the Lord, is hidden within each one of us.

Many people could ask, how did these people become martyrs for God? Where did they find the strength to resist such tortures, internal as well as physical? What about the enormous weight on their conscience? How did they rise after apostasy and treason? How did they arrive to Christ, when for many, their previous ideals had been social and political, rather than spiritual?

Firstly, until their arrival in prison, they cultivated an extreme awareness of the value of their own existence. They deeply yearned to give their life a higher purpose, for which they should be prepared to die for, and the One Who named Himself "The Way" of our lives granted them even death for Him.

Secondly, they had continuously fought with sin, struggling for a clean conscience. They had tried to get rid of egotism, endeavoring to live in brotherly communion, by renouncing their own wishes and striving to enlarge their hearts to welcome others in them.

Thirdly, one cannot help noticing the deep intuition of those who did not possess any kind of spiritual enlightenment before suffering for Christ but who cultivated the spirit of sacrifice as a way of living. Their sacrifice for the Christian faith and for the country made them close to Him, Him Who sacrificed Himself for the salvation of human kind. Christ received the Cross and took upon Himself Adam and Eve's sin after their fall from obedience. By willingly receiving the shame and suffering of the Cross – for which they suffered so much – the martyrs proved themselves the followers of the Lord. And because they had endured the torture, the blame, the mutilation of both soul and body, for Christ's name, Christ offered those who suffered through to the end His Spirit, by reviving them spiritually, healing them and offering them the salvation of their souls. "Blessed are you when people insult you, persecute you and falsely say all kinds of evil against you because of me." (Matthew 5: 11).

The sacrifice of those in the Communist prisons was an authentic one, assumed in Christ. It was not the result of their political options, which put them in opposition with the new regime, imposed by force. It was the sacrifice for God and for the people in whose midst they were born, and for which they felt responsible (Corinthians 15: 23). This was what gave Valeriu Gafencu the conviction that he confessed before his death: that their sacrifices will not be in vain[8]. As Father Seraphim Rose said: "there is one law of spiritual life which says that where there is Golgotha – which means, where there is real sacrifice for Christ – there is also Resurrection. This Resurrection first takes place in our hearts and one should not think too much about the exterior form it will take, by God's providence"[9].

Valeriu Gafencu

Among those who understood that the only chance to withstand evil was to be filled with Christ was a man called Valeriu Gafencu, the one to whom this book has been dedicated. When asked about Communism, he replied that "there is no doubt that man's imprisonment inside the system is a bad thing, but nothing is more

---

[8] Ioan Ianolide (2006) *Ioan Ianolide, Intoarcerea la Hristos(Return To christ)*, Bucuresti: Editura Christiana, 80.

[9] Ierom. Damaschin, *Viața si lucrările Părintelelui Serafim Rose (the life and Works of Father Serafim Rose)*, Bucuresti: Editura Sophia, 851.

frightening than the conditioning of the consciousness, which transforms man into a controlled tool"[10]. Satan's tool, one would add. For the hater of mankind wanted man to be his servant in order to take to perdition as many as possible among "the children of the most High" (Psalms 81: 6), by taking advantage of God's dispensation of passing them through the sieve: "but this is your hour, and the power of darkness" (Luke 22: 53).

Due to reasons known only by God's providence, although "a cloud of testimonies" emerged from the Communist prison cells, the one mentioned the most is "Valeriu Gafencu". All those who knew Valeriu mention him with great piety, considering him a saint. Indeed, Father Nicolae Steinhardt, a Jew converted to Christianity in prison, called him in his evocations "the saint of the prisons."

Through his sacrificial love, springing forth from the complete dedication of his life to Christ, the image of his life was deeply imprinted in the hearts of those who met him. It was impossible otherwise: at the end of his life, when, being very sick, any effort (even talking) was causing him a great deal of pain, his friends advised him to spare himself. But he told them: "Do not take this joy from me, because confessing Christ is the only thing I am living for!"

Father Gheorghe Calciu-Dumitreasa, another important Orthodox witness of the communist period[11] exiled by Romanian communist authorities to the USA, said, "I have no doubt he is a saint; he lived God's word

_____

[10]Ianolide, op. cit., 500.

[11] Author of the famous Lenten sermons "Seven Words to Young People".

at a height incomprehensible for us."[12] Another fellow in suffering, Father Constantin Voicescu, was sure that "sooner or later, the Orthodox Church will canonize him."[13]

His most accurate portrayal of the detention period is offered in the book *The Return to Christ* [14] by his best friend, Ioan Ianolide, a survivor of the prisons, who also reached great spiritual heights. Indeed, only a spiritually advanced person, one that leads a holy life, can truly understand and present to others the image and likeness of a saint.

How did Valeriu become this giant of the Spirit?

First of all, his conviction was that only a man who lives in the presence of God acquires the true measure of himself, of life and of the world. In other words, faithful to the Church's Tradition, his fight reaches back through the centuries to reply to Protagoras' atheistic attitude, namely that man was the measure of all things. For Valeriu not man, but Christ is the measure of all things. Indeed, his deep belief, manifested in his actions and attitudes, had prepared a fertile ground for the coming of God's grace. He was aware that it is not enough to follow God's commandments in order to be saved. A deeper understanding of life in Christ was needed.

The Lord never ceased to look upon him. This moment of consciousness (mentioned in the chapter

---

[12]Confession given in October 2005 to Monk Moise.

[13]Multiple authors (2002) *Parintele Voicescu: Un duhovnic al cetatii (Father Voiculesc: A spiritual father of the realm)*, Bucuresti: Editura Bizantina, 28.

[14]Ioan Ianolide (2006) *The Return to Christ*, Bucuresti : Editura Christiana.

"Two Testimonies") ought to be memorable for the spiritual development of every true Christian. Without the guidance of the Holy Spirit, without the coming of God's enlightenment, which bestows upon man the full understanding of his own mortality, man cannot begin his spiritual life. This is the moment when Valeriu realized that, even though prior to his imprisonment he struggled against sin, only from that moment on, he started the conscious fight against it, a continuous battle that does not cease until death.

Valeriu wished for one thing: that through his veins will flow the life of Christ and not that of a mortal man. He prayed without ceasing and had been crucified with Christ in asceticism and in illness. Nevertheless, Valeriu lived no longer, but Christ lived in him (Galatians 2: 20).

It was obvious for everyone who knew him – even guards, doctors and atheists prison mates – that Valeriu was *made for another world*. From several testimonies we find out that many of the signs of his holiness echoed the ones of saints. In Ioan Ianolide's book *The Return to Christ* we can find discussions with him that are true Philokalia pages in the spirit of Saint Nicholas Cabasilas (The *Life in Christ*). His favorite meditation and discussion topics were *the fight for unity with Christ* and *inner purification* – outer reflections of his profound spiritual concerns.

Meekness, along with his joyful sorrow, were at the center of Valeriu's life. This is reflected in Traian Popescu's testimony: at the beginning of December 1951 Valeriu was very close to dying. Peaceful and reconciled with himself, he said his goodbyes to those close to him: "I am happy; I am going to God. Pray with me, for my soul and yours." However, after a few days of agony, he recovered. To those who took care of him, his words reminded of the state Saint Silouan was before death. Asked by his disciple, Father Sophrony Sakharov, if he was ready to die, Saint Silouan told him that he has not yet acquired true humility: "God did not want me, I am not yet worthy of His Kingdom."

Another piece of evidence demonstrating the presence of the Holy Spirit within him is described in one episode during his surgery that took place without anesthetics while in prison. Many were bewildered to find out at the end of the surgery that the administered anesthetic did not work and that he was awake during the procedure. Full of martyrs' grace, he was completely silent for the entire duration of the procedure.

According to Ioan Ianolide's testimony, after repeated practice of the Jesus prayer, Christ gave him His grace. Thus, he acquired the gift of unceasing prayer, even during his sleep. Just like Saint Anthony the Great and many other saints, he often showed his capacity to foresee in spirit, which he received as a gift from above, from the Father of lights.[15]

In the same way as Saint Silouan the Athonite, he reached an adamic conscience, suffering and praying for a fallen world. Though he was a dreamer by nature, he was aware that he was not able to change the course of history. However, he wished to be able to stir "the good uneasiness" in others (as Elder Paisios of Mount Athos said) both through his testimony and that of his prison mates. Valeriu said to Marin Naidim "that even if we will not be able to change the world, at least we could awaken people's interest; we could make it such that it no longer feels good when one is committing a sin and

---

[15] See the testimony of Octavian Anastasescu on 171 of this book.

we could create problems that force people to ask themselves [difficult] questions and to change their path."[16] The grace of God, who never leaves peoples' good wishes unfulfilled, granted the wish of his humble servant. Nowadays the testimony of the Communist prison martyrs bears fruit in the Church and outside of it. Glory to God, Christ took into account the will of His follower, and today the testimony of the martyrs brings a lot of good harvest in the Church and outside of it.

Valeriu lived his last years filled with the Lord's grace, enlightened by the greatest blessing which can be bestowed upon man on this earth: to know the Way. Because he bore witness of Christ with his very life, he already reached the age of the Beatitudes. He climbed up the ladder of repentance in full, without missing a step - as God avows in His Beatitudes in the Sermon on the Mountain (Mathew 5: 12) - while also receiving the greatest gift – to be persecuted for Christ and thus become the light of the world (Mathew 5: 14-16).

The best expression of the height of Valeriu's inner state belongs to one of the Fathers who heard his confession near the end of his life: "Christ lived in him"[17] as Apostle Paul had said.

One night, during the last Christmas of his life, as had happened to Saint Seraphim of Sarov and to other saints, the Mother of God appeared to him and encouraged him. Then, two weeks before his passing into eternal life, God Himself let him know about the day of his death, and so Valeriu asked one of his prison mates

---

[16] Nicolae Trifoiu (2003) *Studentul Valeriu Gafencu: Sfantul Inchisorilor din Romania (The Student Valeriu Gafencu: The Saint of prisons in Romania)*, Cluj-Napoca: Editura Napoca Star.

[17]Ianolide, op.cit., 142.

to help him prepare for the burial.

As he was living in extremely harsh incarceration conditions, while being seriously ill, his inner peace and happiness were clearly a gift from God. His spirit was no longer affected by the strains of imprisonment and illness, as Valeriu had become a true disciple of Christ. His heart, purified as the "purified gold" in the fire of prayer and suffering, had healed from its natural, human desires. Through Christ, he conquered fear. Christ has offered us a new, paradoxical perspective over suffering and death, when, a few days before Golgotha, talking about the passions awaiting Him, He told his disciples that the Son of man would be glorified (John 12: 23-24). Like God, Valeriu felt the same in the face of death: he was not awaiting death in fear, but in joy and hope of glorification.

It is often said that the face of a deceased person speaks for the value of his life. In the morning of 18 February 1952, Valeriu confessed and then received the Eucharist; he made peace with everyone around him and asked all for forgiveness. After several hours, filled with love and the grace of resurrection that flooded everyone around him, his pure soul left to meet his beloved Groom, whom he had longed for during all the years he had spent in this Valley of sorrow.

Father Sophrony of Essex said that the Christian spirit has not and will not win over but an insignificant part of mankind. But maybe this chosen part of love-afflicted people will show the true sense of history, which God has laid out since Creation. God's design for man can be seen in their lives: how man should live, how he should fight for his salvation. History will not be able to lead us to salvation unless we live it with the conscience of the eternal life.

Any human being saved by Christ has everlasting

value, Father Sophrony said. That is because, as was mentioned at the beginning, history needs to be understood in a theological way. Hence, everything will find its rightful purpose and place only on the great day of the final Judgment.

This book is about the immortal value of man that has reached its fullness in the holy being of one of those who loved God to the end. A book to stimulate, to comfort, to set an example, written with love for all our brothers who are, even without knowing, seeking the true Joy: our Christ the Lord.

Father Ciprian Grădinaru

Before Prison

Valeriu Gafencu was born on January 24, 1921, in Bessarabia, in the town of Sângera, near the city of Bălți. His parents, Vasile and Elena, were wealthy peasants. After completing high school, his father took classes at a technical school for electricians, and after World War I enrolled in the College of Electro-Technology in Iași. He did not follow the coursework through to graduation, but returned to his native village to teach. During World War I he was mobilized into the Russian Navy. On March 27, 1918, the National Council voted to unite Bessarabia with Romania; Vasile was a member of the Council.

In his notes from the colony at Galda,[18] Valeriu says a few words about his parents. "When she married, Mama was about 24 years old. Tuța[19] was about ten years older than she was and had loved her in secret for a long time. Mama was a simple girl with an elementary school education, without any wealth other than her spiritual and physical purity. Tuța was an honest man, healthy and robust, with a good upbringing; he was a student at the Polytechnic University, well-regarded by all men of value in Bessarabia. With a little more schooling he would have become an engineer, but after coming into contact

---

[18]In 1946-1947, Valeriu was taken to the colony of Galda for forced labor (Ianolide's *Intoarcerea la Hristos*, 60). Gafencu and Ianolide, his friend, could enjoy an increase in freedom, since they were working outside, in nature. (O.G. note)

[19]Tuța (pronounced TOOT-sah), an affectionate nickname for one's father, equivalent to the English "Dad" or "Daddy." (Translator's note)

with 'high society' and realizing its decadence, he renounced all prospects opened for him and went back to the village to farm and teach. He wanted to establish a pure, beautiful home, to have a wife, children, a farm…. And he married Mama. Mama once asked him: 'Why are you taking me as your wife since I have no education, no money… while you…? Why didn't you choose an educated girl from Iaşi, since so many girls wanted you for a husband?'

"He answered her, 'Lena, so many times I look at you and I think that I am not worthy of you. You have something special. You have purity. And that's why I love you.'

"Before marriage, Tuţa had sinned with other women. He had, however, a sense of spiritual honor. He was totally sincere in recognizing his own sinfulness. That's why he was so dear to me. In my last year of high school, I was troubled by thoughts and anxieties regarding relations with women. I asked him one night: 'Tuţa, I'm a bit embarrassed but please tell me honestly, what's the best way to deal with women? Among my friends I advocate abstinence, but I meet with great opposition. The environment in the schools is very bad.' Tuţa answered me: 'The best thing is to abstain. I sinned in my youth because of a misunderstanding. I had reached the age of 21 and was still a virgin, still pure, but it was rumored among the boys and girls my age that I was impotent and that that was why I didn't have relations with women. I was angry, and I tried to find out who had invented this rumor. I discovered that it had started with a girl who was intrigued by my honorable and pure behavior. I sinned with her, out of spite. Later on, I was sorry.'

"Oh, how much my father's confession helped me! His advice protected me from so many temptations and falls.

"'After you were arrested, Valeriu,'" my mother recounted, "I was home alone. One night during the winter of 1944, I left Bălți on foot for Sângerei. The frost was terrible. A man driving a sled caught up with me. I prayed him to take me into his sled, and he did. He was from a village farther away. We arrived in Sângerei late at night. Since it was winter, I put him up in our house. After I fed him, I thought, 'Now I must prepare the bed so that he can sleep.'"

"And my good mother thought it would be best to prepare the bed in the bedroom for him while she would sleep on the cot in the kitchen. [20] And that's what she did. During the night, Mama heard the doors of the house opening one after the other. Alarmed, she woke up at once. The man opened the door of the kitchen slowly, and Mama asked him, with her gentle voice: 'What do you want, Mister?' 'I thought you might be cold and would like to warm up,' he answered. Mama looked at him and replied: 'I have taken you in and sheltered you in my house, offering you the most honorable place, with my thoughts towards God. And just as I have one God, Jesus Christ, I also have only one husband.' The man cast his eyes to the ground in shame and closing the door behind him, went back to his bed.

"I kissed Mama and she told me that throughout their married life, both she and Tuța were faithful to each other. What a wonderful thing in which God is

---

[20]The kitchen was in a separate building in order to minimize the risk of fire. (Translator's note)

well pleased! They lived all their lives so beautifully. They loved each other. And we, their children, never saw them arguing. I know that Tuța loved Mama; he protected her. For example, he would get up early in the morning, prepare everything for the field and prepare the household for the day. Then at sunrise, when he left for the fields, he would wake her up. He always let her sleep in so that she could rest. I can still hear him saying to her affectionately, 'Hey, Lena, lazybones, get up!'"[21]

The fruit of the love of these exceptional people were their four children: Valeriu, Valentina, Eleonora, and Elisabeta. Valeriu started school at Sângerei then went on to Ion Creangă High School in the nearby town of Bălți.

While a student, Valeriu distinguished himself. He received high marks in his classes, was loved by his fellow students, and was highly appreciated by his teachers. He was demanding with himself and also with the education of his sisters. As an older brother, he supervised them closely regarding their friendships, lessons, and such. Being a sensitive person, he loved literature and wrote several pieces that were published in the school's periodical.

He graduated from high school in the summer of 1940 and enrolled in law school in Iași. During this period, Bessarabia was handed over to Soviet troops. The Gafencu family crossed the river Prut and took refuge in Iași. Valeriu, together with his father, went back to Bessarabia in order to resolve matters having to do with their abandoned homestead. When they crossed the river Prut back to Romania, they had to

---

[21]Nicolae Trifoiu, *op. cit.*, pp. 229-231

keep clear of Soviet troops guarding the border from the river bank. A touching scene recounted by Virgil Maxim occurred here. "After a short rest on the right bank of the river,[22] the old man stood up and gave thanks to God for His help in bringing his family to safety. He then embraced his son and made the final confession of his life: 'I brought you here so that you can take care of your mother and sisters. I charge you with this responsibility before God. I have to return to my people, my village.'

"Valeriu was troubled. The old man noticed his emotion and continued. 'What would all of our Bessarabian brothers say? How could I raise my eyes to heaven if I and others like me, who until now have struggled to preserve the Romanian spirit in this land, would now flee from the path of the oppressors and not take part in the suffering that awaits us?' Valeriu understood his father and didn't try to dissuade him. He realized how strong his father's sense of duty was and resolved to be faithful himself, as a son worthy of the same faith in God and in the future of his people.

"'Better times will come, but now we need sacrifices,' added the old man. Once again embracing his son and making the sign of the cross, he headed for the shore and swam across the river into his beloved Bessarabia. A short time later he was arrested and sent with a group of fellow Bessarabians to a camp beyond the Arctic Circle.[23] He died a year later amid horrible conditions, placing his hope in God to Whom he had

---

[22]The two had already crossed from what was now the Soviet Union into Romania.

[23]Valeriu Gafencu's father was part of the first waves of deportees to Siberia.

27

entrusted his loved ones. Someone who hadmiraculously escaped from the camp later related these things to Valeriu."[24]

As a student at the law school in Iași, Valeriu came to the attention of his professors as an honest young man full of decency; fellow peers also appreciated Valeriu for setting an example of benevolence and upstanding behavior.

In the fall of 1941, the reigning political regime declared the Legionnaire movement illegal; Valeriu, a member of the Legionnaires, was arrested and sentenced to 25 years in prison. He was 20 years old.

---

[24]*Ibid*, pg. 88

Valeriu and Legionnaire Education

Before discussing what happened with Valeriu during his imprisonment, one must clarify an aspect that remains difficult for many: his involvement with the Legionary Movement.[25] It must be said from the onset that, before all else, the Legionary phenomenon was a wave of feeling or sentiment, a state of spirit. It has been observed that Romanians are generally not receptive to doctrines but to spiritual states. This is certainly true with respect to the Legionnaire movement. According to those who experienced it, it was rather a spontaneous phenomenon, a state of spiritual resonance, a response to internal searching, than a collective adherence to a doctrine.[26] The Legionnaires were convincing to others

---

[25]The historical sources on the Legionary Movement are few and often written from a partisan perspective. Communism demonized the movement, identifying it with Nazism, even if the movement was exonerated in the Nuremberg Trials. On the other hand, the legionnaires present it in legendary terms. The task to clarify the role of the Legionary Movement during the 20th century remains difficult, but much is needed to understand a troubled period during the history of Romania and of Europe. (note OG).

[26] Strictly speaking, the Legionnaires did not have a doctrine or a program in the sense in which we speak of a political party having a doctrine, an ideology, or a program. Their point of departure was something else. From the very beginning they defined themselves as a community united in feeling and sentiment. Codreanu himself said, "Another characteristic of our beginning, beside the lack of money, was the lack of a program. We did not have a program. And this fact, of course, will give rise to a big question. A political organization without any organized program, conceived in the mind of one man or also in the minds of others? *But we did not bond with those who thought as we did, but with those who felt as we did. Not with those who had the same way of thinking, but with those adhering to the same spiritual framework*. It was significant that the statue of

through their manner of living, through their example, through what they transmitted. They had a faith and a decisiveness that others found stimulating.

But where did this manner of living come from? What gave rise to this spiritual state that "contaminated" thousands, if not hundreds of thousands, of people? What exactly kept up their zeal? Historical, sociological, or political explanations have been offered, speaking of a localized echo of European unrest and upheaval, [27] partially referring to long-standing repression of the Romanian people, who were growing dissatisfied with corruption in politics. Without disputing the fact that these did play a role in the sense that the Legionnaires had their origins in the problems of the day, the response they had vis-à-vis these concerns was rooted in their faith in God. Although they departed from historical causes, if we consider things from a spiritual perspective, their orientation toward God and toward Christian values – although admittedly not always affirmed or defended by the most evangelical methods – as well as their yearning for renewal and purification could not have been merely a social phenomenon. I believe that it was also a spiritual phenomenon, a spiritual calling addressed to this nation to return to

---

another goddess – Reason – would be shattered [by the Legionnaires]. In the service of God and for the meaning of life and instead of that which the world has raised up against God, we, without throwing it out or despising it, put something else in its place... If we, therefore, had neither money nor program, we had, rather, God in our souls, and He inspired us with the invincible power of faith." (Corneliu Zelea Codreanu, *Pentru Legionari*, ninth edition, Ed. Scara, Bucharest, 1999, pg. 232)

[27] It was often seen as a local echo of Nazism or Fascism. Codreanu of the Legionnaire movement distinguished it from the other political trends.

God, a deepening of certain meanings, an incentive toward Christian renewal, and especially the call of this generation of Romanians to martyrdom.[28]

It is true that not everyone - and especially not from the beginning – was aware of the spiritual finality of this calling. Many were left behind on the way, at different stages, according to the measure of their capacity for spiritual understanding and growth. But a good number of them were enlightened, they were purified, and through suffering – like Gafencu – penetrated deeper into the sense of this calling and proceeded toward martyrdom. The road was not easy; there were slips and falls, but also enlightenment and moments of spiritual uplift. Demonstrating a virtue dear to Paisios the Athonite, self-sacrifice with soulful boldness, Legionnairism was, from a spiritual point of view and in spite of all human shortcomings, a preparation for martyrdom. This was clearly reflected in the Legionnaires' behavior in Communist prisons, where they showed the true measure of their worth. Of the hundreds of thousands of political prisoners, a significant number came from among their ranks. In any case, the finest and largest number of Orthodox prisoners were Legionnaires. [29] For all of these men,

---

[28]Gheorghe was asked whether he saw the Legionnaire movement as being from God or from men, he replied, "Considering how many martyrs came from among their ranks, I believe that it was from God; but being human, they also made mistakes." When asked the same question, Father Papacioc

[29]Out of the 207 martyrs commemorated in the publication of the Biblical Institute and Mission of the Romanian Orthodox Church, entitled *Martiri din România perioada comunistă (Martyrs for Christ in Romania During the Communist Regime)*, Legionnaires constitute a significant percentage.

training in the Legionnaire movement was a preparation for the difficult trials to which they would later be subjected.

After wandering off in different directions, Codreanu and other young people, troubled by the need to do something for their country, realized that what was needed to instigate a profound change in society was not so much a new party or a new political program – as they themselves had been tempted to believe – but rather an education of a Christian and national character that would lead to moral renewal. "This country is perishing from a lack of people, not from a lack of programs. This is our opinion. It is not programs that we must create, but people, new people.... Therefore, the cornerstone from which the Legion sets out is humankind, not political programs. The reform of people, not the reform of political programs. Therefore, the Legion of the Archangel Michael[30] will be a school and an army rather than a political party. The Romanian people, at this point in history, do not need a great politician, as some mistakenly believe, but a great educator and leader to vanquish the powers of evil and shatter the ranks of evildoers. In order to do this, however, he must first overcome the evil in himself and in his brethren."[31]

---

[30] One of the official names of the Legionnaire organization. (Translator's note)

[31] Corneliu Zelea Codreanu, *op cit.*, pp. 238-239. Codreanu considered Jewish social and political activities to be the true cause of the moral decadence and the majority of the misfortunes which had befallen the Romanian people. Although this generalization may well be exaggerated, the significantly disproportionate involvement of Jewish individuals and organizations controlling commerce and the press, involved in Freemasonry, in the spread of Communist

In order to form a Legionnaire elite, the best from among the youth were selected, beginning with those of high school age. This organization of young men was named *Frăţia de Cruce* (FDC), the *Brotherhood of the*

---

ideas, in the influencing of political decisions and other anti-Romanian activities cannot be denied. For example in 1944, 30% of the Communist Party was Jewish according to historian Dennis Deleant, although they represented less than 4% of the population. During the height of the terror camps, the highest office in the parliament (Ana Pauker), the head of security service (Alexandru Nicholschi), Moscow ambassador and later Pauker's replacement (Simion Bughici) and the head of finance (Vasile Luca) were all held by Jews. Moreover, long before the Legionnaires, scholars such as Mihail Kogălniceanu, Vasile Alecsandri, Vasile Conta, Mihai Eminescu, Nicolae Iorga – to mention only a few – had sounded an alarm regarding the pernicious role that Jews were playing in Romanian society. It is difficult to believe that all these people, and many others, were all afflicted for no good reason with irrational anti-Semitism. Considering the anti-Semitic sentiments prevalent in the first half of the 20th century, real but absurdly exaggerated (see the report by the Wiesel commission on the Holocaust in Romania), it is natural for us to wonder if the behavior of Jews themselves did not play a role in provoking them. Romanians, generally a tolerant people, have never been known to be aggressive or resentful even towards those peoples with whom they have been in conflict for centuries, such as the Turks or Hungarians! Why would they suddenly and inexplicably turn against the Jews, who had settled among them in significant numbers only since the 19th century? This question acquires even more legitimacy when one considers the fact that anti-Semitic sentiments have appeared not only in Romania, but in every country in which Jews have dwelt. Was their own behavior not a factor? Of course, speaking in a Christian manner, the excuse of provocation does not exempt one from guilt, but it does modify responsibility. At the same time, as far as we, Romanians, are concerned, we ought to consider whether this domination by another people was permitted by God because of our sins. In this sense, even the history of the Jewish people themselves in the Old Testament, led into slavery for having departed from the ways of God, is full of significance.

Cross. [32] Those targeted were screened according to certain criteria: faithfulness and church attendance, good academic achievement, respectfulness toward others, love of country, honesty, etc. Candidates were not admitted to the FDC automatically but in accordance with certain requirements. It set out to be an elite organization that would accept only the best.

Those who were accepted found an atmosphere of love, seriousness, and enthusiasm, an atmosphere highly suitable for their spiritual growth. They received a primarily moral and spiritual education, along Christian ideas; they were encouraged to participate in the sacrament of confession, to adhere to a prayer schedule, to fast, to avoid bodily sins, to be merciful, correct, punctual, sympathetic, ready to help others, obedient, and studious. Since work played an important role in Legionnaire training, [33] work camps were

---

[32] The principles of selection and education of the brothers of the cross, as well as their form of organization, are considered in *Îndreptarul Frăţiilor de Cruce (Guidebook of the Brotherhoods of the Cross)* by Gheorghe Istrate. Ion Gavrilă Ogoranu also gives a vivid and very picturesque description of the atmosphere within the FDC, derived from his own experience as a youth, in *Brazii sefrâng dar nu se îndoiesc (Fir Trees Break But They Don't Bend)*, volume 5 (subtitled *StridingThrough the Brothersof theCross*), Ed. Mişcării Legionare, Bucharest 2006.

[33] The law of work was one of six laws of the organization. The others were as follows: "*The law of discipline*: Be disciplined, Legionnaire, for only in this way will you be victorious! Follow your leader in good times and in bad. *The law of work*: Work. Work every day. Work with love. Let the reward of your work be not your pay, but gratitude that you have put a brick in the progress of the Legion and in the prosperity of Romania. *The law of silence*: Speak little. Speak only when necessary. Your speech is the speech of deeds. You act. Leave it to others to speak. *The law of education*: You must become a different person. A hero. Know the Legion well. *The law of mutual help*:

organized in which, along with Legionnaires, *brothers of the cross* participated in the construction and repair of churches, schools, roads, bridges, levees, etc. They worked in an atmosphere of youthful enthusiasm, while the camps also provided an opportunity for the formation and strengthening of spiritual ties.

Their meetings began with a prayer commemorating those who had died for the Legionnaire cause, followed by a reading from the New Testament. At every meeting, those present took turns introducing a theme having to do with faith, morality, national history, culture, etc. Legionnaire songs were sung and memorized; participants took turns reciting from Legionnaire writings, while the final portions of meetings were reserved for decision-making regarding new goodwill projects that needed to be undertaken, such as help for someone in need, collection of assistance for the family of an arrested Legionnaire, or similar work for the benefit of their brethren.

The young men who gathered together in the FDC made up a real family; they were taught to love one another and to help one another in time of need. The friendship that existed between them sprang from an impressive degree of love and sincerity. The most original part of the meetings was the moment of friendship or sincerity, a form of public "confession" of all mistakes made since the last meeting. This did not replace the sacrament of confession – each of them also

---

Help your brother who has fallen in misfortune. Don't abandon him. *The law of honor*: Proceed only on the paths indicated by honor. Fight and never be cowardly. Leave to others the paths of infamy. It is better to fall fighting on the path of honor than to win through infamy. (Corneliu Zelea Codreanu, *Cărticica şefului de cuib* (Denmaster's Booklet), Bucharest, 2000, pp 6-7).

confessed to his spiritual father; rather, it was an expression of the trust and sincerity that united them.[34] After they all confessed their mistakes, each of them reported what mistakes they had noticed among the others who were present. Then each of them received a "penance."[35]

These moments of sincerity were very important for strengthening their spiritual bonds. Within the safety of love and understanding given by the other *brothers of the cross*, each of them found the power to struggle against their own mistakes and defects. All the natural noble aspirations of a young soul - friendship, sincerity, love, sacrifice for lofty causes - found fulfillment in the warm atmosphere of the FDC.[36]

---

[34] According to Father Voicescu, this public confession also served as a preparation for the sacrament of confession. "I admit that I learned how to confess properly in the *Brotherhood of the Cross*, from those moments of friendship. During those public confessions [that we concluded our meetings with], we told each other our sins and I began to perceive the subtlety of thought." (*Părintele Voicescu - un duhovnic al cetăţii*, pg. 299)

[35] Because it is not easy to correct one's faults, according to the testimony of former *brothers of the cross*, tension among members appeared. It could also happen that a confession was superficial and insincere. In any case, what is worthy of being retained apart from the problems that arose during the practice of it, is the idea, the principle.

[36] Considering the love and sincerity that cemented the spiritual bonds uniting the Legionnaires, we can better understand the harshness with which they viewed betrayal. Mihai Stelescu, a former Legionnaire who made an attempt on the life of Codreanu even though Codreanu supported and promoted him to the rank of deputy in Parliament, was killed by his former comrades from the same *brotherhood*. The fact that these young men considered their love and sincerity violated by Stelescu's betrayal, as well as the cult they had for Codreanu, are extenuating circumstances that must be taken

In addition to educational activity, the *brothers of the cross* participated in the political activity of the Legion through the distribution of leaflets and posters and through occasional involvement in electoral propaganda. They also participated in the collection of funds for imprisoned Legionnaires and their families. The training of the *brothers of the cross* continued along the same principles even after they became Legionnaires.

The moral-spiritual component of this education was interwoven with a national-heroic component. The accent was placed on love of country and a knowledge of Romanian history and personalities. There was pronounced consideration of historical struggles and national heroes, the Legionnaires identifying with these heroes and looking to them as models. The intention was to cultivate the heroic and soldierly qualities of these young men: courage, strength of will, steadfastness, a spirit of sacrifice, discipline, the ability to confront danger, etc.[37]

The Legionnaire organization and its discipline were of military inspiration, but those involved assumed

---

into consideration but which, from a Christian point of view, do not justify the crime nor absolve them from the sin of killing.

[37] Expeditions in the forest or in the mountains, on difficult roads or in inclement weather were organized with the intention of developing their physical condition. Physical exercises proved to be helpful as well as soldierly instruction that did not involve the use of weapons. Ideally, there should have been a balance between the spiritual and the nationalist-heroic components of this training; in reality, there were differences among the youth as well as among *brotherhoods* in terms of temperament and spiritual structure. There were those who were much more attracted by the musketeer-soldierly aspects of the Legionnaire movement than by the moral-spiritual side.

it freely, so it did not have an air of dryness and barrack-like rigidity for them. The harshness was alleviated by their spiritual relationships and their state of spirit. The conduct of a *brother of the cross*, like that of a Legionnaire, had to be like that of a soldier: dignified, firm, disciplined, and orderly.[38]

We could draw a parallel between the heroic component of Legionnaire training and the spirit of the medieval knight of Western Europe. Faithful toward God, moral, of strong character, dignified in conduct, ready to sacrifice for faith and country, "for the Holy Cross, for the fatherland," as phrased in the Legion's anthem, the Legionnaire was a kind of knight, free of moral stain or fear. Defender of the oppressed, determined to fight all manner of injustice, no one and nothing could deter him from his incorruptible code of conduct. An outlaw with the soul of a saint.

A very important trait for both Legionnaire and knight was a sense of justice. While being obligated by their code of conduct not to do anything that would tarnish their sense of honor or that would prevent them from supporting a just cause, this very sense of honor also required them to act when someone offended them. This kind of conduct is debatable from a Christian point

---

[38] The military character of the Legionnaires, clearly seen in photographs and recordings from that era where they are, shown marching in green shirts with belts and diagonals, although tempered by the brotherly love shared between them, does not quite express the spirit of our Romanian Orthodoxy, with its characteristic sense of discretion and balance. It is more typical of Western orders of knights. Even though this was only a stage, it would be interesting to compare the ethos of traditional Romanian Orthodoxy with the decisive, offensive, and sometimes overly impetuous behavior of the Legionnaires.

of view, which advocates humility and requires that one turn the other cheek when struck. In the Communist prisons, when the Legionnaires encountered Christianity in all its profundity, this concept of honor turned out to be a source of great difficulty for them, as they realized that the passion of pride can lie behind it. "Vanity hid itself within us under the secret cloak of 'honor' and it was a difficult struggle until this so-called dignity and 'honor' were spiritualized, passing through a process of purification."

Many youngsters were attracted exactly by this "musketeer" aspect of the Legionnaires: uniforms, training songs, military discipline, manly conduct, the call to sacrifice and heroism. Firm and steadfast characters, single-minded men with a fighting spirit, found an environment well-suited to their spiritual framework. Youthfulness and impetuosity pushed them toward complete engagement, while at the same time they were sensitive to offenses and injustice. In these kinds of situations, they did not turn the other cheek, but took action: "Our law is clear and precise. If he respects me, I respect him. If he strikes me, I strike him. We do not start fights, but we end them."[39]

Those attracted to the Legion by this outlaw aspect gradually reached, each at his own pace, a deeper level of understanding.[40] Someone once spoke to me about

---

[39] Alexandru Ştefănescu, *Comentar la monografia oraşului*, Ed. Babel, Bacău, 2003, p. 69.

[40] A complete analysis of the Legionnaires must be mindful of their spiritual growth, not only of their errors and acts of violence. For example, it must be considered that Codreanu had a particular mind frame at age 25, when he took revenge on the prefect of police Manciu, and a quite different one when he expressed himself in his journal during the last months of his life while imprisoned at Jilava.

such a young man whose life had been changed by meeting Puiu Gârcineanu, a Legionnaire with a profoundly Christian lifestyle, in a work camp. "Seeing Gârcineanu, I was ashamed of my superficial understanding and came to realize the spiritual transformation to which I was being called." There would be others like him, but most would change during the long, hard years of prison when, maturing through suffering and confronted with the limits of their own strength, without the hope of release, they would balance honor with humility. The Spartan component of their training would then prove to be of great use to them, helping them to brave the difficulties of imprisonment.

Because measures were taken against the Legion such that they were almost constantly persecuted, the education of the *brothers of the cross* did not follow its natural course. Forced to meet in secret, sheltered from the far-reaching sight of the authorities, without experienced guides, these young men were not always able to benefit from a solid spiritual education.[41] Moved

---

The same can be said of other Legionnaires who, in their youth, were carried away by enthusiasm yet carried themselves very differently after having matured as a result of being imprisoned.

[41] Apart from external causes, there are some aspects of the education of the *brothers of the cross* and of the Legionnaires thatare questionable from an Orthodox point of view. In Gheorghe Istrate's *Guidebook of the Brothers of the Cross*, as well as in other Legionnaire writings, we find exaggerations alluding to a cult-like appreciation of Codreanu; vague spiritual terminology; philetistic tendencies (philetism being the heresy of putting one's people or country ahead of the Church); justification for acts of revenge or for anti-Semitic attitudes; oaths and agreements that were ambiguous from a theological point of view, etc. All of these things show that, at that time, the Legionnaires, although embraced by the Church, were often

primarily by enthusiasm and sincerity, they nevertheless lacked a profoundly Christian vision, which most of them would acquire in prison. The seeds sown through training in the Brotherhood of the Cross, despite their shortcomings, were significant because these young men received a spiritual foundation based on Christian principles that was much more solid that any training offered in traditional academic milieus. The Christian conduct they later displayed in prison found its source in these principles which formed their characters, principles which cultivated the virtues of steadfastness, solidarity, and a spirit of sacrifice, while many non-Legionnaires, as Steinhardt noted, lost their balance, their humanity, and their self-control.[42]

Bearing in mind this dimension of Legionnaire training which, in spite of its shortcomings, prepared a great many people for martyrdom, it can be understood why Father Constantin Voicescu called the Legionnaire movement "The love story between Christ and the Romanian people," while Father Iustin Pârvu saw it as "The highest form of the manifestation of Romanian genius."[43]

---

confused from a theological point of view and did not always think or conduct themselves in an Orthodox spirit. In their later lives, many of these shortcomings would be corrected.

[42]The Legionnaires' behavior in prison pointed to the effectiveness of their character building.

[43]We can speculate why the Legionnaires did not succeed in bringing a Christian political system to power in Romania. There are those who blame this failure on acts of violence which, in turn, caused God to turn His face from the Legionnaires. However, taking into consideration the fact that the satanic Communist regime was allowed by divine providence even though it was responsible for millions of crimes, I believe that the real answer is something else entirely. But who can know the thoughts of God? Along with the fall

After this lengthy digression about the Legionnaire movement, necessary for a more comprehensive understanding of the political and spiritual context, let us return to Valeriu Gafencu. Having an enthusiastic and idealistic nature, he completely found his place in the *Brotherhood of the Cross*, which he joined while still a high school student in Bălți. In 1937 and along with other *brothers of the cross*, he participated in an electoral campaign for the Legionnaires' political party which named itself *Totul pentru Țară* (Everything for the Country). He posted placards and campaigned with much enthusiasm, at one point being retained by policemen.

While a college student at Iași, he became the leader of a group of *brothers of the cross* from the city's high schools. After January 1941, he organized the high school students of Iași to protest against Antonescu. For this action, he was arrested and sentenced to three months in jail.

---

of the last Christian political system in 1917, the Russian Empire, the gift of a society based upon Christian principles was taken away from the world because of the sins of humankind. "For everything there is a fitting moment and a specific time for every occupation under heaven," says the Holy Scripture. In the apocalyptic phase that the human race entered in the 20th century, the Christian order that the Legionnaires sought to establish could no longer exist. They answered what they thought was a political calling, when it was in fact something much more transcendental: Martyrdom. Therefore, any attempt to resuscitate the Legionnaire movement today as a political party seems to me anachronistic. The time is no longer propitious for such a thing. The gift we have received from the Legionnaires – and it is by no means small – is the spiritual inheritance from which each of us can benefit in our work toward salvation.

After this episode, although the *Brotherhood of the Cross* had been officially abolished and any *Brotherhood* activities declared illegal, Valeriu, who had put his whole being into the education of these young high schoolers, had no intention of giving up. The students loved him very much, although he was a bit older than them, and they all bonded in genuine spiritual communion. Their activities together were educational rather than political.

In the autumn of 1941, Valeriu was arrested during a meeting of the *Brotherhood of the Cross* held at a military high school in Iaşi. At the trial, his professor of civil law, Angelescu, stepped forward in order to offer this defense: "It is a sin to send this kind of person to prison, for it will be a loss for society if he is taken out of its midst. He is one of the best students I have had during the whole of my teaching career."[44]

Nevertheless, Valeriu was sentenced to 25 years in prison. He was sent to Aiud. It was January of 1942.

Hundreds of students were arrested during this period and sentenced to long, hard years in prison; they were arrested either because they participated in *Brotherhood of the Cross* groups or because they had assisted Legionnaire prisoners and their families.

---

[44]Nicolae Trifoiu, *op. cit.*, p. 105

The Ascetics[45] of Aiud

During his time at Aiud (1942-1948), Valeriu befriended a group of prisoners who cultivated their spiritual lives very seriously. The "mystics,"[46] as they were called – sometimes in admiration, sometimes in derision – considered their main concern to be a life in Christ, according to the teachings of the Holy Fathers. The atmosphere of this group not only played an important role in Valeriu's spiritual cleansing and growth but also contributed to the birth of philocalic spirituality in Communist prisons. It is appropriate, then, to say a few words about these prisoners, and to mention a few in particular.

Most of them were very young students sent to prison for the same offense: the continuation, in one form or another, of Legionnaire activity after January 1941. As was true of Valeriu, these students did not

---

[45] *Ascetics* are those who practice *askesis*, i.e., physical endeavors such as fasting, prostrations, and vigils for a spiritual benefit. (Translator's note)

[46] The term "mystic" comes from Greek, where it has the sense of someone initiated into mysteries, aware of things supernatural, a seer of things that are not seen. In Latin, its meaning was secularized by popular culture and scholastic thought. From Latin, it came to be inherited by the Romance languages, where its meaning came to be out rightly misconstrued after the French Revolution in the 18th century and the Bolshevik Revolution in the 20th century. Unofficially yet most effectively, and under the aegis of an exclusively rational and atheist society, the term "mystic" came to mean crazy, mentally unbalanced, absurd. The "mystics" of Aiud were called thusly by people who held them in high regard, in the sense that Christianity gave this term: A person with a lofty spiritual life, aware of divine mysteries. By others, they were called "mystics" derisively, in the sense of the atheistic mentality mentioned.

participate in assaults or conspiracies; instead, they were found guilty of attending meetings held to promote the moral and spiritual education of young people. "We did not consider ourselves guilty in a legal sense," one of these men, Marin Naidim, later said, "because we had not been actively involved in incriminating deeds. We had not killed, we had not stolen, we had not oppressed anyone, yet we were sentenced to long, hard years in prison because we joined an organization, we sang Legionnaire songs, and we were good students. For such deeds, any man of good faith would have congratulated us. But it is apparent that God permitted the judges in court to hand out punishment for sins quite different from those of which we were aware.

"Nevertheless, we were guilty of one thing, the doing of all these good deeds as part of a forbidden organization. But for this reason, to condemn a few people, a few boys, to 25 years of hard labor? It is clear that this was a case of passion, not of fair judgment."[47]

Though hard to believe, this was the reality of the times. As a travesty of justice, the trial of two of these young men, Virgil Maxim, still a high school student, and Marin Naidim, a high school graduate, lasted only minutes and their attorneys were not permitted to speak; the two youths were sentenced to 25 years in prison. Their offense? The continuation of Legionnaire training in the *Brotherhood of the Cross*. Another young man, Nicolae Mazăre, also a *brother of the cross*, was arrested for delivering a letter to a certain address. Nicolae carried out this action at the request of an acquaintance of his, a Legionnaire who was under police surveillance.

---

[47] In the periodical *Puncte Cardinale*, nr. 11/59, November 1995, pg.p. 11.

For delivering this letter whose contents he discovered during his interrogation, he was sentenced to 20 years in prison.

After January 1941, hundreds if not thousands of young men were arrested and convicted for reasons just as contrived. Driven by earnest aspirations, idealistic but a bit confused, open toward spirituality but without a solid spiritual foundation, they matured through suffering and were spiritually purified in prison. At Aiud, the most earnest of these young men came together in a group of ascetics centered around the lawyers Traian Marian and Traian Trifan.[48]

The second of these two men, "Badia"[49] Trifan, came to be a genuine spiritual figure for the others by virtue of his age, his manner of living, and his wisdom. Unyielding in the face of compromise, "Badia" Trifan was, as Father Papacioc describes him, "[A] man with a profoundly Christian manner of living, a great and upright character, a gentle advisor, wise, comforting,

---

[48] The group that came together around these two men differed in no way in terms of hierarchy, rules, or organization from the other prisoners. It was the spontaneous gathering of a group of men who, although structured differently, had common spiritual affinities and ambitions. The nucleus consisted of Traian Trifan, Traian Marian, Anghel Papacioc, Father Vasile Serghie, Valeriu Gafencu, Marin Naidim, Virgil Maxim, Nicolae Mazăre, Iulian Bălan, Constantin Pascu, and later Ioan Ianolide. This list is not complete, mentioning only those of the inner circle; there were other participants.

[49] The moniker "Badia" is used in many regions of Romania when addressing an older man and conveys a friendly, informal respect. (Translator's note)

seemingly wanting to express entire pages in a single word."[50]

Born in Lancrăm into a family of twelve children, Trifan raised himself up through his own efforts, eventually becoming a lawyer and a professor of law. He was appointed prefect of Braşov county during the brief Legionnaire administration, and at the time of the so-called rebellion of January 1941, he refused to allow the army to take over the prefect's office in Braşov, awaiting confirmation from Bucharest and requesting that, just as he was appointed by decree, he also be removed from office by official decree. He was arrested and sentenced to 16 years in prison.

At Aiud, he stood up to prison leadership who, at the order of Antonescu, promised the Legionnaires freedom on the condition that they disassociate themselves from the movement and agree to go to the battle front, thereby "rehabilitating" themselves from their past mistakes. Although the idea of going to the anti-Bolshevik front may well have appealed to the Legionnaires considering their patriotism and opposition to Communism, it was rendered unacceptable because it was presented as "rehabilitation" for errors. In front of the other prisoners and prison leadership, Trifan openly rejected this proposal with dignity. "Traian Trifan has the rank of captain and serves his country as a soldier, but the Legionnaire commander Traian Trifan has no reason to be rehabilitated in the eyes of anyone."[51]

---

[50]*Mărturisesc ... robul 1036 (I bear witness ... slave 1036)*, edited by Virgil Maxim, Ed. Scara, Bucharest, 1998, pg.p. 103.

[51]Virgil Maxim, *op. cit.*, pg.p. 87.

Dumitru Bordeianu, in his book *Mărturisiri din mlaștina disperării* (*Confessions From theMire of Despair*), gives us the most beautiful account of the life of this *avva* seemingly descended from a *Paterikon* of the prisons. At Gherla in 1955, Bordeianu happened to be in the same cell as Trifan during Lent. During Holy Week, Bordeianu saw how much Trifan lived and felt with all his heart the torment of Golgotha alongside Jesus Christ, weeping like a mother who had lost her only son. "I saw Trifan," he confessed, "from Monday until Holy Saturday. What I saw in him was more than impressive. On Monday morning I wanted to speak with him about spiritual life during Holy Week. To my great surprise, however, when I approached him, I noticed that he was crying. Streams of tears were flowing from his eyes. At his request, the others in the cell had reserved the corner of a bunk for him. I was ashamed that I had disturbed him and for the rest of Holy Week I did not have the chance to speak to him. He retreated into this little corner and wept continuously, seeing with the eyes of his soul and feeling with his heart the sufferings of the Son of God crucified on the cross on Golgotha. He had created such an impression on the others in the cell that, for them, that entire Holy Week was one of mourning."[52]

A man of prayer, gentle and humble, winning over many souls with his way of life and his wise counsel, "Badia" Trifan passed through his long pilgrimage of 21 years in the desert of the Communist prisons with the serenity of a saint. Regardless of his former accomplishments and status in civil society, after

----

[52] Dumitru Bordeianu, *Mărturisiri din mlaștina disperării*(*Confessions from the Mire Of Despair*), second edition, Ed. Scara, Bucharest, 2000, pg.p. 393.

his release from prison, he divided his time between church services and unskilled labor at a small enterprise that manufactured boxes for packing fruit.

Alongside Trifan, the young Anghel Papacioc, later Father Arsenie, "walked without a moment's hesitation upon the well-worn path of those who, through physical and spiritual striving, achieve cleansing and enlightenment for their souls." [53] Inheriting the manly and steadfast nature of his Macedonian-Romanian ancestors, Anghel Papacioc felt attracted to the Legionnaires from a very young age. His testimony is a welcomed supplement to what was said in the previous chapter.

"The Legion helped me enormously; it was truly a severe and intimate struggle for us to give birth to a new man in us. [This rebirth] was something necessary in my life. The principles of Legionnaire training were extraordinary. It was a system of training that engaged you. This brought me out of a latent adolescent state, where I felt I wanted something but didn't know what. This is when the Legion appeared, with its fervor, with its valor, under the protection of the Archangel Michael. This aspect of the movement won me over completely, since I knew the troparion of the archangel from childhood.

"I knew Codreanu, I had many discussions with him, and I held him in great esteem. We cannot consider the Legion apart from the will of God; therefore, it was the will of God, even though it sprang from certain secular, historical causes.

"I was not in agreement with murders of revenge," said Father Arsenie about the violent acts of

---

[53]Virgil Maxim, *op. cit.*, pg.p. 183.

the Legionnaires. "Perhaps this big mistake affected the entire Legion, [not just those who carried out the murders]. I had a brother, a Legionnaire, who was shot by police soldiers. When the Legionnaires rose to power, I could have avenged my brother's death. I thought this would be a big mistake. I was given the chance to kill [the man who shot my brother]. I reasoned that if I don't kill him, God is indebted to me. And my brother is indebted to me. If I do kill, they are no longer indebted to me but I to them. I sent a message to my brother's murderer not to be afraid because I would send him protection so that no one else would be able to harm him."[54]

Looking back on these long and hard years of imprisonment, Father Arsenie sees them as a blessed opportunity for strengthening his faith. "There were no other means of preparation that could offer such possibilities for growing in one's faith, for a spiritual deepening, for a living relationship with God as were offered by the tribulations of imprisonment. I bless that period of time. I spent years in the wilderness without coming upon the possibility to deepen my thoughts of eternity, of the divine nature; this possibility was accorded me in daily torture [of life in a Communist prison]. Suffering also united us. Those of us who succeeded in knowing each other on the cross, so to speak, remained united."

"The image I have of my imprisonment," recalls Father Arsenie referring to his fellow prisoners at Aiud, "is very much bound up with that of the little group in which I felt very well. There was a great camaraderie

---

[54] Testimony given to monk Moise by Father Arsenie in January 2005. He fell asleep in the Lord in July 2011.

among us. Everyone was prepared for death. I would like to canonize these men, Gafencu, Trifan, Marian, all of them, Maxim, Pascu, others. Was one really better than the others? What matters is the way in which each one accepted suffering. I would like to canonize all of them because they were sincere and did not hesitate to sacrifice themselves. All of them sacrificed. They all died, one by one. With a joy that is difficult to explain, I commemorate them all at the Proskomide[55] as spiritual fighters, alongside the great warrior princes of our country."[56]

We cannot speak of those imprisoned at Aiud without mentioning Virgil Maxim. Arrested in 1942 at the age of nineteen while in his last year of high school in Buzău, he was sentenced to 25 years in prison for belonging to the *Brotherhood of the Cross*.[57] He was

---

[55]Proskomide - a short service performed by an Orthodox priest before the Liturgy to prepare the bread and wine for Holy Communion. (Translator's note)

[56]*Ibid.*

[57]Again, the farce of his trial reveals much regarding the lack of objective justice toward the young *brothers of the cross* under Antonescu's reign after January 1941. "The trial was a mockery. In just a few sentences, the prosecuting attorney accused us of being psychologically unwell and affirmed that society needed to be cleansed of this kind of element. Manea, [the prosecuting attorney], only asked us if we had participated in the Legionnaire *Brotherhood of theCross*. The defending lawyers were given only one minute to speak for the entire group of defendants. Popescu [one of the defending attorneys] said this much: 'Your Honor, my clients are not common-law delinquents but political prisoners. As such, they can only be sentenced in conformity with provisions of the International Code for political prisoners, which stipulates the privation of freedom by obligatory house-arrest or light detention for a limited time, but in no case penal punishments of hard labor or hard imprisonment, as the prosecuting attorney has requested.'

liberated in 1964, having served 22 years, after an amnesty decree for political prisoners. As a result of his attitude and way of life, even though imprisoned, Maxim was regarded as a saint in the eyes of the other prisoners, becoming a symbolic figure of these [Communist] prisons. In his memoir *Imn Pentru Crucea Purtată* (*Hymn for the Carried Cross*), he testifies to his prison encounters and experiences. This book is truly a spiritual chronicle of prison life in Aiud, with ample reference to the group of spiritual strugglers who had been formed around Trifan. Since Maxim spent two years in the same cell as Gafencu and was also with him in the colony at Galda, his testimony, after that of

---

"'Enough!' Manea stopped him. Addressing the other attorney, he asked him, 'Have you anything to add?'

'I would only like to add that since the prosecution did not see fit to draw up trial documents for these six minors brought here today, Your Honor does not have the right to sentence these children to prison without good reason. I am speaking of Constantin Voicescu, Ion Mocanu, Constantin Ilie, and Teodor Iamandi, sixth graders at the grammar school in Buzău and Vlahopol Stroie and Lucian Rădulescu from the high school in Râmnicu Sârat.'

'Are you a Legionnaire?' insinuated Manea.

'Mr. President, I am the defense attorney,' the lawyer responded smiling, 'and cannot be questioned here about my political affiliation. What I would like to tell you, Your Honor, is that you are committing an error in form and in content, a fact which I am pointing out in defense of my clients.'

Beating the desk with his fists, Manea spat out, 'I will request the Presidency to repeal the right of civil lawyers to plead in military trials.'

Then, to the court clerk, he said 'State the sentencing.' (Standard protocol is for sentencing to be read by the President after deliberation.)

"The court clerk removed a list from an envelope and read our sentences. That is how long our trial lasted and how it unfolded." (Virgil Maxim, *op. cit.*, pp. 68-69)

Ianolide, is the most important source of information about that period of time in which the "saint of the prisons" was confined at Aiud.

Throughout the book, Virgil Maxim shows himself as not only a steadfast confessor of Christ, endowed with an admirable spiritual foundation and solid theological knowledge, but also as a man with a profound awareness of reality, armed with a singular capacity for bringing out the spiritual meaning of the events he describes. Speaking about him, Father Arsenie Papacioc affirms: "Maxim had a perfect intuitive understanding of the state of things. In fact, many did, but he presented it in detail, in all of its meaning. A very competent individual once said about him that he was the only one of us who was capable enough to be the spiritual patriarch of the country. I, who have known [Maxim] since childhood, agreed."[58]

In the same time period as Virgil Maxim, another member of the group of mystics, Marin Naidim, was arrested and convicted. This is how someone who knew Marin during his first years in prison described him: "Shy as a girl, of great spiritual purity, obedient." Naidim had a spiritual structure similar to Valeriu's and was his closest friend during the Aiud years. Gabriel Bălănescu, who knew Marin while working in a lead mine in the Nistru Valley in the fifties, describes him well:

"Marin Naidim dominated by the way he carried himself, his breadth of knowledge (acquired in prison!), and his great capacity to love all of those around him. In

---

[58]Testimony given to monk Moise by Father Arsenie Moses in January 2005.

the dormitory where Naidim was assigned, there was an atmosphere quite distinct from the other dormitories. That same atmosphere could also be found in the work teams to which he was assigned. Conflicts were frequent in prison, but such a thing was impossible around Marin Naidim. He would rise above conflict with the skill worthy of a career diplomat. Unlike other *brothers of the cross* who had spent a long time in prison, Naidim was able to maintain a certain balance by conducting his religious life in a way that was decent and humble. Only a very watchful eye could discern Naidim's moments of absence in which he said his prayers or the days in which he fasted. He was extraordinarily discreet in all of his actions, while in religious discussions he did not seek to impose his point of view. Rather, he imposed his point of view with his actions, with no ostentation. That is how a Romanian peasant is. Marin Naidim had all the qualities of a Romanian peasant, but reinforced by an intellectual refinement which Sandu Mazilu called "a restrained force." In all domains - philosophy, literature, theology, art - Naidim had accurate information which he conveyed in a quiet, modest voice; he was a ready listener, lacking any desire to argue."[59]

Later, around 1945, Ioan Ianolide joined the group of ascetic strivers. He was arrested in October 1941, while attending law school in Bucharest. Just like Gafencu, he was the leader of a *Brothers of the Cross* group.

Eugen Cristescu, the general director of State Security, needed to come up with a plot planning to take the life of Marshal Antonescu. His purpose was to

---

[59]Gabriel Bălănescu, *Din împărăţia morţii – pagini din istoria Gărzii de Fier* (*From the Kingdom of Death –Pages from the History of the Iron Guard*), Ed. Gordian, Timişoara, 1994, p. 165.

unleash a compromising scandal against the Legionnaires. He staged a clandestine meeting of the *Brotherhood of the Cross* in the forest at Băneasa, set to coincide with an aerial demonstration carried out by German pilots. At that meeting, seventy-eight people were arrested; forty-eight were detained and twenty-one were sent to trial. Cristescu achieved his objective with this staged scandal, having no concern for what happened to the victims. Nonetheless, in order to cover his tracks, eight of the 48 detained, including Ioan Ianolide, received prison sentences on account of having Legionnaire books and brochures in their homes.

During his interrogation, Ioan Ianolide was brutally beaten to make him give to the police the statements they were seeking. At his trial, he was sentenced to 25 years in prison.[60] He was released after 23 years and, according to Father Voicescu, "[A]lthough relatively young, he had acquired the philocalic wisdom of a great avva."[61]

Ianolide was the only member of the group of spiritual strivers at Aiud who accompanied Valeriu to Piteşti and later to Târgu-Ocna. His confessional book *Întoarcerea la Hristos (The Return to Christ)*, to which we will often refer, has Gafencu as its central character.

Many of those who, while free, had considered the Legionnaires to be nothing more than a group of adventurers changed their opinion after coming in

---

[60]Sourced from the appeal made by Ianolide in 1941, in the archives of the *ConsiliulNaţional pentru Studierea Arhivelor (National Council for the Study of State Security Archives)*, Penal Fund, File 327, vol. 12, pg.p. 280.

[61]*Părintele Constantin Voicescu – un duhovnic al cetăţi(A spiritual father of the realm)i*, pg.p. 26.

contact with them at Aiud. This was the case with Romulus Dianu, assistant director of the newspaper *Curentul (TheCurrent)*, who had published venomous articles about the Legionnaires. In the mines at Baia Sprie, he admitted to Nicolae Goga, "I want you to know that I had a mistaken notion of the movement you belong to; after I met Legionnaires at Aiud who had been arrested in 1941 - Gafencu, Ianolide, Maxim, and their whole group - I completely changed my mind. I could not imagine that such high moral values could exist in the Romanian people."[62]

Among the ranks of prisoners sent to Aiud after 1941, there were different opinions regarding Legionnairism. The approach adopted by Trifan's group, although gradually coming to be appreciated by most of the prisoners, stirred up considerable controversy at first. Following the teachings of the Holy Fathers, these ascetics concentrated all their attention on spiritual growth and transformation. The spiritual part of life was the only part they valued. Those who took a more combative stance, displaying dignity and intransigence, considered them traitors to the Legionnaire movement. The combative attitude of these prisoners was based more upon advancing their own moral strength and power than upon attracting the grace

---

[62] Nicolae Goga, *Triunghiul morții(Triangle of Death)*, Ed. Marineasa, Timişoara, 1995, pg.p. 78. Immediately after saying these words, Dianu added, "I would like to suggest something. Knowing the West as I do, I do not think they will ever recognize your sacrifice and that of your generation. The debt would be too great for them to pay; therefore, they will not acknowledge it." Unfortunately, Romulus Dianu proved to be prophetic. It is sad that their sacrifice is ignored by the West, but even more so that it is ignored by most Romanians.

of God through repentance. This stance led them to wear themselves out needlessly, continually being provoked by prison administrators, and ultimately leading to stumbling or reorientation.

Those who gathered around Trifan, however, pursuing their path of spiritual growth with no ostentation, avoided everything that could divert them from this path, crowning the steadfastness of their witness with the garb of humility. "The characteristic trait of these seekers was humility,"[63] said Virgil Maxim.

Devoting themselves to the Jesus prayer, studying and learning texts from the Holy Scripture, the Philokalia, and other patristic writings, these prisoners were to form, in the Communist prison at Aiud, a philocalic way of life. United in their desire to sacrifice themselves for Christ, these monks in spirit – for as we shall see, they lived a high level of asceticism at Aiud – supported each other, preparing themselves for the difficult trials which were yet to come. Forged in the hearth of Aiud, after their group was scattered in different directions, these young men were to become true spiritual beacons in the darkness of the Communist prisons.

Precisely by assuming an ascetic lifestyle, the ascetics played a direct or indirect role in the spiritual cleansing and transformation of those who were imprisoned after 1948. Father Iustin Pârvu testifies to it:

"From a spiritual point of view, prison was a blessing for us. There were so many spiritual people gathered together in one place whom we couldn't possibly have found outside of prison. At Aiud, where I arrived after my trial in 1949, and also in other places, I

_____

[63]Virgil Maxim, *op. cit.*, pg.p. 183.

came to know those who had been arrested after 1941 and who, by that time, had been imprisoned for a long time. Some of them had achieved great spiritual awakening. For those of us who were arrested in 1948 or later, these prisoners were our saviors. Disoriented by the long and difficult interrogations we had gone through, our contact with them clarified things for us. They made us aware of the Christian significance of our struggle, of the fact that we were engaged on the Christian front against the apocalyptic beast. We thought we were paying for our sins, but thanks to them we realized that Christ called us to the war front in the name of the Romanian people. Once we understood this, the fact that we were in prison became a joy for us. For this reason, I say that they saved us; they showed us the path of survival. It is interesting how, even after 7 - 8 years in prison, having been arrested at a very young age, most around 17 - 18 years of age, they had preserved their innocence and purity, their child-like traits, as if the time spent in prison had left no [malevolent] trace on them. They seemed to be younger even than those of us who at that time, [in 1948, some 9 years later], were 17 - 18 years old. They were very serene, very lively, very mature, and very wise. Very rich from a spiritual point of view. They were a light for us. By that time, several volumes of the Philokalia had been translated. These young men knew entire pages by heart. Simply by their presence, by their behavior, they changed the other prisoners."[64]

In addition to that of Father Iustin's, other testimonies could be given that speak just as

---

[64]Testimony given to monk Moise by Father Iustin Pârvu January 2005.

convincingly about the spiritual influence of these young men at Aiud. Comparatively, I would liken what they did with the spiritual work of the disciples of Paisii Velichkovsky,[65] who went wherever divine providence carried them, spreading the philocalic flame kindled in their souls at Neamț[66]. In like manner albeit in a different context and to a different degree, those from Aiud, while constricted by the diabolical severity of Communist prison in which not even the slightest expression of religion was tolerated, set in place a treasury of spirituality that was the foundation which enabled them to tolerate successive prisons or adverse conditions.

God, who knew their sincerity and purity of thought from the onset, worked in a wonderful way, and transforming the evil intent of those who had condemned them into something beneficial, brought the Aiud ascetics together in the lavra[67] of Aiud so as to prepare the salvation of many other souls through these ascetics' transformation and spiritual growth.

---

[65]Paisii Velichkovsky (1724-1794) - monastic leader originally from the Ukraine who attracted a very large following in the late 18th century. He was the leader of a monastic renaissance in northeastern Romania.

[66]Neamț - monastery in northeastern Romania near Piatra Neamț. Founded in the 15th century, it served as one of the primary centers of activity for Paisii Velichkovsky.

[67]The term lavra is a name given to large, rich monasteries of importance that enjoy special privileges and are cultural centers in the regions they occupy.

They Found This Path an Hour Earlier

One more witness should be added to the portrait I have sketched of the ascetics of Aiud, that of someone who, at that time, regarded them with reserve if not hostility. I have already mentioned that after 1941, the Legionnaires who were not quite won over by the movement's spiritual aspects did not give much credit to the ascetics.

One of those who adopted a resolute position, interpreting their humility as weakness and a departure from the combative stance of the Legionnaires, was Vasile Turtureanu. Arrested during Antonescu's time for his activities in the *Brotherhood of the Cross*, he spent his entire youth - from the age of 19 until 42 - in prison. Of an intransigent nature, forever bearing witness to his Legionnaire stance and indifferent to consequences, he passed through his long period of imprisonment without compromise. Although at the time he disagreed with Trifan's group – "they seemed to me too mild, too soft" – the sufferings that divine providence laid before him brought him to the point of being of one mind with those "who even now serve as models for me."

Although he only had a tangential connection to Valeriu's group, a very condensed account of the adventures of Turtureanu – difficult to cover in a single book, impossible in a few pages – will prove interesting. Apart from the sincerity and courage with which he bore the cross of his faith, the authenticity of Christian thought resonates in his testimony, facts which even the most ardent of Legionnaires cannot deny if he were honest. The statements of Turtureanu, stemming from sentiment rather than reason, confirm the fact that

Legionnairism was a spiritual state of being more than anything else. Any sincere reader cannot help but notice the connection between the Legionnaire creed and the spiritual experiences that this tormented soul finally achieved. Of course, this happened with many others, at different times.

"I am not worthy to thank God for giving me this suffering. For me, prison was a font of gold in which I received, to a great degree, the gift of love toward God and country. There, undergoing those terrible trials, I came to know God and to feel His intercession. When there was no longer any humanly-possible way to escape, He seemingly put His hand on my head and moved me from here to the beyond. I have this great joy: God helped me and I never compromised.

"I endured prison with love. During my trial, I smiled when they sentenced me to 25 years. My soul accepted this condemnation with joy. 'Look at that hoodlum,' they said. 'He got such a heavy sentence and he's smiling.'

"Knowing that I was legally innocent, I accepted even the most difficult trials with the sense that this was the will of God. I never despaired. I considered that I was suffering for my own sins and for the sins of my people, and that perhaps God had ordained prison for me as a path of salvation.

"I was arrested as the result of a betrayal, for activity in the *brotherhood*. I want to emphasize something: I never acted according to reason; I did what I felt. What I did, I did because that's how it came to me. When Antonescu was handing out long prison sentences, for singing a song or reading a Legionnaire book, when everyone was running away or hiding, I

61

assumed leadership of the *Brotherhood* in the Suceava region. Why? Because that's what felt right.

"That's how I understood the *Brotherhood of the Cross*, as being a brotherhood until death, gathered around the cross, of all of those who felt the spark of love for God and country in their souls.

"Among those things that led me to follow this path of sacrifice were the words of Corneliu Zelea Codreanu: '*Christ is risen. In like manner, the righteousness of the Romanian people will also arise. But in order to achieve this, its best sons must willingly accept crowns of thorns, must take the cross upon their shoulders, must ascend Golgotha on their knees and, withtears in their eyes, let themselves be crucified. Legionnaires, may you be these children!*' These words, ending with '*Legionnaires, may you be these children,*' made me say, 'Lord, make me worthy to be one of these children!'

"And truly, God gave me suffering, God gave me everything. He filled my soul with joy in difficult moments and fills it even now. I was indeed one of the children that confessed the Legionnaire creed. Even in the most difficult situations, I always stated openly that I was a Legionnaire, regardless of the consequences. I didn't even think about the consequences. A sorting was done in prison. Those who had renounced the movement were on one side, while those who had remained faithful were on the other. Without a moment's hesitation, without caring about the consequences, I joined the ranks of those who had remained faithful to the Legionnaires.

"In prison, I was again put on trial and sentenced to 20 more years for Legionnaire activities while in prison, for holding meetings, for singing and such. Considered a fanatic, I was brought to the mental hospital, drugged, chained, isolated – to say nothing of the hunger and cold – for openly affirming Legionnairism. But I never compromised.

"I have nothing to hide. Today I maintain the same position, openly declaring myself to be a Legionnaire. After 1989, they called me to witness at the *Memorialul Durerii(The Memorialof Pain)*. I said to them:

"'Do you realize that if I come, the first thing I will say is that I am a Legionnaire?' After which the whole thing fell apart. 'Oh no, not that, not that. You don't need to say that!' 'Then I won't participate. That's not my way, I don't do anything half-way.'

"In the fifties, in the [coal] mines at Baia Sprie, I had an accident. The ceiling caved on top of me. Two stone slabs propped themselves up, one against the other, and I found myself in the space underneath them. That's how my life was saved. It was a miracle, one of the many miracles that God worked with me. But there were smaller rocks that had fallen on top of me. I had a cracked spine and a few broken ribs. I was in a cast for seven months. It was a difficult time. I was in a lot of pain and was unable to move. I was alone, with no one to talk to, only a sour and morose common-law prisoner who brought me food. It was difficult for me to eat. I couldn't lift my hands to my mouth. I stretched out, took my plate, lifted it up to my mouth and, from a distance, I poured what was in the spoon into my mouth. That was my life for seven months. Prayer was my only support.

"God gives you one kind of suffering in order to deliver you from another. The accident at the mine got me out of 're-education' at Pitești. Those at Pitești [who knew of me] asked about me, but I couldn't be triaged there because I was in a cast. I had an angel that watched over me.

"While in prison, I was not slovenly or careless. I was always attending to my spiritual improvement. I sought to bring about the new man within me, the man who would be a genuine Legionnaire, the new man who lives his life for Christ. The Legionnaire man, as I understood it, is born of pain and sacrifice and shines ever brighter, scalded with the tears of repentance - confession and Holy Communion. He has sincere love for his neighbor and unlimited faith in the victory and resurrection of the Romanian people, guided by the light of the holy teachings of the meek Jesus. The elite Legionnaire is a hero with the soul of a saint. He struggles with faith, sacrifices out of love, and serenely accepts death's torments in the hope of resurrection.

"All my life I sought to be ever more sincere with myself. My prayer would be, 'Lord, help me to do Thy will in order to be worthy of Thy love!' I prayed for the dead a great deal. I prayed for one, and then I would remember to pray for another whose voice I seemed to hear saying, 'Pray for me, too!' I also prayed for him.

"I was set free after 22 years, 2 months and 2 weeks. When I arrived home, it was a tragedy. My mother cried, she caressed me, she kissed me, and cried, 'Where is the other one? You came back, but where is the other one?'

"I had a brother who died at Pitești, in re-education camp. They tell of a young man who, around the time of Pascha, was crucified and martyred because he didn't want to renounce Christ and blaspheme. I later discovered that it was my brother.

"For me, the Legionnaire movement was everything. It filled my soul completely. Before I was arrested, a few of us decided to stand guard at the grave of a *brother of the cross* who had been shot during the time of King Carol II. It was summertime and there were a lot of mosquitoes. I was so captivated by this Legionnaire movement that, in this cemetery full of mosquitoes, as long as I stood guard, I didn't move. I was standing guard at the grave of a Legionnaire, so whether the mosquitoes bit me or not, I didn't move!

"I was receiving dues from the other *brothers of the cross*. My aunt once asked me to give her small change from that money, to exchange. I had been told that this was the Legion's money not mine, and that I cannot touch it. 'Aunt,' I said to her, 'it's not my money. I can't touch it. Folded, torn, however it may be, that's the way I got it and that's the way I'll pass it on.' She marveled at my fanaticism.

"During my first years in Aiud, I got to know Trifan's group. At that time, it seemed to me that their style, so mild, so soft, was not the true Legionnaire line. They sometimes had a sectarian tint of isolation. Later on, they weaned themselves from this. But until they found their balance, it could be said they were guilty of exaggeration. They didn't exercise good judgment in the beginning. They had too many varied concerns and were extremist. Ioan Ianolide and Virgil Maxim write of essential, mature Legionnaire attitudes after things had been sorted out properly; but they went through much turmoil before they were cleansed. They final attitudes were gained through their toils. They had good intentions; they were sincere and God granted them grace.

"Their luck lay in the fact that God allowed them to remain near each other when they were shifted around in prison; in fact, they were almost always together. Because of this, they were able to help each other. They shared the suffering and supported each other. However, tensions also appeared. It was difficult for eight men to inhabit a cell built for two. They rubbed against each other too much. They no longer had privacy. It was very difficult.

"There were different personalities among them. In time, things leveled out, they arrived at a common denominator. Trifan and Father Arsenie were born leaders. Trifan was the oldest, a mature man who was respected at Aiud. Father Arsenie, as I saw him, was a determined, intransigent Macedonian. Suffering changed him. Maxim was cerebral and of a combative nature, but around the others he calmed down, he followed the others. Mazăre was more rational, he did not have the native inclination toward mystical things as did Gafencu. Structurally, Naidim was closest to Valeriu. Shy as a girl, obedient, markedly pure of spirit.

"Gafencu burned with a spiritual yearning. Like many Bessarabians, he had something special. He was close to the Slavic spirit, with much affection and warmth. Having in his soul this Slavic component, it may have been easier for him; he had something that predisposed him toward mystical things. It was more difficult for the others, even those in his group.

"I did not believe that Gafencu, as I knew him in around 1943, would reach such spiritual heights. Although we were the same age, I considered him a child. I did not consider him to be a combative Legionnaire who would confront anything for the sake of this ideal. In the beginning, he also didn't see things clearly and he went off in many different directions. It was only with difficulty that he earned the grace that was later showered upon him. Naturally, his troubling concerns encountered the others' worries; by living together and helping each other, things worked out in the end.

"I was forced to come to some conclusions on my own. I was harsh toward others' mistakes, during my time of freedom as well as in the first years of imprisonment. Suffering made me sense the presence of God and become very forgiving. Before, I was intransigent. I spent most of my time in isolation.

"I did not understand those in Trifan's group at the beginning. But in the end, I had to admit they were right. Now, they are role models for me. The greatest joy for me was when I fell on my knees and cried for my sins. I came to understand that the greatest satisfaction a Christian can have is to be able to shed a tear. Trifan's group discovered this path one hour before the others. The others had a hostile attitude toward them, but later many came to think the way they did.

"Now that I have arrived at the threshold of death, I ask God in prayer: 'Grant me, O Lord, tears of longing for heaven! Allow me, O Lord, to have the joy of tears shed for the forgiveness of sins! Lord, grant that the lamp of love and forgiveness for others may always be lit! Amen."[68]

---

[68]Testimony given by Vasile Turtureanu to monk Moise in May 2007.

The Path of Blessedness

Weak in faith and spiritually impoverished by a lifestyle full of comforts, modern man understands only partially and with difficulty the sufferings of those who endured life in prison. Many testimonies seem unbelievable to those of us who, as a poet once said, were not with them in the prison cell and do not know the life of darkness.[69] We cannot imagine how they endured so much suffering. What is even more difficult to understand, if not beyond our comprehension, is the nostalgia felt by prisoners when they look back at the time spent in prison.

"It is impossible for someone who was not in prison to understand," Father Gheorghe Calciu tells us. "We are now free and we are very happy that we are free, but we have a kind of nostalgia for prison. And we cannot explain it to anyone else. They say we are crazy. How can you miss prison?

"Because in prison I lived the most spiritual life. I attained to spiritual heights that I am not capable of reaching in freedom. Isolated, anchored in Jesus Christ, I had a joy and an enlightenment that the world cannot offer. I cannot find the words to express precisely the feelings I

---

[69]"You were not with us in the cells
To know what is the life of darkness
In the claws of beasts, with insatiable mouths,
You do not know what is man, when he starts to howl,
Clamped by chains on his ankles."
Radu Gyr, *You Were Not With Us In The Cells*, from the volume *Last Night Jesus Entered My Cell – Poems From Behind Bars*, Ed. Elisavaros, Bucharest, 2005, pg.p. 65.

had in prison. Those that did not live this experience cannot understand how we could be happy in prison."[70]

Valeriu Gafencu lived such happiness - beyond our understanding - in spite of suffering. Virgil Ioanid remembers how, on the road between two prisons, in a police van, worn out by tuberculosis, his cheeks bright red with fever, Valeriu spoke of "the joy of suffering for Christ and of enduring, like the first martyrs, the persecution unleashed by the enemies of the faith."[71] Likewise, in a letter sent to his family, he confessed, "Today I am happy. Through Christ I love everyone."[72]

One does not easily reach such a state of blessedness. The journey full of struggle, searching, and suffering that enabled Valeriu to achieve such a state will be the subject of what follows.

By nature, generous and enthusiastic, Valeriu was idealistic from the time he was young. "Referring to my high school years, my essential thought at that time was to become a man who could add value to society. I understood this to meant a man who would play an important role in history, a man who would give something to his people. I wanted to do a lot of good in the world...."[73]

"I lived a normal life as a student. I was one of the more popular students, loved by everyone and with an

---

[70]The monks John Marler and Andrew Warmuth, *The Youth of the End Times – The Last and True Revolt,* Ed. Sophia, Bucharest, 2006, pp. 184-185. See also Father Calciu's *Interviews, Talks, and Homilies.* St. Herman of Alaska Brotherhood, 2010.

[71]Nicolae Trifoiu, *op. cit.*, pg.p. 123.

[72]Ioan Ianolide, *op. cit.*, pg.p. 235.

[73]*Ibid*, pg.p. 233.

uncommon thirst for one ideal: a new world in which love, justice, and perfect harmony would reign."[74]

Imbued with such thoughts, he was naturally attracted to the *Brotherhood of th eCross,* where he fully found his place. Very much loved by the students he eventually mentored, he bonded with them in true communion. He was then arrested and sentenced to 25 years in prison. His only offense was his heartfelt involvement in the education of the *brothers of the cross* – albeit within the ranks of a forbidden organization.

After arriving at Aiud, he lived under a harsh regime. For a long time, as he later confessed, he lived in isolation, being taken out for a walk of only an hour and a half per day. The beginning was not at all easy. "And, dear Mama," he said in a letter, "I'd like you to know that I suffered very much. During the first winter I would wake up at night and in the solitude of my cell, in cold and in hunger, I looked into the darkness and whispered quietly, so that only I would hear, but loud enough for God to hear, 'Mama, I'm cold and I'm hungry.' At the beginning it was very hard."[75]

The suffering was all the more oppressive because, believing in his innocence, he did not understand his imprisonment. "From the very beginning, I wondered why I was locked up. In my former social life, in my relationships with people, I was considered a very good person, an example of moral conduct. If I had conflict with anybody, it was for the sake of Truth."[76]

---

[74]*Ibid*, pp. 233-234.

[75]*Ibid*, pg.p. 234.

[76]*Ibid*, pg.p. 231.

In the midst of this spiritual grinding, he sought an answer in the books that were circulating in prison. "At the beginning, he studied and read very much, but soon his attention was drawn to Christianity, which appeared to him in its true light, in its spiritual intent. Valeriu dedicated himself to intense theological study, undertaking a careful examination of Orthodox spirituality. Among the books he read were the *Paterikon, The Salvation of Sinners, The Lives of the Saints, Imitation of Christ.* He read St. John Chrysostom, St. Basil the Great, St. Gregory Palamas, St. Gregory Nazianzen, St. Ephrem the Syrian, St. John Damascene. He also studied Pascal, Bulgakov, Berdyaev, Papini, as well as all the courses offered at the School of Theology. His reading concentrated especially on Holy Scripture."[77]

Spiritual books helped him to see things more deeply and to turn more toward himself. In the solitude of his cell he prayed very much, seeking to understand the meaning of suffering. After a time of tormenting unrest and struggle, through the grace of God he experienced a state of enlightenment and saw his soul filled with sin. "After a time of much uneasiness, after experiencing a great deal of pain, when the cup of suffering had filled up, there came a holy day, in June 1943, when I fell to the ground, on my knees, my head bent, my heart shattered, in a burst of tears. I prayed to God that He grant me light. At that point I had lost all faith in people. I realized perfectly well that I was in truth, but then why was I suffering? Within my zealous soul only love had remained. No one understood me.

"During this long period of weeping, I began to do prostrations. And suddenly – O Lord! How great art thou, Lord! – I saw my soul full of sins, I found within myself the

_____

[77]*Ibid*, pg.p. 43.

root of all the sins of mankind. Alas, so many sins, and the eyes of my soul, hardened by pride, had not seen them. How great is God!

"Seeing all my sins, I felt the need to shout them out loud and cast them away from me. And a deep peace, a deep wave of light and love, poured into my heart. As soon as the door opened, I left my cell and went to those who loved me and to those who hated me and to those who had most wronged me and I confessed to them openly, 'I am the most sinful man. I do not deserve the trust of even the last among men. I am blessed!'

"Everyone was astounded. Some looked at me with disdain, others with indifference. Some looked at me with a love that they themselves could not have explained. A single person said to me, 'You deserve to be kissed.' But I fled quickly back to my cell, threw my head into my pillow, and continued my weeping, thanking and glorifying God."[78]

This moment of enlightenment was a true rebirth for Valeriu. The most immediate benefit of the awareness of sins is the understanding of the meaning of suffering. "Suffering, no matter how difficult it may be, has no other meaning than the cleansing of souls thirsting for salvation."[79]

From this moment forward, Valeriu was preoccupied with the problem of sin. "In June 1943, when I experienced my first spiritual upheaval as a result of a greater awareness of sin, I realized that the more deeply I looked into myself, the more sins I discovered."[80]

---

[78]*Ibid*, pp. 231-232.

[79]*Ibid*, pg.p. 25.

[80]*Ibid*, pg.p. 229.

As a result, he began the work of spiritual cleansing. "From that moment on, I began a conscious struggle against sin."[81]

The awareness of sin to which Valeriu had attained brought about the movement from a moral approach to a spiritual one. In the *Brotherhood of the Cross*, Valeriu was trained to understand a renewal of life as based on Christian morals. Codreanu himself had considered the Legion a spiritual school to train the new man, to recreate him as a moral hero. Judged according to a Christian-Legionnaire morality, Valeriu was the epitome of a man who aspires to a renewed life: Devout, honest, studious, generous. In a word, a man of irreproachable conduct. Because the moral consciousness of such a man can find nothing reproachable within, this new man does not understand the meaning of suffering.

However, Valeriu looked at things differently after he acquired a spiritual consciousness. He realized that God's grace exacts more profound demands than those of [civil] morality. "I saw that I was a sinful man. I trembled at the thought of my sins, at the thought of my powerlessness. I realized that I, who wanted an ideal world with all my heart, am a sinner. Therefore, the first thing necessary was for me to become a pure man, a new man."[82]

The new man toward which Valeriu was now striving required a transformation much deeper than that of the moral hero, as was typically understood in Legionnairism. This was the spiritual man who, renewing himself through repentance, cleansed the robe of baptism of the filth of sin.

---

[81]*Ibid*, pg.p. 232.

[82]*Ibid*, pg.p. 230.

Although this struggle exceeded the demands of morality, this does not mean that the training Valeriu received in the *Brotherhood of the Cross* was of no use to him. It was a stage that formed his character, protected him from sin, and developed the spirit of sacrifice and communion. Many young people who were trained in this way made impressive sacrifices in prison, although they did not attain to the same level of spiritual awareness as Valeriu. All of these sacrifices had value.

The spiritual awareness to which Valeriu had now attained did not lead him to disavow what he had received in his training, but rather led him to a deeper and more spiritually profound understanding of Legionnairism. Therefore, he did not deny his past. Later, at Târgu-Ocna, in a discussion with Ion Popescu, he said, "I entered prison as a Legionnaire. I can't deny this before the administration and say that I no longer am one, because it was as a Legionnaire that I was convicted. But spiritually speaking, I have gone beyond the threshold from which Legionnaires normally understand things. This does not mean that I am breaking my ties with them, but rather that I am no longer interested in politics, only in spiritual life. But to each his own. First and foremost, I think the Legionnaire movement has to have a nucleus in its midst, a spiritual community that lives a lofty spiritual life which will inspire others to live as Christians."[83]

At Aiud, where most prisoners understood faith from a moral level, Valeriu was the cause of much perplexity. "Valeriu was shocking because of his awareness of sin, which he confessed with humility both personally and collectively, at a time in which we, although we were Christians, did not yet have a true spiritual life.

---

[83]Testimony given by Ion Popescu to monk Moise, April 2005.

Vainglory was hiding in us under the secret mantle of 'honor,' and it was a hard struggle until our so-called 'dignity' and 'honor' were spiritually cleansed."[84]

Striving to cleanse his soul, Valeriu spent much time in prayer. "He often fell with his face to the ground and cried, asking for mercy, help, heavenly enlightenment. He gradually replaced study with prayer. At night he read the Paraklesis to the Mother of God; during the day, he read various akathists. He attended services regularly, humbly confessed his sins, and received Communion with joy. He respected the priests although he had not yet found a spiritual father who could understand the dimensions of his soul. He liked to sing prayers and psalms. He did many prostrations, in accordance with his physical condition. The silence was complete, the isolation from the world almost total. In other words, ideal conditions for spiritual activity.

"Love caused him to pour out his heart to his friends at a spiritual level that was both deep and sincere. He strove to perfect the virtues within himself, a process that he would bring to completion over the coming years. He always sought the advice of those who were of like mind and together they struggled to cleanse themselves spiritually.

"From day to day he created order in his soul, he became a new person, he accustomed himself to life in the Spirit in accordance with Christian teaching. His progress was harmonious, seeking to realize the new man. Through the grace of God, he went down the path of the most authentic Orthodox spirituality.

"Valeriu was in isolation under solitary confinement until 1943, living within a severe regime, without books,

---

[84]Ioan Ianolide, *op. cit.*, pp. 43-44.

without contact with family, with an inadequate supply of food. Here he dedicated himself completely to the prayer of the heart, continuously repeating, 'Lord Jesus Christ, Son of God, have mercy on me, a sinner.' His orientation being clear, he built a good foundation, such that this time in his life was of significant spiritual benefit.

"The first years had been a time of searching, the years that followed a time of tears and repentance. But now there came a time of conversation with God, living with God, and union with God on the path of prayer. The guidebook at his disposal was that small book by an anonymous author, *The Way of a Pilgrim*.

"All other concerns had disappeared, to be replaced by prayer. Along with the discovery of the internal light, along with spiritual order, along with the light of grace, prayer made manifest to him all the problems which had preoccupied him. Now they were not a discovery, but a gift."[85]

In letters addressed to his family, Valeriu spoke of his struggle with sin and of the serenity that was settling into his soul little by little. "I fight against sin. The more deeply I delve into myself, the more new sins I find. But with God's help I overcome them. I have acquired a permanent spiritual serenity and I am content with the gifts that God gives me, for they are priceless. I confess to you the same thing again: I am experiencing a state of blessedness, I taste it especially in tears and in pain. There I find it to be sweeter, deeper. I live with the awareness that I am a sinful man. I live in God, the Source of all the joys of life. (…) I tell you truly, I am blessed. I understand and forgive everything. If anyone offends me personally, I forgive him.

---

[85]*Ibid*, pg.p. 47.

"The Mother of God fulfills my prayers. I live as if propelled by true waves of love which overwhelm my whole being. I am permeated by the awareness of my nothingness on earth. I fall on my knees before the icon, imploring mercy, help, and love for myself and for all those I know, my parents, relatives, friends, benefactors, enemies. (…) I am as you know me. I keep quiet and meditate for hours and days on end. I send my thoughts far away, and when I wake up to reality, I smile. I sing and I pray. I am spiritually joyful. Daily life is monotonous. My interior life is simple, lively, full and great, with longings and dreams that I experience and feel vividly in my soul."[86]

"In that most secret corner of my heart I have found the inexhaustible spring of life, which is love. I realized that I've disregarded this gift. I said then, 'I have sinned!' In the soil of my sins, I had buried the most precious things that God had sown in me. For the spurning of love, that holy gift, I feel responsible for all the sins of my fellow men, at all times and in all places. But I am a blessed man, the most blessed man! I feel the love of God at every step, I feel His protection and care for me. I no longer want to live for myself, but for love, and with the grace of God to contribute to everyone's happiness. May I save my own soul through the salvation of my fellow men. Ah! How blessed I am! How can man, this little creature, endure such happiness?"[87]

---

[86]*Ibid*, pp. 226-227.

[87]*Ibid*, pg.p. 229.

Life in the Lavra of Aiud

Built during the time when Transylvania was part of the Austro-Hungarian empire, the prison at Aiud was the largest prison in Romania between the two world wars. Beginning with November 1942, several thousand Legionnaires tried by the Antonescu regime were sent to this prison. They were all gathered together at Aiud for one reason: at the command of Marshal Antonescu, the prison's administration intended to cut them off from the Legionnaire movement and to send them to the Soviet front so as to "rehabilitate" them.[88]

It was with this goal in mind that in March 1943 the prison commander, Major Munteanu, a sworn enemy of the Legionnaires, began to implement severe measures: isolation of the prisoners, suspension of the right to receive packages and guests, shutters on the windows, a decline in the quality of the food, and corporal punishment for nonexistent infractions of rules.

In the prison courtyard, Munteanu gave a speech promising freedom to the Legionnaires on the condition that they go to the battle front for rehabilitation. The speech ended with the ominous question, "Is there anyone here who does not want to go to the front?" In the silence that followed, Traian Trifan stepped forward and parted the waters, showing that he did not accept being subjected to pressures and threats. "Traian Trifan holds the rank of captain and serves his country as a soldier, but the Legionnaire commander Traian Trifan

---

[88] The Legionnaires who accepted this assignment were grouped into special battalions and were sent to the foremost ranks of the Soviet front, along with the order that they be given the most difficult missions, those in which death was virtually certain.

has no reason to be rehabilitated in the eyes of anyone."[89] Most of the prisoners followed his example.

In June 1943, the Legionnaires were called to the administrative office of the prison to sign an [already-written] request to be sent to the front for rehabilitation and an [equally contrived] declaration of disavowal of the Legionnaire movement.

"Valeriu and a few others," Ianolide remembers, "said that they had no need for rehabilitation beyond the demands of their own conscience. We wanted to fight against Communism. We were striving to unite the country, but not as prisoners, not as men found guilty. We did not have anything to 'rehabilitate' in our souls and therefore we turned down the front.

"We also refused disavowal of the Legionnaires, but not because we had not made mistakes from which we needed to disassociate ourselves, but rather because we were fully aware of our errors without having them pointed out to us by a political elite whose representative was a monster like Major Munteanu."[90]

As a result, Valeriu's response was very firm. "I am what I am. I have nothing from which to disassociate myself. I believe in the ultimate victory of truth and goodness."[91]

The fact that he refused to break his ties with the Legionnaire movement did not mean that Valeriu necessarily shared all the opinions of the other Legionnaires. "After the 'rehabilitation' episode, Valeriu adopted an equally noble attitude in a different

---

[89]Virgil Maxim, *op. cit.*, pg.p. 87.

[90]Ioan Ianolide, *op. cit.*, pg.p.44.

[91]Nicolae Trifoiu, *op. cit.*, pg.p. 187

situation: Seeing that political struggles put an emphasis on punishment and revenge, he asserted that revenge belongs to God. No one has the right to administer justice on his own. A Christian forgives, a Christian places himself on the firmament of love, the only virtue that brings peace, the only approach that overcomes and is not overcome.

"Powerful voices rose up against this point of view and Valeriu, in his attempts to justify himself, found himself increasingly alone. Nevertheless, he remained unshaken in his convictions; in time, many came to agree with him."[92]

As a result of their refusal to disassociate themselves from the movement, several hundred prisoners were isolated in Zarcă, crowded into cells measuring only 4 x 2 meters, exposed to harsh conditions, fed inadequate food. There were no beds and they slept on the floor with only their ragged clothes on their backs. Many became sick in these conditions. This continued until the summer of 1944.

After August 23, the newly-installed regime issued a decree freeing all political prisoners except the Legionnaires. The war front was approaching in September, so the prisoners were evacuated on foot to Alba Iulia. The journey was made in a single day, in difficult conditions; the prisoners were weakened physically, exhausted by heat and thirst. In October, they returned to Aiud.

Since confusion reigned in the country and the Communists assumed power only gradually, life at Aiud was less harsh for a time. The prisoners enjoyed a certain freedom, moving about unrestricted within the

---

[92]Ioan Ianolide, *op. cit.*, pg.p. 46.

prison. They were able to keep in contact with each other, going from one cell to another, from one floor to another, even going to other buildings within the prison without having to give account to prison officials.

Apart from the Holy Scripture, other theological writings were available and were a source of real spiritual nourishment for the prisoners.

According to Virgil Maxim, those gathered around Trifan made use of this time of lesser restrictions to strengthen themselves spiritually.

"In order to establish a program of study, meditation, and prayer, we drew up a schedule of meeting times. Instead of being locked by the guards, we constructed our own interior bolts. When a door was locked, that was an indication that the lamp of the heart was lit and was burning for Christ. You had to return at the day and hour indicated on the door.[93]

"It started to get cold in the cells because the radiators were not emitting heat. We decided to organize ourselves so that several of us would stay together in the same cell, the warmth of our breath softening the harshness of the cold. In the winter of 1944-1945, I stayed with Anghel Papacioc, Father Vasile Serghie, and Valeriu Gafencu; Marin Naidim stayed with Trifan, Marian and Ion Schiau; Nicu Mazăre stayed with Iulian Bălan, Petru Foti, and Avram Sebastian.[94]

"During the winter, under obedience to Father Vasile, Serghie, Valeriu and I read very much. I studied *Dogmatics* and *Apologetics*, *Biblical Archaeology*, *Symbolics*, *Mystics*, *Ascetics* thoroughly…. Anghel Papacioc combined his program of study with hours of prayer,

---

[93]Virgil Maxim, *op. cit.*, pg.p. 106.

[94]*Ibid*, pg.p. 108.

meditation, and exegetical discussions. I have never felt as fulfilled as I did at that time.

"Father Vasile Serghie, a graduate of the School of Theology at Cernăuți, was a man who vividly experienced the truths of Christian life. All of his actions reflected an unusual seriousness of purpose. Life for him was 'Christic time,' not something governed by chance or a series of events from which one does not know what to choose. Along with Anghel Papacioc, who had an uncommon zeal for a virtuous, pure, and holy life and was a fervent advocate of hesychastic prayer, he was a source of light and inspiration for us as we travelled on our paths of integration into the body of Christ.

"Valeriu Gafencu, as someone inspired directly by God, did not need to be guided by Father Serghie, because holiness sprang up from his soul as though its roots were in his very being. He submitted, however, in complete obedience to the program of study, exegesis, prayer, and the exercise of moral self-control. He was like a big brother: I tried to hold onto his coattails along the road of knowledge and experience of Christ.

"From time to time, once a week or once a month, knowing from the counsels of the Holy Fathers that true humility requires one to reveal one's thoughts to a spiritual father rather than directing oneself spiritually, we would gather in Trifan's cell or in our own. Sometimes all of us were present, other times only a few; here we revealed our perplexities to each other and debated the problems that had given rise to questions of conscience in light of the Holy Fathers and the canonical decisions of the Church. We raised our minds to the level of divine meditation. We walked down the road of holiness, guided by the light of grace, by '*the wise men of God, who served not the creature, but rather the Creator.*' The

Paterikon, our fundamental guidebook, enabled us to intuitively understand how to put into practice eternal truths, saving our strength for the acquisition of virtue."[95]

"In the spiritual program, apart from prayer, study, meditation, and exegetical conversations, one day a week was reserved for complete silence to create a space for a deep and private encounter with God. Later, in confession, we would scrupulously analyze all the moments and actions of our lives, deepening our confession even further and trying to find solutions of healing, correction, or reconciliation, as was the case."[96]

"In March, when the weather started to get warmer, in order to carry out a spiritual experiment we decided to arrange ourselves so that each of us would have his own cell: The experiment was to intensify the practice of hesychastic prayer and to have as much time as possible to study the patristic literature we had at our disposal. With Father Serghie's blessing, each of us organized his own priorities, subject to the control of periodic meetings among all of us.

"Father Vasile Serghie completed his prison sentence and was released at the end of April, leaving us without a divinely-inspired teacher. The other Legionnaire priests, although they were models of Christian living, were mainly preoccupied with the maintenance of spiritual life at the level of enduring suffering and the practice of prayer. Trifan and Anghel Papacioc became the supervisors who monitored our spiritual lives. We also consulted those among us who had theological training: Straja – a future priest, Radu

---

[95]*Ibid*, pg.p. 110.

[96]*Ibid*, pg.p. 115.

Leonte, the priests Ion Marinescu and Ion Florea, Traian Belu, the deacon Grebenea."[97]

"We spent the summer of 1945 in prison, in a state of semi-freedom, moving freely between the workshops and the cells. Trifan was of the opinion that we should experiment with the lifestyle of a monastic community and occupy ourselves with weaving baskets, a handiwork that could be done while we practiced prayer of the heart."[98]

These prisoners who were monks at heart, clothed the conditions of prison life in monastic garb.

"Prison created special conditions for you," says Virgil Maxim. "Your cell became a sanctuary of prayer, of nourishment, an opportunity for ascesis, solitude, renunciation of material goods and joys of life, an opportunity to live as paupers, in purity and chastity. The chronic uncertainty of our situation enabled us to put our trust in the will and providence of God. Obedience requires a superior – a father confessor – to whom one submits, and God also offered us this gift through the presence of our priests. We were also obedient to the program imposed by worldly authority, as an act of divine pedagogy, in which your will enters consciously into submission to the divine will.

"Is this not the way of a monk? Renunciation of the world, taking up the cross, and acceptance of the will of God?"[99]

Valeriu established a special spiritual connection with three members of this "community" of ascetics.

---

[97]*Ibid*, pg.p. 117.

[98]*Ibid*, pg.p. 119.

[99]*Ibid*, pg.p. 109.

"They were in the same cell for a while and they confessed their sins to one another. They opened their souls to each other. They struggled together. They prayed together. They held all things in common.

"This restricted community was ideal, but not without temptations and frictions. Their souls were troubled by subtle forms of pride and envy. Their attempts to resolve their differences through group confession sometimes rendered good results, but at other times inflamed their tempers. They felt the need of an experienced counselor, someone with authority.

"They also understood that no matter how great the desire for communion, every man is unique, every man has his own life, his own evolution, his own specific traits that cannot be confused with those of another but only communicated – even communicated according to certain guidelines imposed by the human personality.

"In spite of all the temptations, love and good intentions never disappeared from among us. We learned the practice of Christian spirituality, for spiritual teaching and direction is an art or, if you will, a science.

"Tensions appeared out of nowhere, perhaps from a bad thought. I came to understand that not every bad thought is a sin; only those that the mind succumbs to and that then turn into passions. It can happen that the temptation aroused by a bad thought can endure for a long time and yet never be fully succumbed to. In this case, it is not a sin and does not need to be confessed, unless perhaps this confession serves to alleviate the unseen war with evil spirits.

"Gluttony was one of the temptations – although not the most difficult to overcome – and confession in common worked well against it. Laziness sometimes disturbed our peace, but as soon as we sounded the alarm against it, it disappeared as if by miracle.

"There are those who might imagine that we experienced certain physical temptations, but they did not exist among us. But each of us struggled individually, a struggle in which mutual help was of great benefit. We learned that if you do not let your mind follow the desires of the body, the body submits to the spirit. And a restrained body is a great help toward spiritual progress. (…)

"Virtues that seemed firmly established in the soul when we were living in solitude proved fragile in the company of others. It often happened that we felt an upsurge of anger or irritation if someone said something uncalled for, if someone spoke too much; even for a rash gesture, for an exaggerated wish.

"Our little community was a school of perfection. We learned that every passion can be replaced by a virtue, and in doing this, it is God who acts within us. Our internal horizons broadened. We learned to love each other, to be tolerant with each other, to be patient with each other, to see ourselves within the framework of a broader human understanding and, not allowing ourselves to stumble, we ran toward the ultimate goal of the glory of God.

"In this manner, we achieved self-denial, the death of the ego. We forced ourselves to be obedient to each other, to submit to each other in the same way as we submitted to God. Satan tempted each one of us, but the Holy Spirit also worked within us and was victorious. (…)

"In fact, our communion was, on the one hand, an encounter between us and, on the other hand, an encounter between us and God. We ran toward the same archetype-Christ and each one of us rounded off his personality such that we realized unity in diversity. The spiritual force behind this struggle was always love. We entrusted ourselves to God, we offered ourselves to Him, and we lived through Him and in Him.

"In most instances, Valeriu was the one who was not deceived, he was the first to see the light, he burned like a flame in our midst – and this was so simply by virtue of our circumstances, because nothing had been established among us in the sense of a specific hierarchy.

"Valeriu was the man in whom I saw Christ dwelling. Thanks to him we were successful in our efforts. Thanks to him I believe we were protected by God."[100]

---

[100]Ioan Ianolide, *op. cit.*, pp 58-60.

The Work Camp at Galda de Jos

From 1946 to 1948 Trifan's group, along with other prisoners, found themselves in the work camp at Galda de Jos. Virgil Maxim, who worked alongside them, describes conditions there:

"Around March 25, they started sending us to the work camps in Unirea near Ocna Mureş, to Ciuguzel on the hills near Blaj, and to Galda de Jos near Teiuş. The prisoner-workers formed spontaneous friendships according to spiritual affinities, already-existing friendships, or by virtue of the logistics of projects underway in the work camps. The work camps were also called colonies. Unirea was populated with prisoners from a peasant or agricultural background. Prisoners sent to Ciuguzel tended to be those who were from hilly regions, wine-growers and fruit farmers, as well as those who were spiritually bound to them even though less experienced with this particular work, and the more sickly prisoners who were being cared for by the other prisoners. Galda, where I was sent, was a work camp that required a varied work product, and so the prisoners assigned here were skilled in several areas.

"In 3 or 4 days, roughly 100 - 150 men were sent to work in each colony. About 100 men remained in the prison, some of them doing odd maintenance work, while others simply did not want to go or, for personal reasons, were unable to go."[101]

"At the beginning of May, I left with the last group scheduled for Galda: Traian Trifan, Marian Traian, Anghel Papacioc, Ion Schiau, Valeriu Gafencu,

---

[101]Virgil Maxim, *op. cit.*, pg.p. 129.

Gheorghe Dragon, Victor Ţâru, Vasile Jacotă, Nicolae Mazăre, Constantin Pascu, Iulian Bălan, Marin Naidim, Ion Iordache, Sandu Ştefanescu, Andrei Popescu, and Costică Dumitrescu.

"We wrote our families and they sent money or care packages, or they made plans to come and visit. From the get-go we formed a community similar to those in the early Christian times. We shared everything. It was not a Communist, but rather a Christian community. The colony functioned like a Legionnaire work camp. Each member was selected for a team based on his skills and aptitudes. In order not to waste our energy – and we did not have much energy – we put together teams that worked continuously in the local villages, hoeing corn, harvesting, working in vineyards, cutting hay, lumbering. We worked for a share of the harvest, were paid in material goods, and were thereby assured of an ample supply of potatoes, beans, fats, and even meat. [...]

"When the weather did not permit work outdoors, we transformed the colony into a monastery, with a program of prayer, study, meditation, and spiritual conversation. Father Arsenie Boca of Sâmbătă-Făgăraş Monastery gifted us the first three volumes of the *Philokalia*, spiritual nourishment that enlightened our souls with the teachings of the Holy Fathers of the Church."[102]

In the autumn of 1947, some thirty-six or so prisoners were temporarily transferred to the colony at Unirea. An incident occurred here on account of being forced to work on a Sunday.

---

[102]*Ibid*, pp. 133-134.

"We mowed the hay with the intention of gathering it the following week. On Sunday, those of us who had arrived from Galda were getting ready to attend church services in the village. Two of the guards stopped us and told us to go and gather the hay. We reminded the guards of our right not to work on Sunday. They got angry and began to threaten us and insult us. They took out their pistols and accused us of starting a rebellion in the colony. Valeriu Gafencu answered them:

"'Put your pistols away! We'll go to work! But know that God will not help you!'

"We took up our pitchforks and rakes and set out, a distance of 3 kilometers to the field. We got there at 9 in the morning. We started gathering hay and piling it up into haystacks. The sound of bells floated through the air, announcing the beginning of the Liturgy. We stopped working for a moment and said the *Our Father* and *Hail Mary*. Trifan, Marian, and Gafencu were the last to get up from kneeling. There was still a lot of hay to gather, but we needed to take a break anyway because it was getting close to lunchtime. Cooks usually brought food out to the field in kettles. In order to finish quicker, we didn't break for lunch. We even forgot about the meal, which wasn't brought to us that day anyway.

"We finished at around 3 or 4 o'clock in the afternoon. Only then did we sit down and rest a little. From the top of a hill a man, a guard, approached us. He told us to wait for three big trucks and seven wagons in which to load the hay before evening.

"A breeze was blowing dandelion wisps in the air, along with dried leaves from the nearby cornfields. The sky clouded over; the wind picked up, turning into a storm, and tore the tops off of the haystacks. The wind became more forceful and blew away all the haystacks, carrying them like plucked birds over the peaks of the hills. In less than a quarter of an hour, there was not one piece of hay left on the ground and a fine rain began to mist. It was getting dark and lightning was slashing the sky, accompanied by violent thunder. The guards looked at us desperately, as if it were up to us to rescue the situation. We lined up and set off for the colony without being ordered to do this. The guards followed closely behind us. Then the rain stopped. When we arrived at the colony, it was already dark. The trucks and wagons were still on colony grounds, waiting [to depart for the hay fields]. The guards told the deputy what happened out on the field.

"A report was drawn up stating that, because of the storm, the gathering of the hay had been disrupted. We were asked to provide confirmation and we did so, specifying that this calamity had taken place on a Sunday, with no additional commentary."[103]

"In the winter of 1947- 48, we were feeling more secure since we had sufficient provisions necessary to ensure survival, so our time in the colony was marked by intense spiritual activity. We read many writings of the great Orthodox theologians as well as those of Western theologians, both old and new. But we studied the *Philokalia* and the *Paterikon* constantly. At Aiud, under the guidance of Father Serghie, everyone had pored over Father Stăniloae's work *Jesus Christ and the Restoration of man,* the *Hristoitia* by Nicodemus the Athonite, and many other works. At least once a week, Trifan was besieged by younger prisoners to help them deepen their understanding of the words of the Holy Fathers.

---

[103]*Ibid*, pg.p. 137.

"We started to learn Scripture by heart, especially the *New Testament*, and we came to realize that this was the way to arrive at a more thorough understanding of it. The mind enlightens the soul with the meaning of the divine word, which not only no longer seems difficult to retain and, but becomes the soul's own property, thus giving sense and meaning to other kinds of knowledge and becoming permanent spiritual nourishment for the mind and soul."[104]

The testimony of Ioan Ianolide will now complete this description of spiritual life at Galda. He gives an account of several events that occurred in connection with Valeriu during his time in the work camp.

"Valeriu worked and prayed. Worked and sang. Worked and glorified God. He felt spiritually bound to a girl he loved and now he had the opportunity to write to her. By this time, the girl had gotten engaged and was soon to be married. His suffering was deep, but he pulled himself out of it by deciding to become a monk.

"Up until this time, he had prepared himself for secular life, even though he had acquired much learning from the Holy Fathers. From this point on, however, he betrothed himself to Christ so as to serve God completely. The immense joy [following this decision] overcame the pain stemming from the separation with the girl. His entire life, he would respect this girl, understanding her. One can see here how thin the line is between a man and a monk.

"I can see Valeriu at Galda even now, on the hills at evening, singing, collecting flowers, uniting the blue of his eyes with the blue of the heavens. I see him night and day on his knees in the chapel, praying in a state of

---

[104]*Ibid,* pg.p. 170.

rapture, with his hands clasped together like a child and his eyes shining with joy. I see him giving his bread to someone weaker than he. I see him playing with children and trying to be like them. I see him immersed in himself, preparing for confession. I see him beaming with joy after receiving Communion. I hear him speaking enthusiastically to all those who were seeking the word of God. I see him wearing himself out, striving to fulfill the quota. I hear him singing carols, church hymns, or songs that he wrote himself. He was full of longing for holy things. There was something angelic within him, something preternatural. He was the most beautiful man I have ever met.

"For some, however, he was a stumbling block.

"One night, as he was sleeping outside, a thief who had escaped from Aiud attempted to rob Valeriu even though he was in rags and tatters. Valeriu woke up, asked him what he wanted, then took him by the hand - like one does a child - and brought him to the boss. In his other hand, the thief had a sharp knife.

"'What are you doing with that knife?' asked the boss.

"'I intended to use it to defend myself in case I got caught.'

"'But, you were caught and you did not use it. Why not?'

"The thief replied that he forgot about the knife and he did not know what overcame him in those moments.

"Another time, Valeriu was standing guard in a wooden watchtower in the vineyard when he was attacked by some evildoers, who shot at him from a short distance away. The bullets, however, passed by him, leaving no mark; the hour of his death had not yet come.

"In 1948, a Soviet agent came to the work camp to bring Valeriu back to the USSR since, having been born in Bessarabia, he was considered a Soviet citizen. [105] Valeriu, however, adamantly refused.

"'You will be free [in the Soviet Union],' the agent told him.

"'My freedom is in my soul!'

"'You will be able to continue your studies.'

"'I will continue to study [regardless of where I am], if that is God's wish!'

"'In our country, the church is free [from the influence and control of the state].'

"'The church is in the souls of men!'

"'But here you will remain in prison!'

"'[It is] the prison of my soul that frightens me!'

"'So you don't consider yourself a Soviet citizen?'

"'I am a Romanian citizen and I wish to remain in Romania.'

"'Soon Romania will belong to the Soviets!'

---

[105] There are different variants of this event. Based on information from Marin Naidim, Nicolae Trifoiu tells of Valeriu being taken to Vacaresti in the spring of 1945, where he appeared before the commission on repatriation. On the way, thanks to the goodwill of the guard escorting him, they made a side trip to Sâmbăta de Sus Monastery to visit Father Arsenie Boca. Virgil Maxim also speaks of a visit Valeriu made to Father Arsenie Boca, but places it in a different context. Regarding Valeriu's repatriation, Virgil Maxim states that "Valeriu was called before the commission," without specifying whether the commission came to Galda or Valeriu was taken to Bucharest. Such differences among writers appear in descriptions of other situations as well; considering the time lag between the events themselves and the time they were recorded, the differences seem quite normal.

"'The future belongs to God!'

"'So you will stay here?'

"'Yes.'

"Later, the propagandist walked up to him and said, 'I admire your intelligence, but I can only weep for you. You must understand that you are defeated and you will not escape. If you resist, you will be crushed. We also resisted and today we are in chains, like bears. You believe in God. I would also like to have a God with which to confront prison and death, but my soul is empty, my mind is full of slogans, and I totally exhaust my strength working for the Communist cause.

"'We don't stand a chance. Hitler appeared before us as a savior, but he was defeated. All those who supported Communism – as you Romanians also did– are much more to blame for what will happen than we, who were born in the USSR, are! I have confidence in a man like you. I admire you. I think I understand you and that makes me even more unhappy. I also regret that I do not know Christianity. But I assure you that you will stay in Romania!'

"'This is a great moment in my life,' responded Valeriu. 'You have given me wings, for you have a soul with a remarkably strong faith. Please accept this cross from me.'

"And Valeriu took the cross from his neck and gave it to the Russian, who was clearly moved. So it happened that Valeriu remained in Romania."

At the beginning of May 1948, the Galda prisoners were sent to Aiud. Here, they found the churches defiled and the furniture [inside the churches] destroyed. A few days later, they found locks on the church doors. The regime of freedom they had enjoyed until that time had changed. They were subjected to a detailed search; every book, every sheet of paper, every pencil was taken from them. The search was particularly directed toward Holy Scripture and religious books.

The prisoners were required to work in the two sections of the prison's factory: mechanics and woodwork. But a short time later, changes were made. At the end of May, following an order from Bucharest, there was a general triage of political prisoners, [grouping them based on their age at the time of their arrest]. Adolescent prisoners were sent to Târgşor, university students to Piteşti, former civil officers to Sighet, laborers to Gherla, Legionnaires – apart from those in the above categories – to Aiud.

Valeriu, a university student at the time of his arrest, was sent to Piteşti.

From the Testimony of Marin Naidim

Marin Naidim was sentenced to prison at the same time as Virgil Maxim. He arrived at Aiud in 1942. His spiritual character was similar to that of Valeriu, and they soon became good friends.

"Valeriu was an enthusiastic sort. He was one of those people about whom it was frequently said that he walked around with his head in the clouds. He did not have a practical nature. I never saw him sewing or knitting, and he did not know how to wash his clothes, which usually fell apart in rags. He was very much preoccupied with spiritual concerns and he was very vigilant with himself, [with his thoughts and actions] he had a watchful spirit. He had the soul of a poet. Some thinkers believe that on the ladder of perfection, poets occupy the lowest rung, followed by heroes, prophets, and finally saints. I read this somewhere – Iovan Ducici – and I think it is true. Poets that fulfill their vocation as they should beautify life and elevate man. Valeriu even wrote poetry. He wrote in blank verse but also in classical form.

"Valeriu showed us the path that leads to salvation; this [could only be] Christian love. Love was a byword for him; he said it in all circumstances, whether verbally or when writing. He used it instead of hello and good-bye.

"When he arrived in prison, he was wearing a suit made out of some kind of English fabric. It looked good on him, but he did not like wearing stylish clothes and tried to get rid of them.

"While in the colony at Galda, one day he happened to run into a poor man; afterward, he returned to the colony without his clothes. When I asked him what happened to his clothes, he replied quoting the Paterikon: 'I sent them on ahead.' In other words, he gave them as alms in order to find them in heaven when he got there. I scolded him and accused him of exercising poor judgment because his family was in need. 'It would have been better to have given your clothes to one of your sisters so she could make you a jacket.' He remained convinced that he had done something good, saying that God took care of his family.

"Around this same time, a gypsy woman came up to him and asked him for a match. He put his hand in his pocket and promised that he would give her all the coins he had if she would throw away her cigarettes and crush them under her feet. The woman did as he requested and took the money. He realized that she would only use the money to buy more cigarettes. Still, he was satisfied that he had tried to prevent evil, that he had given the woman something to think about, namely that smoking is a sin.

"Those imprisoned at Aiud speak of the years in which prison rules were more or less followed. Until 1948, we were allowed fresh air outdoors, about an hour per day, after which, little by little, the time was reduced to 10 - 15 minutes per day, and later on, this was reduced to no time out of doors for days. In the courtyard of the prison, there was a barren flower bed. There was grass growing, but no one took care of that either. In the middle of the flower bed bed, there was a troiţa [106] crafted and placed there by prisoners who came before us. One night, it disappeared. The Communist guards or prisoners had broken it and took it away. The flower bed was left with neither flowers nor the cross. One day, Valeriu returned from a walk around the flower bed and brought back a clump of grass along with a daffodil and some shepherd's purse. He

---

[106] *Troiţa* - a large, elaborately engraved wooden cross. (Translator's note)

showed them to me with a radiant face and said, 'Look what beautiful flowers I brought!' He saw beauty even where there was none. Or maybe there was, but we didn't see it. He had eyes to see it. Nature is indeed beautiful, but you must be gifted with special antennae in order to pick up on the hidden mysteries of creation. Valeriu had this capacity to perceive the beauty of nature because he loved nature, and nature reveals itself only to those who love it sincerely.

"In the colony at Galda, he would get up before dawn on Sunday and go out on the field to gather flowers. He would come back with his legs wet from the morning dew and his arms full of flowers. He brought them to the church. He encouraged me to do the same. I myself had gathered some field poppies, but I felt somewhat embarrassed to walk through the village with my arms full of flowers. Valeriu did not. He did this very naturally, he didn't feel any discomfort, he did not feel silly. He, himself, was an element of nature. He was part of the picture.

"He was a kind of incorrigible dreamer. A kind of Don Quixote. I often heard him reading a paradox from Cervantes, 'I am running through the prisons toward liberty.' The verses referring to the death of Don Quixote suited him very well: 'But I, close to death, beside an old candle / Will hear Sancho crying as well as the priest / How could a dream so big fit / In a body so frail and weak as that of Don Quixote?'

"He sang. He often hummed Schubert's Serenade or various religious hymns - *The River of Babylon, God is With Us, Lord of Powers*, etc. He even improvised his own melodies, but they were always in minor key. I never heard him sing worldly songs. He did not seem to be a part of this world.

"He had read much in his life, but now - as much as he was able to read in Aiud until 1948 - he read only one book, the Bible, and other books related to it: the *Philokalia*, the *Paterikon*, *Imitation of Christ*. And he prayed. In the colony, he would go to the ruins of an old abandoned church on top of a hill, out in a field– it had no roof, it was exposed to rain and bad weather – and he prayed there.

"When family would come visit, he would always bring up issues of faith, trying to convince everyone of the importance of salvation. He told me that even if we do not succeed in changing the world, at least we can stir up interest, we can make it so that people no longer feel right when they do something bad, we can create tension, we can raise questions so as to make people change their ways.

"He tried very hard to increase people's awareness of sin because there were many who considered fornication, theft, and crime to be the only sins. They didn't consider themselves to be sinners because they were not guilty of these and so accorded other sins no importance. They did not recognize that there are still other sins, some of them even more serious, such as pride. 'God sets Himself up against the proud and grants grace to the humble.' The Lord deprives the proud man of His grace; without Him, he comes to realize that he can do nothing; then he cries out to God. From Valeriu I acquired the habit of confiding everything I had on my conscience in a brotherly manner. We practiced brotherly confession. 'Confess your sins to one another.' Taking his advice, in this way I cultivated moral courage."[107]

[107]Nicolae Trifoiu, *op. cit.*, pp. 82-85

Valeriu Gafencu: A Light!

We will bring closure to our description of Valeriu's life at Aiud with excerpts from Virgil Maxim's testimony addressed to the Commission for Canonization of the Holy Synod entitled *Valeriu Gafencu: a Light!*, followed by the poem *Burnt Offering*.

"God bestowed upon him the grace of beauty. Physically, he seemed like an archangel, at times carrying the fiery sword of the divine word, at other times carrying the lily of purification, full of mysterious perfume. Morally, he was beyond reproach, uniting humility with the tenacity of his decisions. Spiritually, he was always transfigured, almost continuously in a state of ecstasy. It was impossible to tell whether something he said was inspired by the Spirit or whether the Spirit was speaking through him. His life was a flight toward heights that one could follow only with difficulty.

"When we were together with Father Serghie Vasile, under whose direction we practiced hesychastic prayer, Valeriu emitted warmth of an intensity that was difficult to understand and to express. Words were inadequate to convey the reality. He had a divine gift that placed him beyond my possibilities of understanding.

"I was young, a beginner on my spiritual journey, and many times I felt I was about to go crazy. Father Vasile Serghie loved me very much and gauged my spiritual state like a barometer. With an exceptional pedagogic tactfulness, he built a connecting bridge between the two stages of spiritual life, mine and Valeriu's, aware of the need to lower the hurdle to a level complementary to my capacity for spiritual experience, both interior and exterior.

"In common prayer I felt like a chick that had fallen from the nest, trembling underneath wings barely powdered with the dust of faith, while I felt Valeriu to be an eagle soaring high, pulling me along.

"Valeriu was not a conformist. He broke conventions with spiritual boldness, without sacrificing truth for personal whims, which would be thereby making himself guilty of breaking canonical decisions. In the freedom of his spirit, everything was naturally included in the archetypal pattern of Christ, God, and man. This direct ascent to Christ, like an entry into your own house where the laws and rules regarding behavior and appearance excuse you of all formalities, seemed to be defiant toward God. For this reason, very few among those who knew him were able to understand him in the beginning.

"Later on, when God granted me the joy of deepening my spiritual life, I understood that you cannot judge at a worldly or even a religious level great spiritual men through whom and in whom [God's] special graces work. You can come to understand only when you, yourself, begin to partake of the understanding that these other souls have arrived at, little by little, thirsting for unconditional integration into Christ, with Christ leading you on the same path but at your own pace.

"Valeriu had this spiritual freedom of which the Holy Apostle Paul speaks wonderfully, a freedom of no longer judging yourself in what you do but in letting Christ judge you, a stage at which you yourself do not toil, but in which grace works in you and through you.

"His presence in any meeting among those of us who were spiritually close – who were called 'mystics' by some in a positive sense but by others sarcastically – as well as among those less initiated into a spiritual life was a cause of joy and respect, but sometimes of anxiety and fear.

"The joy came from those things which Valeriu uttered, beyond the tumult of daily problems. His words removed you from the present earthly time and made you capable of overlooking human misery, sublimating suffering and accepting it as a saving gift. Respect came for the beauty of truths expressed at a level that each of us could understand. Each of us was able to partake from the being of Christ that part that was the sweetest, the most suitable. [There was] fear of that which is holy. We had a holy fear stemming from, the thought of your own lack of fulfillment, from the awareness that your involvement in things confessed as truths that condition your life as existence bestowed by God, will require isolation, pain, and death, sacrifice and offering of self.

"Valeriu personified the Christian fighter who simultaneously finds himself on the mountain (renunciation of passions, the stage of purification), and in the forest with wild beasts (the struggle with evil spirits, enlightenment), and in the swamp of despair (splitting it in two with the cross as weapon, which is carried conscientiously), accepting 'not as I will, but as Thou will,' the stage of unification, perfection). His person gave confidence to every soul, making it aware of its longing for spiritual advancement toward perfection.

"Once again I say, Valeriu Gafencu burned.

"He burned… .an ignited offering in the presence of everyone, like a beacon of light toward whom and from whom each of us gathered spiritual and physical strength. His words conveyed the spirit. His gestures were blessings and embraces. His deeds, discerned and discovered rarely or late, were integral gifts of his being.

"Valeriu did not just give; he gave [offered] *himself*.

"The capacity for sacrifice expressed in the words of the Savior - 'But whoever strikes you on your right cheek, turn the other to him also,' 'If someone wants to sue you and take away your tunic, let him have your cloak also,' 'And whoever compels you to go one mile, go with him two,' 'Love your enemies,' and 'Greater love has no man than this, than to lay down one's life for his friends' - was for Valeriu something so natural that he would have troubled, even scandalized, many people if he had not behaved according to these Christian entreaties secretly.

"At the beginning of our friendship, when examining my conscience in order to confess my sins and receive Communion, I found myself in a state of doubt regarding the sincerity of Valeriu's spiritual endeavors. It seemed to me that some of the forms in which he clothed his spiritual life were sometimes rather artificial, even ostentatious. With guilt, I revealed to my thoughts to him. He listened to me attentively. At the end, he embraced me, crying, and we prayed together. Valeriu took upon himself all the trouble that he had caused me: 'I am guilty before God of all the trouble that I have caused you. I thank you for showing me a flaw of which I was truly unaware, for it is not only through sin, strictly speaking, that someone can be led astray, not only by things on the left, but also by things on the right, by virtues when they are not practiced with a spiritual gentility, with concern for guarding the conscience of one's brother who can be led astray because of your freedom while you, yourself, are confident that you are doing good.'

"I grasped the idea from the epistle of the Holy Apostle Paul to the Corinthians, Chapter 8. Later on, I would come to understand that the Holy Fathers had turned this message into a rule of life in monastic communities and especially in hermitages.

"It was July 1946. We had started the second tilling in the vineyard. Nicolae Vişean and Paul Vilescu were two comrades who were well-liked by all of us for their good dispositions wherever they found themselves. They teased each other, without ever degenerating toward harshness or vulgarity. Their regional backgrounds supplied them with enough material for amusing disputes. Vişean was from Oltenia, while Vilescu was from Prahova.

"One day, their verbal darts started to turn bitter. Their jokes degenerated from indirect subtle barbs to sarcasm and mockery of a personal nature, until finally they began to direct insults at each other. What other work does the devil have than to disrupt peace and friendship among people? Each one accused the other of lacking good sense, responsibility, and other such offensive accusations. Nevertheless, their discussion was still carried out quietly, [so that the others couldn't hear]. The wind was carrying bits of their cutting remarks to the ears of those were working closest to them. We were uneasy and looking at each other helplessly, not knowing how to assuage the tension between them.

"Valeriu Gafencu was [working closely] behind them, on an adjacent row, and heard the argument in its entirety. When they got to the end of their rows, Valeriu put down his hoe, stood in front of the two comrades, got down on his knees, and implored them with a voice full of emotion, 'I ask your forgiveness. I heard the words, beautiful as the words of a psalm, that you spoke to each other.' With tears streaming down his cheeks, he kissed both of them and went back to work. The two men fell into each other's arms. With suppressed voices they asked forgiveness from all of us.

"This was the Spirit, working through Valeriu in our community, the holy life of love within the mystical body of Christ.

"Oh, love so holy, how well you know how to crush the work of the evil one with the simplicity of your actions! (…)

"At Aiud in 1945, I was sitting with Marin Naidim in a cell when Ioan Ianolide came in and told us, on the verge of tears, that he felt the need to be near us and to partake of the same mystical joy of the Savior Christ. I did not know how to proceed. I asked him to go to Valeriu and share these wishes with him. Up until this time, Ioan had had a somewhat defiant attitude toward provocations from prison administrators and had suffered the consequences. Ioan thought that [in sending him to Valeriu] I was trying to get rid of him and not considering him in good faith. Nevertheless, he [went to Valeriu] and revealed the state of his soul and all his conscious concerns.

"Valeriu did not let him speak but embraced him as a brother whom, at the threshold of his soul, he had waited for a long time. With his love, Valeriu raised Ioan up to a level where he could transcend his excessive scrupulousness, a place so uncomfortable for Ioan as though he were on the edge of a knife, undecided whether to abandon an imaginary style of life that was subject to chance in favor of an orderly life in Christ, confirmed by the results of withdrawal from sin, growing obedience, and continuous submission to Christ in His Church.

"Within my soul, I have always carried the image of Valeriu as a young hermit, consumed in the Prayer of Fire. This materialized into a poem I wrote for him:

BURNT – OFFERING
Dedicated to Valeriu Gafencu

…There rises up within me a hermitage
In which a gentle hermit became sanctified…
He built up heavenly virtues in a frail body
And bore in his eyes a humble joy.

From long vigil – white flower –
He leaned on the edge of a windowsill
And the moon kissed his holy cheek
When it heard his word, like a gentle breeze:

"O come, thou wicked servant, sleep, and bring
Along with you the dream over the still waters…
For one hour take me up in a streak
To the Kingly Wine-Cellar, fruit of the vine!…"

He hangs from the living cord of hope
And in prayer climbs up a high ladder…,
He unlocks the highest points of the senses
And the angels behold him face-to-face.

They have clothed him with heavenly armor…
They sprinkled him with snowflakes of wisdom,
Deliberately purifying his soul
That it be like theirs in image and likeness in might!…

An angel…made a sign in heaven!…

He sees the Face of the Unseen world…,
He hears the words… unborn,
With his heart he melts the layers of frost!...

How many times the earth, without a spleen,
Goes, like a black bull, somersault,
How many times they fire at him, in vain,
Horned demons, ever vigilant.

The sky is a scroll tied with a knot
The earth, the last letter of the alphabet…
The Living Altar of the Great Prophet
Receives the sacrifice, the Burnt-Offering!...

In the fire of Prayer, he falls asleep…
Late, the light of the oil-lamp goes out…
An angel steals into the room
And snows a fine halo upon his forehead;
The demons moan at the doorstep on their horns.

A pile of sand stands beside the door…
The rust ever grew upon the bolt,
The oil flourished in a pitcher,
But his body stayed on his knees, even though it was
ashes…

On a bench nearby, more several books
Were arranged. On a page in his service book,
He had written his holy charter
In four lines, golden words:

"Forgive me, Fathers, I ask you,
For, having little work today with the Lord,
Sleep overcame me in prayer,
And I have left you my ashes, as security…"

But not believing that he was really dead,
I touched his vestments with my hand...
His hot ashes scattered,
And kissing them...., I wept deep in thought.

It is difficult to imagine and impossible to convey in words what Valeriu did for every soul with which he came into contact with throughout his long years of detention and what he lived through experience is difficult to imagine and impossible to convey in words. The account that of everyone who knew him gives suffices: He was a saint. He is a saint."[108]

---

[108]Virgil Maxim, op. cit., pp 180-187

The Prison at Piteşti and Re-Education

Among the many prisons of Communist Romania, Piteşti is a particular one. It became famous for the horrible atrocities that happened there as a result of the implementation of that satanic experiment known as re-education. Valeriu did not undergo re-education; he was transferred to Văcăreşti, then to Târgu-Ocna before the experiment at Piteşti began to be applied on a large scale.

Re-education was also attempted at Târgu-Ocna, but it was thwarted by circumstances in which an important role was played by the attitude of the prisoners, as influenced by Gafencu. Let us now examine what constituted this experiment of re-education – the most loathsome of all methods used in Communist prisons to destroy a man.

In the first part of the year 1948, following an order from Bucharest, the prisoners were grouped according to their age at the time of arrest. All university students were sent to Piteşti. In the first phase, the prisoners, most of them Legionnaires, lived under a rather lax regime. In a short time, however, things changed and [what can be identified as] a program of extermination was initiated. The guards became very strict, doling out harsh punishments to the prisoners for perceived offenses. The quality of food deteriorated and they were given just enough food to keep them alive. Beatings, cold, and hunger lowered their physical and moral resistance. All of these measures represented only the preparatory phase, so that when re-education was later unleashed, exhausted prisoners would be that much easier to subdue.

A group of prisoners was brought to Pitești from Suceava, led by Eugen Țurcanu. Turcanu was to become famous for crimes and torture committed at Pitești and later at Gherla. Eugen Țurcanu and the other Suceava prisoners had joined the Communists [while in prison], and they were chosen by the prison administration as the tool by which re-education would be implemented. It must be stated from the beginning that re-education was conceptualized at a high level, by leadership in the Ministry of the Interior, Țurcanu and his group essentially being the instruments. When the experiment was called off, they were executed by the very Communist government they had served, while those who were truly guilty, those in the shadows, went unpunished.

Initially, the Suceava prisoners were scattered throughout the cells, mixed in with the others. They succeeded in gaining the others' trust with their well-meaning attitude. After some time, at the beginning of December 1949, the Suceava prisoners, together with other prisoners who were purposefully selected, were brought back together, to inhabit the same cell. One day, Țurcanu and his group announced to the others that they had changed their ideas, that they had given up Legionnairism and had been re-educated, adopting communist ideology. When they recommended to the others that they do the same, there was objection and laughter. Țurcanu and his followers attacked. Armed with broomsticks and wooden clubs hidden ahead of time under mattresses, they began beating the others. Soon thereafter, the prison leadership - director, officers, guards - joined Țurcanu, severely beating the ones who would not renounce Legionnairism. This moment marked the beginning of the re-education program,

111

which meant continuous beatings and torture. The prisoners, closely supervised by Ţurcanu's group, were subjected to a regime of constant terror without the possibility of escaping or committing suicide.

The torture was well-planned; it stopped only when the prisoner was about to die. There were various kinds of torture: beatings, hunger, being forced to maintain the same position 17 hours a day – legs extended horizontally, hands on knees, chest at 90 degrees – and at the slightest wavering, the supervisor would respond with a club. The prisoners were forced to drink urine and to eat excrement from buckets that served as toilets in the cells. They were forced to drink highly-salted water and then left to dry out from thirst; these were some of the many other tortures devised by the sick minds of the torturers. Those who caved were required to "unmask," i.e., to reveal everything they had not confessed at their interrogation, to betray those prisoners who had helped them in prison or those guards who had treated them humanely. Likewise, in order for the destruction to be complete, each one of them was required to profane the memory of whatever had been most important to him in front of everyone in his cell. For example, perhaps someone loved his mother or wife very much. In front of everyone, he was required to denounce them, to make the most obscene and absurd statements about them. Whatever was clean and good in the mind of the one being tortured had to be slandered and dirtied.

Theological students and those who were devout – "mystical bandits," as they were called – were forced to apostatize, to deny God, to curse everything that had to do with the Christian faith. At Christmas and

Pascha,[109], they were forced to sing carols or well-known religious hymns with altered words which profaned Christ and the Virgin Mary. They were forced to participate in blasphemous processions and to celebrate "liturgies" using human waste from buckets in the prison cells, and were then forced to swallow it as "Communion." Some of them were "baptized" in tubs full of excrement. I believe that these things provide sufficient proof of the satanic nature of re-education.

After the prisoner "unmasked" himself, in order to prove that he had been re-educated, he was required to become a torturer himself and to convince others to give up "all bourgeois rottenness" and to accept communist ideology. Through the use of terror, the prisoners were truly brainwashed. The tortured, no longer able to endure the incessant torment, unable to commit suicide, always closely supervised, finally gave in and were transformed into robots, their hearts turned to stone and, from being victims, they became executioners. Not even after being re-educated did they escape the terror, for at the slightest sign of solidarity with their victims, they were subjected to torture once again. And thus, living in a constant state of terror, always suspicious of one another, they broke down completely, foregoing the possibility of returning to a normal state. Dumitru Bordeianu, who lived through this experiment, described the experience in his book *Mărturisiri din Mlaştina Disperării* (Confessions From the Mire of Despair). He says that at a particular point [in the relationship between] the torturer and the tortured were brought together , a demonic "communion." was

---

[109] Pascha - the most common Orthodox term for Easter. (Translator's note)

created. For example, if Țurcanu asked him what he was thinking, he was unable to lie because Țurcanu would have sensed it immediately. From this came the fear of even thinking something which could be considered bad by Țurcanu: You could not hide anything if you were questioned, and if you told the truth you were punished.

Another satanic aspect of re-education was that everything that the prisoner managed to keep hidden during the interrogation - those things which acted as bulwarks against his internal collapse - began to torment him so much that it was the prisoner who would in the end request to "unmask," feeling a sense of relief afterward akin to the relief felt after sacramental confession, even though the things confessed were held against him. A strange process occurred, resulting in mutations to the personality of the one tortured, who came to disavow his former beliefs and to accept whatever Țurcanu imposed upon him with the conviction that he was doing good. In the process of brainwashing, "his mind was enlightened," he experienced a sense of relief, he "understood" everything that he had previously rejected and he set out, in full confidence, to bring others into the same state of "enlightenment." For those of us who have not passed through similar demonic states, these things are incomprehensible.

Most of those who tortured others did so under the dominion of terror, without experiencing the mutations I referred to above. The system was planned in such a way that, as a result of the continual torture, very few were able to hold out to the end. In general, most of them compromised, some more, some less, according to the structure and stamina of each.

114

From Piteşti, the system was extended to Gherla and the Canal,[110] but due to the fact that word leaked out and there were international protests, the re-education experiment was stopped. If the secrecy had been maintained, re-education would have been applied to every prison in the country.

onsidering re-education from a spiritual perspective, both those who directed this experiment from the shadows and those who applied it were nothing but instruments of the devil in the destruction of souls. Father Gheorghe Calciu, who went through Piteşti, said, "In order to understand what Piteşti was, we must remain above the facts and get at the roots of this evil, and try to see the internal mechanisms of perversion and its metaphysical dimension. I believe that Piteşti was a diabolical experiment. What occurred there was a struggle between good and evil, in which the executioners and the victims were simply instruments. It was a diabolical experiment that took place in our country more than in any other place in the world."[111]

The satanic character of re-education was clearly seen in the words of Ţurcanu, preserved in the memory of one political prisoner: "If Christ would have passed through my hands, He never would have made it to the cross. He would not have resurrected. Christianity, that great lie, would never have existed, and the world

---

[110]The Danube-Black Sea Canal is known as the site of labor camps in 1950s Communist Romania, when, at any given time, several tens of thousands political prisoners worked on its excavation. It became notorious for the barbaric treatment and crimes committed at this work camp.

[111]In the periodical *Puncte Cardinale*, no. 9/165, September 2004, pg.p. 5.

would have lived peacefully! I am Țurcanu! The first and the last! No one has ever been born who could replace me. No one can lie to me the way that I lie to you fools. I am the true gospel! I am writing it now. I have something to write on - your carcasses. What I write is true, it is not a bedtime story for children."[112]

Although the devil may have imagined that he won the battle through terror, he had few decisive victories among those who compromised. After the torture stopped, most of those who had acquiesced gradually returned to God. Considering the subsequent evolution of the re-educated, the devil won a battle at Pitești, but not the war. According to Father Calciu, most of them returned to Christ more vehemently than before their trial by fire.

---

[112]Gheorghe Andreica, *Mărturii ... Mărturii ... (Testimonies ... Testimonies ...)* , Ed. 2000, pp. 70-71

Valeriu at Piteşti

Valeriu was at Piteşti approximately a year and a half, until the end of December 1949. He did not undergo the re-education program, but he did experience the introductory phase, the intended extermination regime implemented before the torture began. As a result of a national campaign to combat tuberculosis, Valeriu, along with a group of 40 other prisoners suspected of having tuberculosis, was transferred to Văcăreşti for medical examinations before the re-education program was enforced at Piteşti. A few testimonies worthy of being included in a Paterikon have remained from Valeriu's time at Piteşti.

***

"Tall, stooping forward a little," remembers Traian Popescu, "because the burden of years spent in prison had left their mark, he used to wear a crocheted cap that looked like a flattened medieval helmet that covered his forehead. An ascetic figure, that of a Byzantine martyr, but with a face that was luminous and smiling, that passed easily from smile into laughter, laughter that was invigorating, not ostentatious, but powerful and stimulating. He seemed to have descended from a medieval painting so as to spread peace around him.

"It seemed to me that I saw in this man how his spiritual powers became stronger while as his physical powers diminished. Although he had become skeletal and could hardly get out of bed, he continued to explain to us the meaning of the parables of the Gospel. He was getting thinner by the day, and becoming more and more physically exhausted. There were four of us [in the cell] and there were two beds, so we slept two in each bed. We decided straightaway to take turns keeping watch over him, giving him a bed to himself, every now and then helping him turn over from one side to the other. Toward the end, during those harrowing moments, the strength to open his eyes having left him, he did not stop smiling discreetly. He was like this for about three weeks. One evening, in the beginning of December, he asked us to rub his legs gently because they were cold. Outside, frost covered the ground. The cells were unheated. Valeriu was beginning to get cold from the legs up. It was after midnight when, aware of what was happening to him, he whispered to us:

"'I am happy. I am going to God. Pray with me for my soul and yours.' We were horrified, in despair, frightened; but we were also disconcerted because we found ourselves far from being able to accept Valeriu's death serenely. We were not ready to go down this road. We felt shaken, powerless, abandoned. Valeriu continued to display the same restful smile, he whom Steinhardt would later name, in a blessed way, 'the saint of the prisons.'

"But the miracle of this man continued. Toward morning, he started warming up and a gleam of light flickered about him. I reported the seriousness of Valeriu's condition and asked for medical assistance. Later, I don't remember if it was the same day or the next, an orderly came and gave him calcium, sufficient for the sorry plight he was in. This agony lasted for several days in which, extraordinarily, I heard him say serenely: 'The Lord did not want me. I am not yet worthy of His kingdom.'

"He opened his eyes half-way. He saw our troubled, disturbed faces. 'Don't be afraid,' he told us.

'There can be no greater happiness than to go to Him, Whose name you have uttered in prayer so many times, Whose help you have requested and to Whom you are prepared to entrust your soul to. Pray with me!'"[113]

*

"It was in the month of May 1949," recounts Florian Dumitrescu, "when I awoke in the middle of the night, amid sounds that indicated intense activity. Suddenly, the cell door opened and two colonels who resembled each other - the same thick fingers, the same enormous neck - entered. They were accompanied by a jailer who usually carried out the distasteful orders of his superiors and so, immediately upon entering, started performing a barbaric search. During the search, Traian Popescu, Octavian Voinea, and Mircea Selten came in to the cell [which we all shared]. Valeriu and I were had been brought in beforehand.

"Looking at us with hatred, the colonels said, 'So, you want to escape?' Voinea intervened unabashedly, 'That is a falsehood, Colonel.' The discussion began to slide into shades of mutual distrust.

"'But what do you want?' insisted the colonel. Gafencu's response: 'I want religious assistance, which is guaranteed to us by law.' 'What are you saying? You want us to bring a priest here?' 'Yes! That's what I want. It's my right.' 'This is foolishness!' 'Truly. I am a fool-for-Christ!'

"Valeriu had a perfect state of peacefulness and utter harmony between his words and his actions."[114]

*

---

[113]Nicolae Trifoiu, *op. cit.*, pp. 150-153.

[114]*Ibid*, pg.p. 110.

When a prison guard informed us that we had the right to one pair of underwear and one shirt, but not a priest, we each had different reactions to this decision. I prepared his bundle of clothes to hand over to the storehouse while the rest of us simply looked at what was happening.

" 'We have to defend ourselves from criminals, Voinea,' cried out Valeriu.[115]

*

"Mircea Selten was fond of jokes and there was a particular song which amused him and which he hummed almost daily. The words went like this: *I am the long-handed outlaw, wanted in seven counties....*

"I had the impression that this song disturbed the prayer of the heart that Valeriu practiced as a monastic, hesychastic exercise. Having been a colleague of Mircea at the university and knowing him to be understanding, I asked Valeriu if he would like me to ask Mircea to sing this song less often. Valeriu responded in his usually calm and peaceful manner: 'What gives us the right to take Mircea's small pleasure away from him?'"[116]

*

"One day, Valeriu walked up to the most brutal of the security guards, for whom insults and beatings were common ways of engaging the prisoners.

"'Mr. Georgescu,' he said, 'the chief priest once approached our Lord and with him was a woman who had fallen into the sin of adultery. The priest asked Jesus, *'What should we do with thiswoman who, according to our law, must be stoned to death?'* The Savior answered, *'Let him who is without sin be the first to cast a stone.'* Those who

---

[115]*Ibid*, pg.p. 110.

[116]*Abide,* pg.p. 111.

heard Him disappeared one by one. Jesus said to her, *'Woman, where are your accusers? No one has condemned you? Neither do I condemn you. Go and sin no more!'*

"A few hours later, Georgescu went to Valeriu's cell and told him, 'They had no reason. That's why they didn't kill her!' From that point forward, Georgescu showed a glimmer of kindness and respect toward the prisoners in the isolation cell."[117]

*

"During the periodic searches carried out in the spring of 1949, this same Georgescu found small crosses made of Plexiglas, sculpted with wire or a needle, or [crosses fashioned out of] a scrap of paper. These objects were strictly forbidden and having them in our possession was considered a serious offense. He summoned Valeriu and complained to him, saying:

"'You, Gafencu, you know about these things. You know who made them, but you do not want to tell me!' 'Mr. Georgescu, the small crosses glorify God. Even you were born Christian.' 'It is not allowed, Gafencu. What do you expect me to do? I have to report you to the warden.' 'You are keeping yourself from seeing that which has to do with the Lord.'

"And so, while the rest of us were not even able to speak to this 'brutal person,' [Georgescu] sought out Gafencu, looking to him for a solution to his overburdened conscience that still wavered [between right and wrong]. This was the beginning of this age of terror, the likes of which had never been seen before and never would be again."[118]

***

---

[117]*Ibid,* pg.p. 111.

[118]*Ibid,* pg.p. 151.

121

"Because of our ever-present hunger, unpleasant discussions often started among us whenever the *turtoi*[119] was distributed. Knowing this, Valeriu would restrain and humble himself by taking the last piece, the smallest one. In his mind, he was thankful to be able to make this gesture of love and self-sacrifice. But while some were pleased by his self-restraint, there were others who considered that, when his turn came he should not forego taking the biggest piece.

"He submitted to the order we established in our cell and when he had to choose ahead of the others, he chose whatever piece happened to be in front of him so as to avoid the temptation of gluttony and not cause harm to his brothers. This small gesture would later come to be considered a good example by everyone."[120]

*

"In the daily life of the cell, minor problems appeared, such as airing out the room, how and when and how much it should be done; or establishing what hours the *tineta*[121] should be used; or what having the right each of us had to walk in the space of two meters left unoccupied by the beds. There were opposing interests and opinions that often ended in quarrels. When these kinds of discussions arose, Valeriu kept quiet. Still, others provoked him, 'What have you got to say?' 'I think that whatever the rest of you decide is good. If we cannot live in a brotherly manner in the midst of this suffering, how can we expect people to share the riches of the entire world in a just and loving

---

[119]*Turtoi* - a kind of bread made from corn meal or wheat or a combination of the two. (Translator's note)

[120]Ioan Ianolide, *op. cit.*, pp. 75-76

[121]*Tineta* - a bucket used in place of a toilet in the cells,.

way? If we cannot be kind here, how will we be able to be good when we are powerful and free? With just a little love, we can feel the joy of trying to go along and please others. If we are to live in peace and goodwill, we need to have a broad and deep understanding of man."[122]

*

"Valeriu's attitude toward the authorities was very dignified and wise, such that he could not be accused of counter-revolutionary activities, only of Christian faith. It was his faith that he wanted to defend, so he tried to outwit his persecutors and not be drawn into an unequal battle in which he would easily be defeated. Therefore he forged his weapon of defense from the 'law of Caesar.' He had to make wise use of the few means of warfare that prison allowed him. Some of the others reproached him, saying: 'This approach works for you but it does not suit us! We realize that we are at war with a ferocious and deadly enemy and we want to win this war. We are not 'bandits,' as they call us. They are. And we have to tell them so. Yes, we are in jail, but we will not abandon the fight even if we die fighting!'

"Hearing these kinds of arguments, Valeriu would lower his eyes, sad yet full of understanding, and say: 'Do you believe that I have abandoned the fight? Do you believe that I do not understand you? Must we die like a bunch of fools? Are they not waiting for a chance to strike at us? What, then, should we do? Do we voluntarily allow ourselves to be eaten by these pigs gone mad or do we use this time to save our lives and souls? It is time for us to humble ourselves deeply, to preoccupy ourselves with problems that are truly

---

[122]*Ibid*, pg.p. 76.

meaningful, to cleanse ourselves in order to be worthy of Christ.' The others retorted, 'It is not us but they who are impure! If we give ourselves over to tears of repentance, we make room for tyrants and sinners to rule!' 'This is the time; this is the time of repentance!' Valeriu responded. 'Have faith! People have forsaken us. Deliverance will come from God. The sacrifices we make here will not be in vain.'"[123]

*

"In the fall of 1949, Valeriu had a strong haemoptysis[124] as a result of his tuberculosis. He was bedridden at this time. He was getting weaker by the day. One by one, with tears in their eyes, others came to visit. A friend offered him the bread crust from his ration, which Valeriu refused, saying 'Just because I am sick is no reason for you to get sick.'

"'Nevertheless, as Valeriu later confessed, that noble soul continued to slip him a portion of his ration, sneaking it into Valeriu's knapsack.' In the face of such capacity for self-sacrifice, Valeriu felt protected by God's mercy.

"The haemoptyses continued. It was not considered 'humanitarian' to allow a prisoner to languish and die [without medical intervention]. Thus, he was taken to the hospital in town and locked in a small room, guarded by keepers day and night. The doctors who came to see him were always accompanied by an escort.

"One night, however, a nurse managed to get in unaccompanied. Valeriu had seen her before,

---

[123]*Ibid*, pp. 79-80.

[124]Haemoptysis - expectoration of blood arising from the oral cavity, larynx, trachea, bronchi, or lungs. (Translator's note)

accompanying a doctor, and had seen tears in her eyes. She managed to get the guard drunk so that she could go see Valeriu. She kneeled next to his bed, took his hand, and kissed it.

"'How did you get in here?' he asked her.

"'I put the guard to sleep,' she smiled.

"'What do you want?'

"'I want to be beside you, to help you. I'll do anything you ask me to do.'

Valeriu saw her sincerity and was deeply moved.

"'You have risked your freedom for me. God will reward you. But there is no way that you can help me. If I die here, I ask you to bear witness to people and to my dear family that I was a believer until the end, that I died reconciled, that I gave my life for Christ and for my neighbors. Maybe that is why you had the courage to come to me, because everything that people accomplish enters into the plan of God. I thank you; I will not forget you; I will pray for you.... Now go!.... Do not take risks anymore! I am in the hands of God.'"[125]

---

[125]*Ibid*, pp. 81-82.

"I Miss Târgu-Ocna So Much!"

The prison at Târgu-Ocna was built at the end of the nineteenth century. It was a project initiated and funded by a princess from the Ghica-Comăneşti boyar[126] family, who was horrified by living conditions of the prisoners imprisoned at that time in local salt mines. In those mines, prisoners were allowed fresh air only during great church feast-days, spending most of their prison sentence underground. The project included several buildings, where the prisoners were to be housed, descending into the mines only during working hours. After hard labor in the salt mines was discontinued, Târgu-Ocna became a regular prison, administered just like the others. Between the two world wars, however, at the initiative of Dr. Ioan Cantacuzino, several more buildings were added and the prison became a sanatorium for prisoners with tuberculosis.

Gafencu's group arrived here in February 1950, after a stop in Văcăreşti. They had been X-rayed there, and, out of the 40 suspected of having TB, only 18 cases were confirmed. The healthy prisoners were sent back to Piteşti. When they arrived at Târgu-Ocna, the sanatorium was almost empty, but in the months that followed other groups of prisoners of all ages and political persuasions arrived, most of them young Legionnaires.

After the extermination program at Piteşti, the newly-arrived prisoners found Târgu-Ocna to be a real

---

[126]Boyar: a member of a former privileged class in Romania. (Translator's note)

paradise. They were given adequate and nourishing food, freedom to move from one room to another and to sunbathe in the courtyard, the opportunity to speak with the others, the benevolent attitude of the guards, etc. Father Voicescu, a geography student at the time, arrived at the prison during the month of May and recalls his overwhelming initial impressions.

"I arrived at Târgu-Ocna in the evening. It was a spring evening, there was a scent of lime in the air, and the moon was high in the sky. A few middle-aged guards from the old guard[127] were waiting for us, each one carrying a long rifle. We, the other prisoners and I, moved quickly, being accustomed to hearing words like 'Move, bandit!' and pushing and shoving... One of the guards said to us:

"'Slow down, son, take it easy...!'

"When we heard this word 'son,' we could not believe our ears. We then saw a building full of lights. We were brought in, to a room with eight beds, each one with a mattress! At Pitești and at Jilava, because there were so many of us, beyond the normal limit, we had bunk-beds in stacks of two or three. Here, the windows had no security shutters and there was a bathroom right next door. This was...happiness! The next day we were still dumbfounded. To our amazement, we were brought into the courtyard to meet the others who preceded us there. Grass was growing in the courtyard; we rolled around on it. It was truly magnificent."[128]

But it was not always this idyllic. There were difficult moments even here, with restrictions,

---

[127]Old guard - pre-Communist. (Translator's note)

[128]*Părintele Constantin Voicescu, Un duhovnic al cetății*, pp. 22-23.

punishments, solitary confinement, terror, especially when an attempt was made to implement a re-education program modeled after Piteşti.

Margareta Danielescu, the prison's official doctor, was an extremely soulful woman. Assisted by prisoners with medical backgrounds and medical students, she did all she could to look after the prisoners in her care. Prisoners were not treated for tuberculosis; the treatment, instead, was nutritious food and natural tonics, which yielded spectacular results in some cases. On the other hand, there were many who would have benefited from disease-specific treatment; they did not survive.

In May 1950, a group of prisoners who had undergone the re-education program at Pitesti arrived at Târgu-Ocna. Only a few of them seemed to have gone through the program and remained actively re-educated, while the others, still horrified by the tortures they had experienced, were very restrained. Most of them would heal spiritually in the loving atmosphere that prevailed at Târgu-Ocna.

The arrival of the re-educated disturbed life at the sanatorium. Knowing nothing of the horrors they had experienced, those at Târgu-Ocna did not understand the strange behaviors of these new arrivals. They could not explain the changes that had taken place in those whom they had previously known, those with whom they had been friends and who now behaved so unnaturally. After some of the re-educated made certain disclosures, it became clear that measures had to be taken. They kept an eye on those who were actively re-educated, forestalling any attempt at re-education in the sanatorium, while also seeking, with an attitude full of understanding, to approach those who had not been fully corrupted.

The political officer at Târgu-Ocna was waiting for a suitable moment to unleash re-education. Divine providence, attentiveness, the solidarity of the prisoners, and the attitude of Dr. Danielescu, who expressed considerable objections to the Penitentiary Directorate, thwarted the two attempts made at re-education.

Valeriu Gafencu played an important role in this endeavor and was the pillar around which those opposed to re-education gathered. When he found out about the horrors at Piteşti, he said, "Difficult times also await us," and he asked those around him to pray fervently that they not lose their souls in the trials that were to come. His influence on the others made things difficult for the political officer, who tried to recruit some of the prisoners as informers.

If Piteşti and re-education became symbolic of the demonization of man, torn from his connection with God, defeated and beast-like toward his fellow man, Târgu-Ocna found itself at the opposite pole. Those at Târgu-Ocna found an uplifting, Christian atmosphere, full of love and sacrifice, unique in the history of the Communist gulag. Târgu-Ocna was a Piteşti turned upside-down.

"Târgu-Ocna was more than just a community," said Father Voicescu. "It was a true spiritual family. The relationships formed there were stronger than blood relations. We felt and experienced a holy and authentic joy. Thus, I understood my friend Sami when he said to me, after being released in '54, 'I miss Târgu-Ocna so much!' Because it was there that we could understand what freedom in Christ meant. No one was able to take that freedom and joy away from us."[129]

---

[129]*Ibid*, pp. 28, 31.

"At Târgu-Ocna," remembers Dr. Aristide Lefa, "when the seriously ill began to increase in number, we had to make adjustments to care for them properly. It was decided that two of the less-seriously ill would take turns attending to Room #4, where the seriously ill were located. Alexandru Ioanid and Aurelian Guță volunteered at first; for one week, they stood watch over the ill, which was not an easy task. After them, Ion Popescu and Leonida (Relu) Stratan took over, but seeing how their condition was not good either, it was decided to create teams of two that would change daily, thereby including most of the more able-bodied prisoners.

"The time came when it was necessary to set up Room #5 for those who were seriously ill. There was also a need for medical assistance at night, especially since some of the prisoners were in the final stages of their illness. The potential for infection for the healthy ones, in this environment full of the Koch bacillus, was considerable. Together with my colleague Mihai Lungeanu, we provided medical assistance but, to everyone's surprise, we did not contract the disease. This was truly a miracle.

"Since I was always around Valeriu, I had the possibility to have long discussions with him. I got to know him well. Like the others, I was overwhelmed by his powerful personality and his stalwart Christian bearing, free of ostentation; these qualities of his influenced the spiritual atmosphere of the sanatorium to a very large degree, even though he was permanently confined to bed.

"In room #4, dozens of sick people, most of them young, lived out the last of their days. I sat in their midst and I saw them dying. Not one of them, absolutely not even one of them, rebelled against his fate, and even less

130

against God. They died reconciled, confessing Christ, even Ion Filipescu, an old socialist, the only one among the sick who claimed to be an atheist. And all of this was because of the spiritual atmosphere to which Valeriu Gafencu contributed.

"Room #4, in which each prisoner awaited his end, was a temple of prayer, a temple of the dead. All those who came in contact with the dying were aware of the danger that threatened them, but faith in God gave them the power to overcome their fear."[130]

"The attitude of service that some people had, while of no particular mystical inclination but always extraordinarily helpful, is evidence of exemplary Christian conduct," says Ion Popescu. "Their actions deserve to be made known. I am referring specifically to four prisoners who were ill with a milder form of TB: Mihai Pârău, Sandu Alexandrescu, Alexandru Angelescu, and Ionaş Plopeanu. They decided to do the laundry for those who were no longer able to do it for themselves. There were many more who helped now and then, but these four did this work day in and day out for three years.

"They did the washing outside, in tubs provided by the administration. This work took several hours a day. It was simpler during summer, but in winter the water was as cold as ice, and these men, sick themselves, stood outside in the cold, washing, having their hands red as lobsters. They took up this work for no other reason than as befitting of their Christian spirit. I believe their gesture was important in the eyes of God. It is one thing to give your food to someone who is sicker than you, to sacrifice your portion of meat or jam, but it is

---

[130]Nicolae Trifoiu, *op. cit.*, pp. 106-107.

another matter to wash someone else's personal things. Particularly since it was not so easy, it was rather unpleasant, it was nauseating to wash sheets and clothes belonging to sick people given the fact that they were sometimes saturated with blood, pus, urine, and other things. It was not a pleasant task to do this work every day, especially if you were sick yourself.

"There was an engineer who had been a Communist, Traian Andreescu, a former leader of the regional CFR[131] Moldova. He wound up in prison as a result of mild disagreement among the Communists. Before prison, he had been a freethinker and although he was not against Christianity, he was not involved in any sort of religious activity. Sent to Târgu-Ocna after he became ill, he was influenced by the atmosphere he found there. Something started to change in him. Seeing the attitude of the young people, most of them Legionnaires, he said one day: 'I am sorry I didn't know about the Legionnaire movement earlier. My family, under my influence, has Communist tendencies. I'm sorry for my son, whom I believe I'll never see again; I wish I could tell him that I believed a lie.'

"His sickness worsened and in the final stages he was brought into the same room as Valeriu. Father Gherasim Iscu was also in Room #4. Andreescu wanted to die as a Christian. Father Gherasim heard his confession and gave him Holy Communion, preparing him for his passage into eternity. He died reconciled with God. His soul was won over by Valeriu and by the atmosphere at Târgu-Ocna even before arriving in Room

---

[131] CFR - *Căile Ferate Române* (Romanian Railways). (Translator's note)

#4; he had been at Târgu-Ocna over a year while his transformation took place.

"Another man who returned to God in prison under the influence of the atmosphere at Târgu-Ocna was General Tobescu. This man, before his arrest, had been the national leader of the military police. When his condition worsened, he also was sent to Room #4. Along with the others, I helped him and spoke with him. One day, he told me:

"'Do you know that I used to be a great persecutor of the Legionnaires?'

"'Yes, I know,' I replied.

"'It surprised me that no one here has ever reproached me for doing so much wrong to your comrades despite the fact that I participated in the arrest and killing of many Legionnaires. Now I realize what great mistakes I made and that I did not exercise good judgment. I believed that I was doing good for the country and that by persecuting you I was being patriotic. Now I realize I was wrong. I let myself be influenced by people who did not think well of the Legionnaires. Now I am sorry. Maybe that's why God brought me here, in order to realize my mistakes.'

"He also died in Room #4, having confessed and received Communion. I consider this spiritual transformation a real miracle.

"Gheorghe Soare was a simple boy, a former student at a technical high school. He was also arrested due to his involvement with the Legionnaire movement. He had been imprisoned at Târguşor and arrived at Târgu-Ocna gravely ill. His was a modest family. They did not inquire after him. They never came to see him. They probably did not know he was at Târgu-Ocna. He had a simple, pure soul. Serene and silent, he lived a discreet Christian life, unobserved by the others.

"The day before he died, he told us something that impressed me. 'I was born in 1927. The Legion was founded in that same year. While I was still free, I never thought that I would have the honor of dying for the Legion. God gave me this happiness. I was born at the same time as the Legion and I have the joy of dying for it.'[132] He said this to a few of us who were closest to him. It is a fine thing to die thinking in this way. It seemed to me to be something very special. Even though he did not possess a Legionnaire's bold character, this final thought of his, directed at God, that he was happy dying for this movement, this faith, impressed me. He was a simple boy. There were others like him who, although they did not live lives that were in any way extraordinary, were nonetheless impressive because of their simplicity, their faith, their self-sacrifice. Their commitment to the Legionnaire movement gave them a certain happiness, a certain joy."[133]

---

[132]"Ultimately, what did the Legionnaires accomplish? They languished in prison and changed nothing in this country. So many capable men ended in failure. They got what they deserved because they acted without common sense, they did not accept their position in life and the reality of the historical times, like everybody else." This is the way a person who is "stable" and has "good sense" sees things. Just as a chicken cannot understand what it means to be an eagle, such people bewail the "failure" and "senseless" suffering of the Legionnaires. But in the end, despite all their suffering, most of the Legionnaires did not consider themselves failures. Moreover, their involvement in the Legionnaire movement gave them a sense of spiritual fulfillment – there certainly were many others like Gheorghe Soare – and they died gladly for their faith. Where, then, is their failure?

[133]Testimony given to monk Moise by Ion Popescu in April 2005.

A Blessed[134] Man

Although very sick, because of his love and serenity, Valeriu was the very soul of the spiritual atmosphere at Târgu-Ocna, strengthening everyone with the grace that dwelt within him. "He was the most peaceful and cheerful one among us," recalls Aurelian Guţă, "never uttering a word of discontent. The injustice and hatred that rained down on us melted when faced with the immeasurable love that ceaselessly poured forth from him."[135]

"At that time," recounts Ianolide, "he had arrived at a spiritual maturity. He was serene, balanced, powerful in word, controlled in deed, stable in prayer, intransigent in attitude, full of love, spreading about a mysterious attraction – and all this from the confinement of his bed resulting from his difficult and prolonged illness.

"He suffered from the caverns in his lungs, he had pleurisy and underwent pneumothorax, [136] , he had frequent haemoptyses and lost his appetite. He endured rheumatic pain throughout his body, abdominal pains caused by appendicitis and, finally, he had trouble with his heart.

---

[134] The Romanian word used here is "fericit," usually translated with "happy." However, Jesus' beatitudes from the mountain (Matthew 5:3-12) are also called "Fericirile." The term used in this translation should be taken to also as simply "joy" (OG).

[135] Nicolae Trifoiu, *op. cit.*, pg.p. 117.

[136] Pneumothorax - the penetration of air into a lung cavity as a result of a perforation in the lung or in the wall of the thorax (Translator's note)

"During the last two years of his life, he was no longer able to stretch out on his bed, day or night, but sat leaning on the edge of his bed with his head falling onto his chest. In the beginning of his great period of illness, we were able to bring him out on the terrace on a stretcher, but later he was unable to leave his bed. He was worn out from coughing, he would turn red in the face from this exertion, and he often spit up blood. At times like these, pain took away his pure and wise smile.

"He smiled even when he was sleeping. His sleep blended into his state of prayerful vigil and he often told us that when we thought he was sleeping, he was actually praying. His prayer continued even in sleep and this gave his face a pleasant luster that seemed to spread around him.

"Despite these physical travails, Valeriu was a blessed man due to great internal efforts and especially to God's grace, which was complete and powerful within him, strengthening him to overcome suffering by living in the spirit. The guards and the re-educated, as well as his friends, were impressed by 'something' in Valeriu, but few realized that that 'something' was Christ.

"On his thin face one could detect a certain light that covered the shadows of his suffering. His forehead was high, white, serene, sometimes with a stray lock of hair falling across it. Nothing, however, created a more profound impression than the heavens that were reflected ever more deeply and brightly in his blue, penetrating eyes. There was something in him that was stable, warm, and vibrant and gave him a vivid, intelligent, active expression.

"His hair had once been thick, but had now thinned out and was soft and silky. His cheeks were

136

flushed with a consumptive beauty, such that now and then a touch of purple appeared on the transparent and immaculate white of his cheeks. His nose was in perfect harmony with his entire countenance. His mouth was the very image of his internal joy.

"A smile that was hard to define blossomed on his lips. There was both happiness and pain in his smile, but both of these things spread light, joy, and internal power. When spasms or great pains afflicted him, he clammed up for a while, but by calling mystically upon the name of Christ he transcended the suffering and was reborn with a smile that was fresh, vibrant, shining, coming from another world.

"He often said that things were difficult for him, even tormenting. But he never said that he, himself, was making an effort to master the suffering; rather the grace and mercy of God were lifting him above it and making him happy. His dialogue with God went on ceaselessly and became all the more intense and apparent as the illness laid him low and his life entered into eternity.

"His beautiful and expressive head was supported by a long, thinned neck. Day and night, Valeriu did not rest on a pillow, but stayed awake with his head resting gently on his chest. His skin had acquired an unusual transparency. Although it was thin, it had a velvety quality, or rather, was finely colored in soft and pure shades.

"His hands were thin, as was his entire body. He could not even eat by himself, but when he lifted his hand, his very fingers diffused light. Everyone noticed this light, but in different ways, depending on each person's inner vision.

"His frail, delicate ribs formed bands across his chest. Because his lungs were full of a festering liquid, punctures often occurred, followed by a pneumothorax that caused the swelling to and pressed against his sick heart. Ultimately, it was his lungs and heart that put an end to his life.

"His clothes were worn out and patched, some belonging to him while others had been given to him. He perspired very much and had to frequently changed his the sheets. Instead of shoes or boots he had a pair of overshoes that were quite unusable. He was wrapped up in a grey blanket and a brown tunic."[137]

"Valeriu was very shy and therefore allowed no-one but me to help him with his bodily functions. Now and then, I would wash him with a cloth soaked in a tub of water, while he would wash the more delicate parts. He would smile in a rather embarrassed way, and asking me to be understanding, would say, 'Please, let me do it.'

"Beside his bed there was a metal bucket covered with a bowl for him to spit in. But there came a time where he was not even able to do this by himself.

"Whenever someone helped him, he seemed a bit embarrassed and expressed his gratitude with much delicacy, adding a smile or a gesture that made such an impression that in the end you felt that you were indebted to him. That is why everyone looked after him with such great joy. In fact, his power of love brought out love and self-sacrifice in others. He felt himself indebted by even the smallest gesture of attention and often humbled himself, saying:

"'You are all so good! You endanger your own health that is already so frail in order to take care of us! I

---

[137]Ioan Ianolide, *op. cit.*, pp. 134-136.

do not know if I would be capable of so much self-sacrifice. May God repay you!'

"When he had weakened so much that he could no longer chew, I took the best of the meat, chewed it myself, and made it into a kind of pill, and then gave it to him in his mouth that way. I gave him the other kinds of food with a spoon, as is done with small children. I don't think he ever received a mouthful of food from my hand without repaying me with a smile, a kind look, or a kind word. Although he was withered physically, the intensity of his spiritual life grew day by day.

"There was a time near the end, when his doctors and friends advised him not to speak any more, but he said, 'Do not take this joy away from me, because I live in order to confess Christ. And if I live, I live by His mercy and if I were no longer able to express the love that I have for you, I would have no reason to live. Therefore, do not be afraid! I do not want to tempt the Source of Life, but I want to serve Him until the end! I thank you for your concern, but please understand that I cannot do otherwise.'

"Valeriu was touched the most by the gifts and the spiritual joys that were given to him. He, who was our joy and strength! During the summer, flowers were brought to him daily from the garden, but he, in turn, would ask someone to take one of the flowers to someone else who was sick. Delicate gestures from great and sensitive souls. His favorite flower was always the lily, about which he wrote with great gentleness in his poems.

"He carried everyone in his heart. He knew that he was going to die and he wanted to finish his days in ceaseless self-offering, as he had always done. For each person he found a suitable word or gesture. One of the many gifts he had was that of knowing people, of penetrating into their souls, and of giving them direction in their lives.

"Once he confessed to me, 'I have to struggle hard with some of those who come to me, but nevertheless they are good souls and in the end they arrive at the truth. Others open up like crystal chalices and receive the word of God with love and enthusiasm. There are others yet with whom a simple glance or gesture is enough to understand each other, and our closeness is profound. Priceless pearls from the Kingdom of God have been gathered together here. I sense that even the re-educated look down when our eyes meet, and some of them even look for the right moment to share a good word with me. The wonderful work of God is wonderful!'"[138]

---

[138]*Ibid*, pp. 137-138.

A Confessor of Christ

"When he was feeling better," Ianolide continues , "Valeriu spoke beautifully and with fervor, focusing mainly on his favorite subject: Interior purification and union with Christ. He used to say, " 'Through baptism, we received purifying grace, and when anointed with Holy Chrism, we have been adorned with all the gifts of the Holy Spirit. But this blessed internal state is dormant within us, we are Christians in name only. We live in a world of confusion, of loose morals, of sin. It is considered shameful to be a believer, old-fashioned to be moral. The baptized man, in order to be saved, has to live all his life in the Holy Spirit, but we have not succeeded in doing this. We have believed, we have prayed, we have kept the faith, we have suffered, but in order to be united with Christ, one must purify oneself inwardly through confession and renew oneself through Holy Communion. Therefore, unite yourself to Christ conscientiously and with great steadfastness, making yourself a bearer of His holiness, His power, His love, His light, His immortality. You must oppose sin mercilessly. Then you will be born anew. There is no path of compromise.'

"Another time he said to us, 'The teaching of Christ is so wonderful, so consummate, that if we understand it, we have the most powerful argument possible for the existence of God. When I had this revelation, I wept from pain and from happiness! Those who believe in Him must bear witness to this truth even if it means being martyred. Was not the Son of God killed as an enemy of His people?'

"The seed that he scattered brought forth fruit. Day by day, people drew ever closer and ever more

141

sincerely to Christ, Who became the source and guide of their lives and their thoughts.

"One day, Valeriu was feeling so ill that we thought he was going to die. In addition to all the other illnesses from which he suffered from, he also developed acute appendicitis. He could have been left to die, but that would not have been 'humanitarian.' Humanitarianism is the hypocrisy of cruelty, it brings to light the poisonous and lamentable domain of the Communist revolution, with its slogans and beautiful vestments. The doctor sent a report to prison administration so that he could be transported to the hospital in town for an operation. The penitentiary political agent of the prison came to him and said: " 'Your life is in my hands. If you do not have this operation, you will die.'

"Valeriu smiled indulgently and answered, 'If one man's life depends on another, then this man indeed has great responsibility! But if everyone would realize that their lives depend on God, then everyone would value the life of his neighbor!'

"'You're crazy,' the agent said to him, and sent him to the operating room under strict guard.

"When he came back to the sanatorium, the agent said to him, 'Look, you were face to face with death! You see, we wanted to show you that your life is in our hands. Maybe now you have changed your mind and you will cooperate with us. We will give you streptomycin![139]! You will also get packages from your family. And you who knows what might happen later?... You are an intelligent man and you could be useful to us. We know that you are not interested in politics, but in religion, but are not the

---

[139] Streptomycin was the first antibiotic remedy for tuberculosis.

patriarch and all of his priests on our side now? Why do you not join our side too? You have a lot to gain!'

"'I thank you that you allowed me to have the operation. From now on, my torments will go on even longer…. As for the rest, between you and me there is thre matter of conscience. For the sake of my spiritual freedom I have decided to die. It is good that the truth be told plainly, and I serve the truth. I am not the judge of others, but a confessor of God. There is nothing under the sun that can survive without God. You do not want to accept Christ. I cannot accept spiritual death.'

"'I told you already that you are crazy!' shouted the agent. 'I'm going to file a report. You are a reactionary, a fascist, an enemy of the people, in the service of American bandits! We know how to deal with people like you! You're only fit to die! Go and die with your Christ! I won't be stopped either by Him nor by somebody like you!'

"'You can kill me now, but no one can kill Him any longer. He is the stumbling block for all pride. Understand well that Christ is the only power that can deliver mankind from suffering and sin.'

"'Give up all this nonsense. The truth is on our side!'

"'The truth is love that sacrifices itself for the poor and the persecuted!'

"Look here, you are staring death straight in the face and you're giving me mystical sermons?! You want to convince me too? See, now you have gone too far! You have spread yourself too thin.'

"Valeriu struggled to keep looking at him, because his eyelids had grown heavy. He felt worn out physically, but an internal joy compelled him to speak about faith in order to leave an eternal testimony. The smile of his measureless love blossomed on his cheeks. He prayed in secret for this unhappy man and for God to deliver the world from leaders like him.

"The agent was confused, muddled. He swore a blue streak and then ordered that Valeriu be taken back to his room.

"You cannot say that I didn't behave decently humanely with you,' the agent later added. 'I offered you life, but you want death. To hell with this! Who the hell can understand all this!'

"This is how they parted company. After that, the agent never bothered him again, but he took long looks at him whenever he came back into the room. (…)

"Valeriu realized that he would never get anything from the agents, but he took it upon himself to say to them, 'There are very valuable people here who can be of use to the country, but they are dying because they have neither streptomycin nor news from their families. You can save them!'

"But the agents did not want to save them. In their belief system, the individual man did not matter, because any man could be replaced with another. What counted was the system. The ideas of these prisoners undermined the system, so their prison sentences were permanent.

"Valeriu had a discussion regarding this issue only one other time, with an inspector from Bucharest. The inspector stopped at Valeriu's bed and asked him, 'What's your name, prisoner?'

"'*Să trăiți*,[140], Mr. Inspector. I am Valeriu Gafencu,' he responded, using the required greeting.

"'Aha,' said the inspector, looking at him sternly.

---

[140] Să trăiți (pronounced *suh truh-EETS*) - the obligatory greeting required of all prisoners toward members of prison administration; best translated as "May you live."

"Mr. Inspector, we ask that you grant us the same rights as those that the Communist prisoners used to have!"

"'We will not repeat the mistakes of the past,' answered the inspector drily. 'Our humanitarianism does not apply to reactionaries.'

"'Mr. Inspector,' continued Valeriu, 'the men here are sick, powerless. Every day, one of us dies. Besides this, we are subjected to threats of terror and torture.'

"'How dare you speak to me that way?! We don't want to turn you into heroes! At best, we will make you informers, and your wives and sisters into prostitutes!'

"Valeriu was deeply pained and answered, 'The sins of this world have to be atoned for. We, prisoners here, we are atoning for many sins. All of us, however, are in the hands of God.'

"'You are a mystic bandit! You will die here! Do not think for one moment that you will get out alive! Even though you are sickly now, you too will be forced to undergo re-education!'

"'The way I am is an advantage,' answered Valeriu, 'because I will not be able to last for long. A few blows will be enough to finish me.'

"'Go to hell!' shouted the inspector. 'We will make sure that you die slowly, painfully, until you give up that the Christ that you're trying to scare us with. We hate Him, and you, and all of you! We're going to destroy you all! Here there is no more Christ, dead or resurrected. We'll see to it that future generations don't know His lies or yours! We ourselves are the christs of this world!'

"'May God forgive you,' answered Valeriu and lowered his head in prayer, expecting to hear an order that he be crushed to pieces.

"But he was not killed then. His toil continued for a while longer."[141]

---

[141]*Ibid*, pp. 141-146.

"They Gave Him Gall And You Give Me Honey?"

"One day, during an inspection, a zealous jailer confiscated the cushion that Valeriu used to lean on. Another, being more humane, took the cushion out of the things which had been confiscated and discreetly gave it back. Between those two souls, there was a moment of vibrant spiritual power.

"After the inspection was over, Valeriu thought it would be best to give the cushion to Traian, who could move only with difficulty and had bed-sores. Traian did not want to accept it and gave it to Gheorghe. [Gheorghe] gave it to someone else until, finally, the cushion came back to Valeriu, given to him by someone who did not know where it had come from. Valeriu considered it to be a sign that the pillow was given to him by God."[142]

*

"During all this time, Valeriu confessed and received Holy Communion regularly. His spiritual father was an ordinary priest, but one who had discerned his deep inner spirituality.

"'I am impressed,' he confided to us after Valeriu's death. 'His confession was always a detailed examination, a fine discernment of spirits, and a proof of his steadfastness to the highest degree of Christian living. Although he did not confess sins but rather experiences, some more lofty than others, nevertheless he humbled himself harshly. He said to me, 'I don't want to have even a moment of doubt, so that Satan

---

[142]*Ibid*, pg.p. 136.

will not come at that moment to claim my soul.' Even though he suffered a lot, he was full of mystical joy. His prayer was an uninterrupted sigh, an unextinguished longing, a ceaseless union with Christ. He could never accept even the slightest alteration or compromise of the truth. His judgment was just and sincere. Christ was alive in him.'"[143]

*

"On another day, however, Gheorghe, a bony peasant who had once been a mountain of a man, confronted him and said:

"'It suits you that you are the only one who gets attention and you pretend to be a saint! Why doesn't anyone bring me meat? Why do people not look after me the way they do with you?'

"'Brother,' Valeriu told him, 'because of my negligence, I was a stumbling block for you. I ask you to forgive me. I will do everything I can to ease your suffering!'

"And Valeriu asked us then to leave him alone, to go to Gheorghe more often, and to do everything we could to help him.

"Gheorghe was a peasant whose family had defended their land for generations. He had been at the Canal, where he always exceeded the quota for an extra bowl of soup. That is how he had contracted TB. Now he was on the verge of death. Although there was no longer anything medical that could be done for him, we were at his side day after day. He wanted very much to live and loved his children and his homestead with a robust vigor.

---

[143]*Ibid*, pg.p. 142.

"He changed, however, during the last days of his life. He reconciled himself with the idea of death and his soul became kind and good.

"'Forgive me, I was possessed by Satan!' he said to Valeriu. 'I wanted to live and I was horrified at the thought of dying. What I did was not right, it was not good. I am dying with faith in the God of our fathers. These [Communist] scoundrels [144] have defiled the world! May they be damned!' And he died.

"From then on, Valeriu was careful to never be a cause of trouble for anyone, even if unintentionally."[145]

*

"I remember how Valeriu, when he needed to urinate during the night, waited until someone else called the orderly so as not to disturb him from the armchair in which he rested, even though waiting for this to happen caused him great discomfort, even pain. Such spiritual grace and kindness!

"In the summer of 1951, in addition to the tuberculosis he suffered from, he developed acute appendicitis. He couldn't have an operation at the sanatorium because of the lack of proper instruments and sterility necessary for an abdominal operation. With difficulty, Doctor Danielescu obtained permission for him to be transported to the hospital in town. The surgeon anesthetized him and performed the operation. The nurse who stood by his head noticed that he was perspiring heavily, but concluded that this was caused by his lung disease. At the end of

---

[144]Gheorghe referred to the Communists.

[145]*Ibid*, pp. 140-141.

the operation, in a faint voice, Valeriu said to the doctor:

"'Doctor, I was conscious when you operated on me.'

"The doctor, surprised, told Valeriu to raise one of his legs and when he saw that he was able to do so, he realized that the anesthetic had not taken effect and that the operation had been performed with Valeriu still conscious.

"Why didn't you tell me? I would have given you a local anesthetic and you would not have felt a thing. How did you endure so much pain?'

"This incident made a great impression on those present. With tears in her eyes, the nurse gave Valeriu a handkerchief on the sly. Shortly after the operation, he was packed into a sort of cart with two wheels and, jolting along on the pavement, was brought back to the sanatorium. After he got back, he confessed to me that the journey home was horrible."[146]

*

"Also, during the summer of that same year, one afternoon, Valeriu had a critical episode of atrial fibrillation, along with all of its consequences. We discussed the matter among ourselves and decided to administer a dose of strofantine with glucose, the only major heart medication we had at our disposal. We all waited to see some result, but we did not observe any change in the rhythm of his heartbeat, even though normally the effect of this medication is almost instantaneous. Since closing time was near and I was on night duty, we made a joint decision to administer yet another dose after closing time, even though none

---

[146]Nicolae Trifoiu, *op. cit.*, pg.p. 107.

of us believed he would survive the crisis. He was cyanotic, his eyes were closed, and his hand was on his cross. He was probably praying. I was convinced that only a miracle could save him.

"After we administered the second dose, I took his pulse again, but again there was no change. About a half hour later, I was called by another patient in an adjacent room, where I remained for 15-20 minutes. When I came back, I looked at Valeriu from a distance. I was convinced that he had died. He was no longer cyanotic, but he had his usual wax-like complexion. I was afraid that this was the pallid tone of a corpse. I ran up to him, and when I took his pulse, it was normal.

"I could not believe it, but it was true. The miracle had happened. He opened his eyes and looked at me, smiling serenely, as if nothing had happened. I dissolved some sugar in water and gave it to him to drink. It was the only way to help his tired heart. After he drank it, he looked at me with that unique look in his intense blue eyes and said: 'They gave Him gall and you give me honey?'"[147]

*

"Everyone loved him and respected him. Even the prison administration was impressed by this powerful personality. The so-called re-educated did not dare look him in the eye, especially since they did not work, even though Valeriu would have shown them the same Christian love that he did to all the others. I had many discussions with him and we often found ourselves contradicting each other. I took up the position of the fighter with sword in hand, while

---

[147]*Ibid*, pg.p. 108.

Valeriu that of a dignified Christian attitude and an immense love for one's neighbor as well as one's enemies. In his heart, there was no room for hatred. He convinced me that the most powerful weapon in the struggle against evil is love for one's neighbor; but this was after I had experienced it on my own, and I remained far below the spiritual level attained by those who are called to it. Valeriu was one of those."[148]

*

"Valeriu's prayer and the example of his life worked imperceptibly in the souls of those around him. An example: One day, R. took a few puffs off of a cigarette stub that he had found in the courtyard. Valeriu saw him and said, 'How will you be able to endure the great trials we are engaged in if you can't even resist a cigarette?'

"For R., a young student who was as well-educated as he was well-intentioned, this admonition was enough to make him begin to seriously consider the notion of Christian living and inner striving.

"'Before then, I had not taken any interest in problems of conscience,' he later confessed. 'I owe my true turning to Christ to Valeriu. He revealed to me not only the depths of my own soul, but also a proper orientation toward life and the world.'

"About a year later, Valeriu was preparing himself for confession and Communion. For the sake of humility and in order that nothing escape him, he called R. to come and help him.

"'R., I ask you to be honest with me!'

"'Have I done something wrong?'

---

[148]*Ibid*, pg.p. 108.

"'You haven't done anything wrong and I don't want you to do anything wrong now either. I ask you then, with all spiritual freedom and without sparing me for any reason, to tell me about anything bad or unsuitable that you find in me, either in word or in deed; tell me with all spiritual freedom and without sparing me for any reason.'

"R. was amazed. He had not expected such a request. Therefore, he answered:

"'In other words, I am to be your judge? You're asking me to do something beyond my power. I only know that for me you have always been an example to follow. I hope that you won't doubt my sincerity!'

"Valeriu lowered his gaze and listened, absorbed in thought.

"'Even if you don't see my sins,' he said, 'there are eyes who do see them. I ask you then to go to ten people and to ask them sincerely what they see that is bad in me. Then come back and tell me what they said, without fear.'

"'You're asking a lot from me. But if that's what you want, I'll do it.'

"After some time, he came back and said, 'nobody had anything to say.'

"'Nevertheless,' Valeriu insisted, 'it can't be that no one had any criticism of me.'

"R. hesitated for a moment. Valeriu saw it and didn't let him stifle it.

"'Tell me everything! Why should you hide anything?'

"'I'm not hiding anything, but I don't know if it's worthwhile to tell you about an unfair judgment from a man who is spiritually weak.'

"'Tell me,' Valeriu insisted.

"'It's about X. He's not too keen on helping those in Room #4, and the generosity the others exhibit toward those seriously ill probably troubles his conscience and gives him all kinds of impure thoughts. He thinks that you ought to do some small things on your own rather than expecting others who are sick themselves to do them for you.'

"Valeriu was a bit saddened, but he wasn't troubled.

"'From now on I am going to try to eat by myself,' he said, 'to take my medications by myself, to take care of my bedpan.... But more than that, I want all of you to believe me when I say this, there is not much more that I can do. I always have before me in the most vivid way your great capacity for sacrifice. I do not have any way to repay you, but God will give you reward upon reward!'

"R. then regretted that he had spoken so sincerely.

"'That cannot be, he said to Valeriu. 'I made a mistake telling you the judgment of a foolish man. He thinks immaturely. No one, not even God, thinks he is correct in this. You can't take him seriously. Give up this idea of managing by yourself, otherwise you will grieve us.'

"Valeriu looked at him with love and pain. Things remained as they had been because, try as he might, Valeriu was incapable of the effort necessary for even the smallest of his needs. His friends continued to help him, while he repaid them by bestowing the gifts of his soul on them."[149]

*

---

[149]Ioan Ianolide, *op. cit.*, pp. 138-140.

"When I arrived at Târgu-Ocna, I had the great fortune of being housed in the same room as Valeriu Gafencu. It was the room allocated for the more seriously ill; four of the chamber-mates were permanently confined to bed. The other two, in somewhat better condition, sought to be of assistance to the other four, as far as our physical and spiritual strength permitted. During the long winter evenings and nights, Valeriu called us to come and sit beside him in order to exchange our thoughts about our Christian conscience. On one such evening, he asked me the more most profound and essential question to me, which left its mark on my life forever.

"'What do you believe is the fundamental goal of life?' he said.

"I tried hard to formulate an answer that would be as rich as possible in content, but I don't think I succeeded in capturing the essence of the truth.

"'I consider that the primary goal of our lives,' Valeriu answered, 'must be to continually prepare for the day of Christian resurrection, when all peoples and nations will appear before the supreme Judgment, with their good deeds and their sins, seeking to find their proper place in the heavenly dwellings.'

"Maybe I had previously heard such things or others similar, but they had passed over me like water passes over stones. But the way that Valeriu expressed it, with that thrilling vibration in his voice and the heavenly depth of his look, shook me spiritually and altered my spiritual state for the rest of my life."[150]

*

---

[150]Nicolae Trifoiu, *op. cit.*, pp. 116-117.

"Valeriu's condition worsened. Because of the long months he had spent in bed without moving and because of weakness and inadequate blood circulation, large bed sores appeared on his body, covering a large part of his back, thighs, and shanks, which were impossible to heal. Other patients in such a condition would groan, curse, and revolt, because the pain of the wounds was truly horrible. But I never heard Valeriu complaining, even though on his face one could read pronounced suffering. Tears came to his eyes while prisoners Ion Ghiţulescu, Nae Floricel, and Aristide Lefa, who were also medical trainees, bandaged him for hours on end, with brotherly love.

"From scraps of torn shirts, they fashioned bandages to cover the sores, but lacking necessary medicinal balms, the scraps stuck to the wounds and produced terrible pain when they were removed. Not one groan could be heard from Valeriu's lips, but on one occasion, beads of sweat covered his arched forehead. The doctors noticed. It was a sign that his patience had reached its limit. They stopped for a while and left him alone to recover."[151]

---

[151]*Ibid*, pg.p. 118.

I Saw the Mother of God

During the night of his last Christmas, toward dawn, Valeriu testified to his friend Ioan Ianolide:

"This night, I kept vigil. I was composing my carol. I wanted it to be very beautiful. I sang it in my head. I heard it in the high heavens, from where it descended. Rather difficult for me, since I do not know musical notes and I have to sing by ear. So, I was awake, lucid, and serene, when all of a sudden, I noticed a photograph of Seta – the girl he had loved - in my hand. Amazed by this, I lifted my gaze and at the head of my bed I saw the Mother of God, clothed in white, vivid, real. She was without her child. Her presence seemed material to me. The Mother of God was actually beside me. I was happy. I forgot everything. Time seemed endless. Then she said to me:

"'I am your love! Do not be afraid. Do not doubt. My Son will be victorious. He has sanctified this place now for future life. The powers of darkness are growing and will frighten the world for some more time, but they will be scattered. My Son is waiting for people to return to the faith. Today, the sons of darkness are bolder than the sons of light. Even though it may seem to you that there is no more faith left on earth, nevertheless, know that deliverance will come, albeit through fire and devastation. The world still has to suffer. Here, however, there is still much faith and I have come to encourage you. Be bold, the world belongs to Christ!'

"Then the Mother of God disappeared and I remained overwhelmed with happiness. I looked at my hand, but the photograph was no longer there."[152]

*

Not long afterward, he related to Ianolide:

"'Late last night I was praying. I felt comforted by the grace of God and I secretly rejoiced in the gift that I had been given. I was awake, conscious, and happy. Suddenly I felt that something odd was happening to me, something apart from my own will. Beginning with the extremities of my body, my soul began to desert me. Not only was I not afraid, but I knew that I was not dying, and the more my soul left my body, the more my interior life grew. My soul rose gently toward my chest, toward my neck, toward my head. I felt happy, pure, illuminated by a holy light. My mind has never been as lucid as it was then. I knew that the Lord was with me. I was happy to be in His power. Time seemed to expand. I no longer felt pain in my body. I looked at my body without wanting it or rejecting it. Life and matter seemed to me to be miracles. My soul quickly drew up to my mouth and left my body. I realized then that I could go anywhere I wanted without being obstructed by matter. It was wonderful! An unspeakable joy overwhelmed me. My first thought was to go see my family, but I remembered the Fathers in the Paterikon that counsel you not to entrust yourself to the workings of spirits unless you are under obedience, lest the devil deceive you and you be lost. The thought appeared in my mind of the old hermit to whom the devil appeared as an angel of light. The old man had departed from his obedience to the abbot and the monastery and he considered himself guided by God Himself and thought

---

[152]Ioan Ianolide, *op. cit.*, pg.p. 180.

that the others were jealous of him. Then the 'angel' came to him and told him to call all the brothers to the well in the courtyard of the monastery in order that the power of God be shown to them. They went to the well in the middle of the night. The bright angel appeared and, entering the well, said to the hermit, 'Throw yourself into the well and I will pull you out, unharmed, in front of everyone so that they may see that you are a saint.' The old man threw himself into the well and died like a wretch. Reminding myself of this, I was careful not to fall into temptation and I decided to return to my body. Now, you see, I submit to obedience. Tell me what to do and I will do it!'

"Listening to him, I felt shuddered. I asked for three days off in order to pray. After three days, I went to him and said:

"'I believe that it is a work of God! Your humility is a guarantee of truth and goodness. You submit to me in obedience, but I do not have such a spiritually advanced experiences, nor do I have anyone to consult, nor spiritual books to examine. I feel unworthy of such an honor and frightened by the responsibility. I do not doubt the possibility of miracles, but I also do not believe that they are absolutely necessary for our salvation. But glory to God for those things that are happening with us, with you, through Him! My advice is to be careful. You have proceeded well. Let's not go too far with the prospects that are opening up with this plan, for we have not yet been tested. Let us protect ourselves from temptation!'

"Valeriu listened attentively and accepted everything I said to him without even a shadow of sadness, doubt, or resistance. He remained serene and reconciled with my decision, and it was exactly this humility of his that assured me that he dwelt in a state of grace."[153]

---

[153]*Ibid*, pp. 181-182.

The Testimony of Father Mihai Lungeanu

"I arrived at Târgu-Ocna in the spring of 1950, by a miracle of the Mother of God.

"In 1947, when I was arrested, I was in my fifth year of medical school in Iaşi. I was arrested because of my connection with a group of Legionnaire students at the school. In autumn 1949, I arrived at Piteşti, where I entered the flames of re-education. On the first day, the beating lasted from 7:30 in the morning until noon. Then other beatings followed. I prayed to God constantly. There was only one night in which I didn't pray and I have reproached myself for this all my life. If I had not prayed as much as I did, I would have collapsed completely. Even during beatings, I was praying all the time, 'Lord, get me out of here and I will put my whole life at Your feet!' And I eventually got out.

"After a week or two, along with a few others, I was taken to Văcăreşti. I had had a kidney ailment since Iaşi. Because there was blood in my urine, I thought I had kidney tuberculosis, but it turned out to be something else. The orderly at Piteşti realized that I was sick and sent me to Văcăreşti.

"During the time I spent at Văcăreşti, three groups arrived from Piteşti and after lung exams, the sick were sent to Târgu-Ocna and the rest were sent back to Piteşti. I don't know why, but I, who did not have TB, remained at Văcăreşti. I prayed, 'Lord, do not send me back!' I prayed a great deal to the Mother of God and she helped me.

"After a while at Văcăreşti, without being sent anywhere else, one night I had a dream. I dreamt that the Mother of God said something to me, I don't

161

remember what, but I recall feeling very guilty. Further along in the dream, I found myself in the courtyard at Văcăreşti, along with a few of my colleagues. In that little courtyard, there was a cherry tree in bloom on which some clothes had been hung out to dry. The courtyard was in the shape of a triangle. At the peak was the guard tower, with a sentry guarding us, while at the other side, at the base of the triangle, was the gate to the prison. The gate opened and a guard entered.

"'Which one of you is Lungeanu?'

"'I am.'

"'Pack your bags and leave!'

"I woke up. I wondered what the dream meant.

"In the morning, I was taken out for a walk. In the courtyard, just as in the dream, the sentry in the guard tower and the cherry tree with clothes hanging on it. The gate opened and a guard entered.

"'Which one of you is Lungeanu?'

"'I am.'

"'Pack your bags and leave!'

"Just like in the dream. They put me on the prison bus and I arrived at Târgu-Ocna, where I stayed for three and a half years. Through a miracle, the Mother of God saved me and instead of being sent back to Piteşti, she brought me to Târgu-Ocna.

"At Târgu-Ocna, apart from the administration that could not even begin to compare with that of the other prisons, what was distinctive was the spiritual atmosphere. It was an atmosphere of prayer.

"Here I met Valeriu Gafencu. He was in Room #4, the room for those who were dying. As a medical student, I was put in Room #5, which was connected to Room #4, and I assisted those who were seriously ill. I gave injections, I cleaned wounds, I changed bandages, and so on. Since I was around Valeriu on a daily basis, I had many discussions with him and learned a great deal from him. I perfected 'the technique,' so to speak, of the prayer of the heart.

"Valeriu talked with everyone about faith. In the room with those who were dying, there was a medical student named Traian Maniu. He was paraplegic, paralyzed from the waist down, with sores all over his body – his tailbone was even exposed – and his sores emitted a rotten smell like that of a sewer. Every day I prepared a bandage for him and removed the pus with a stick. I spoke with him. He was not a believer. Valeriu, whose bed was next to his, spoke with him a great deal. He decided that we pray for Traian for a week, and that several times a day each of us would say Psalm 50, *Have mercy on me, O God*....

"After this, Traian returned to the faith, confessed, and received Communion.

"'Mihai' Traian said to me, 'I am in a state of euphoria that I cannot even describe to you. I feel an extraordinary joy.'

"The words of the akathist to the Savior, 'Jesus, joy of my heart' came to me. Traian died in peace.

"The same thing happened with Father Gherasim Iscu. 'Brother Mihai,' he said to me, 'when I close my eyes, I hear extraordinarily beautiful melodies. I cannot find the words to tell you how beautiful these songs are.'

"General Tobescu, who had been the chief of the military police under Carol II and Antonescu, was also there. He had very little interest in God. His warrant officer, Ilie Neagoe, a man whom he greatly trusted, was arrested at the same time. Ilie had a type of faith rarely found in those of his ilk. For an entire year he gave the general a portion of his own food in order to help him. He washed his clothes and spoke nicely with him.

"'General, this is the state of things. We are all dying and we are looking forward to life everlasting. Do you not want to be reconciled with God?'

"'But Ilie, I do not have any sins.'

"'General, we are all sinners.'

"He spoke with the general in that way, day after day, until one day the general said : "'Ilie, I also would like to confess.'

"'Yes, General.'

"These minute things, day after day – the behavior of Ilie Neagoe, discussions with the others, with Valeriu, the atmosphere of prayer – dug into the heart of General Tobescu. Father Gherasim Iscu knelt beside his bed and heard his confession. He then received Communion and died reconciled with God.

"Mitică Duțanu also died in Room #4. He was a student who suffered in silence, meditating on the sufferings of the Savior. One evening I heard him saying softly, as if to himself, the words uttered by Christ on the cross - *Eli, Eli, lama sabachthani* – My God, my God, why hast Thou forsaken me? He died serenely and reconciled with God.

"At Târgu-Ocna, I met up with captain Mircea Cucu again, whom I had been with in re-education at Pitești. I remember that in the midst of a beating, I heard Țurcanu give the command, 'Four men (but who there was still a man?) beat Captain Mircea Cucu only on the head!'

"Mircea sat on the edge of his bunk, making no gesture of self-defense. He only had one leg. He had lost the other on the Eastern front. He had been a career officer, had worked in a tank unit, and had scored many victories. He was decorated with the order of Mihai Viteazul, [154] and I seem to recall that he received a citation to receive a medal from the army. Before this, he had told us many stories from the front. Now Ţurcanu was "repaying" him for his many victories on the eastern front.

"I do not remember even one of the four men who beat him. Just as Ţurcanu had ordered, they clubbed him only on the head. In a short span of time, his head looked like a melon, stained with blood. I was very impressed by the dignity with which he endured the blows. He did not cry out, he did not utter a word. He sat on the edge of his bunk and took it all as if he were not involved, as if he were only a spectator.

"After I parted company with Mircea, I no longer heard what happened to him or how much more he had to endure. We met up again about two months later at Târgu-Ocna. Very thin and weak, he was a mere shadow of a man, sick with pulmonary tuberculosis. He had frequent haemoptyses. He was no longer able to leave his bunk and had been brought in from Piteşti as part of a group of prisoners afflicted with TB. All of them had gone through re-education and had probably given the declaration that had been required of them.

"At Târgu-Ocna, I was able to exchange a few words with him. One day I asked him if he believed in God. He responded in the affirmative and this gladdened me very much.

---

[154]Mihai Viteazul (Michael the Brave) is regarded as one of Romania's greatest national heroes. During his reign, three principalities forming the territory of present-day Romania and Moldova were united for the first time under a single Romanian ruler.

165

"From the way in which Mircea conducted himself at Piteşti and the way in which he confronted suffering and death at Târgu-Ocna, I recognized in him the military career type, the fighter that doesn't make compromises, the hero.

"At Târgu-Ocna, Mircea Cucu stayed in Room #2, in the bed next to Sava Ilie, a student who had also gone through the hell of Piteşti. One day, one of the men who had beaten Ilie at Piteşti came to his bedside. He knelt down beside his bed and asked forgiveness. Ilie forgave him and spoke to him very nicely, as if nothing serious had ever happened between them. Later on, both of them died. The first to die was Ilie, but about two years later the other one also died.

"At Târgu-Ocna I also knew Father Ioja Sinesie. He was a parish priest from Banat who had no special education or any store of knowledge, but who had great faith and a permanent state of prayer. Very quickly, he began to show signs that normally appear in the course of the practice of the prayer of the heart, the warmth, the pain that you feel, the flame that comes forth, and other things that I did not know about at the time but read about later in the *Zbornic*. Those at Târgu-Ocna - Gafencu, Father Iscu, Father Ioja Sinesie, Gheorghe Jimboiu had spoken about these signs, not because they learned about them from books but from their own ceaseless prayer. Father Sinesie, as a priest, heard a lot of confessions at Târgu-Ocna. He died later, in another prison.

"We received a series of packages from home. Some received streptomycin, which at that time was a miracle drug for lung diseases. The political officer, a devil in the shape of a human, summoned a few of us and said,: "'Look, here's your medicine! We'll give it to you if you give us information.'

"In other words, become informers. I know of three who refused: Gheorghe Nițescu, Ion Sultaniuc, and Eduard Masikievich. There may have been more, but these are the ones I know about. All three were of an exceptional purity. They were called one by one.

"'Sir, in the Legionnaire movement I did not learn to do such things!'

"'Go then, and die for Christ and the Legion. Go! March!'

"It is a good thing for these matters to be understood – if not, then you would pass by them as if nothing happened. These men were martyrs. It is a pure sacrifice, and it has extraordinary value. It puts a choice before you: This or that. 'No.' 'Go!' And they died. Nițescu and Masikievich in prison. Sultaniuc lived a while longer, but he did not recover. He had a bone TB of the leg and died shortly after his release, at the sanatorium in Balotești. For the sake of these pure souls, God took pity on the rest of us. For their sake, although it was attempted, what happened at Pitești was not allowed at Târgu-Ocna."[155]

---

[155] Testimony given by Father Mihai Lungeanu to monk Moise in February 2005.

The Day Will Come When Your Heart Will Sing the Prayer

From an account by Octavian Anastasescu: "At the beginning of May 1951, sick with TB, I arrived at Târgu-Ocna. During the three and a half months spent in this prison, I came to know Valeriu Gafencu. The others had informed me that he was a living saint. I myself felt this to be true and I also bear witness to it. I will mention only a few of the many extraordinary events I experienced in his presence.

"In our discussions, he often encouraged me to say the Jesus prayer. He advised me to say this prayer using a certain technique, with my hand on my pulse, every heartbeat accompanied by a word of the prayer. I also tried to say the prayer when I was stretched out in bed and had no other preoccupation. When we met, Valeriu always asked me about the prayer. I would tell him that I was making an effort, but despite all my endeavors, I had not succeeded in saying the prayer as it ought to be said, that is, with the heart.

"'Listen,' he said, 'a moment will come in your life when, without any effort on your part, your heart will sing the prayer on its own and you will hear it.'

"Although I did not pay much attention to it at the time, these words of his turned out to be a real prophecy. After I got out of prison, I was more or less under house arrest. I was not allowed to go beyond a certain distance from the house, a distance determined by Securitate[156].

---

[156] Securitate (official full name *Departamentul Securității Statului*, State Security Department): was the secret service of Communist Romania. Founded on August 30, 1948 with help from the USSR, Securitate was abolished in December 1989, shortly after

One day I no longer took this ban into consideration and I went to visit a friend. When I returned home, I found my worried mother. The Securitate had come looking for me, and since they did not find me, they left word with my father that I should present myself to the office the following day. The next day I went to them. We went into a room that had once been a garage but was now a kind of waiting room. A group of five or six Securitate officers appeared; they sat down and started routine questioning. As I was answering, something unusual happened. I seemed to be enveloped in a kind of luminous sphere. I felt a heavenly perfume, something I cannot describe in words. During this time, I heard my heart singing the prayer, 'Lord Jesus Christ, Son of God, have mercy on me, a sinner.' I felt very light, as if the laws of gravity had been suspended. The Securitate officers did not realize what was happening to me and continued to ask questions. It is interesting to note that I heard what they were saying, but I didn't understand what was being said to me. Likewise, I heard my voice responding, but without knowing what I was saying. This state lasted for three, maybe even four hours.

"At a certain moment, one of them said, 'Enough!'

"At that moment, this unusual state vanished and things returned to normal. The officers left. During the interrogation, a warrant officer responsible for guarding me had also been present. We were left alone and, as we were leaving the room, he said to me :'If there were only a thousand people like you in Romania, the Securitate would not be able to handle it.'

President Nicolae Ceauşescu was ousted. The Securitate was, in proportion to Romania's population, one of the largest and most brutal secret police forces in the Eastern bloc. (Translator's note)

"What questions did they ask me? What did I answer? I do not know. I remembered how Christ told the Apostles not to worry when they would be brought before kings and emperors because they would then be given words that no one would be able to refute. I also remembered that Valeriu had prophesied about this moment in which I would hear my heart singing the prayer of Jesus.

"There were other situations in which I realized that he had the gift of clairvoyance. Once, at Pascha, I was with him in his room. He was stretched out in bed while I was looking at the string of lights formed by the faithful who were coming down from the skete at Măgura with lit candles. From his bed, Valeriu was not able to see this sight and I told him what I was seeing. At a certain moment, I stopped talking. Then looking into my eyes, he started to describe to me what I saw.

"'Look, now they have arrived at a bend in the road, now they are taking a detour.'

"In bed, looking at me, he described with exact precision the scene of faithful returning from the skete with their candles lit. This made an extraordinary impression on me. But this was not the only time.

"One day I recounted to him what I had dreamt the night before. This dream was a repetition of an older dream I had before my arrest. The night before I was arrested, I dreamt that I was in a church. I spent a long time looking at the paintings on the walls. Then I tried to leave the church. I walked all around the inside of the church trying to leave, but I could not find a door. After trying again and again to leave, but without success, I woke up. In the morning, I told my mother about the dream.

"'That means prison!' she said.

170

"The following night, around midnight, I was arrested. At Târgu-Ocna, I had the same dream. It happened that I was in the same church. I recognized the paintings. I tried once again to leave the church. But this time I succeeded. I did not know how to understand this dream. There was no sign whatsoever that I would be freed, and besides, I had heard a rumor that I would soon be moved into a room with a group who had come from Piteşti and who were trying to initiate a re-education program here at Târgu-Ocna. The prospect of this happening horrified me. I even considered suicide. Alarmed, I told Valeriu about the dream and I spoke of the fears I had related to the possibility of being put into the same room with the re-educated.

"'Do not be afraid, Brother Octavian,' he said. 'Tomorrow you will be freed.'

"I was shocked. I looked at him, thinking that he was delirious with fever. I saw no reason to hope that I would be freed.

"'Do not be surprised. Tomorrow you will be freed!' he repeated.

"And that is exactly what happened. The next day, a captain of the Securitate came into the room.

"'Hey, which one of you guys is Anastasescu?' he asked. 'Pack your bags!'

"They took me to Bacău, where I was freed the same day, just as Valeriu had said."[157]

---

[157]Testimony given to Monk Moise by Octavian Anastasescu in February 2006.

Pastor Richard Wurmbrand

Among all of Valeriu's Christian gestures, surely the most impressive was that he saved the life of the Jewish-born Protestant minister Richard Wurmbrand. Some of the sick inmates at Târgu-Ocna received streptomycin from their families, which at the time worked miracles for lung diseases. Among these was Leonida Stratan, whose state of health had recently improved. He therefore decided to give his medicine to Valeriu, who was in a very serious condition. Valeriu accepted it, but, despite the opposition of those close to him, he handed it over to Pastor Wurmbrand. The pastor's life was saved at the cost of Valeriu's life.

We learn more about Wurmbrand from Father Mihai Lungeanu.

"I made the acquaintance of Pastor Wurmbrand around 1950, when I was at Târgu-Ocna. We were there, together, for about three years. I remember a group of sick prisoners that arrived one day, sent from the prison at Văcăreşti. One of them was a blond man, over six feet tall, thin as a rail and held up by two other prisoners. This was Pastor Richard Wurmbrand.

"From the beginning, he was assigned to Room #4, the room that had been allocated for the dying. Anyone who entered that room knew that the next stop was the cemetery. During the three and a half years I spent at that prison, I saw many men die in Room #4. The only one who survived was Richard Wurmbrand.

"I had the opportunity to speak to Pastor Wurmbrand many times. There were details of his life that I learned directly from him. When he arrived at Târgu-Ocna, he had eighteen tubercular bone cavities and a form of pulmonary tuberculosis which had become active and he was expectorating very much. According to what he told me, he had been brought from the Ministry of the Interior, where he had stayed in isolation for a long time, in very difficult circumstances.

"At the Ministry, he had been interrogated by the Securitate colonel Dulgheru (Dulgherber). This man showed a compounded hatred for Pastor Wurmbrand. In the first place, both of them were Jews. Wurmbrand had converted to Christianity long before, entering the ranks of Protestantism sects. As a fervent preacher of the faith amidst of the Jewish community in Bucharest, he had won over many converts. In the second place, Dulgheru hated Wurmbrand because Wurmbrand had once been an illegal activist in the Romanian Communist Party who later abandoned Communism. Wurmbrand had been recruited into the Communist party by the Soviet consulate in Paris. He was then sent to Moscow, where he attended a higher institute of political studies, specializing in Marxism-Leninism. He knew Ana Pauker[158] well, as well as other Communist leaders, both in Romania and outside the country. I no longer remember how long his illegal activity lasted, nor do I remember any other relevant details. But the fact is, he was arrested along with other Communists, interrogated, and sent to prison. He came down with tuberculosis and through the influence of a peasant, he converted to Christianity.

"Before arriving at Târgu-Ocna, he was kept in the warehouse at the Ministry of the Interior. There, he was destroyed physically. He could no longer get out of bed

---

[158]Ana Pauker was the unofficial leader of the Communist Party immediately after WWII in Romania. (O.G.)

and there was no one else in the cell to help him. For an entire month he had no choice but to simply relieve himself in the bed. Imagine what that cell was like. Bedsores started to form. His whole body was covered with blisters of pus caused by his bone cavities, especially those in his spine and ribs. There was no question of medical assistance. During all this time, the interrogator Dulgheru "visited" him regularly, assuring him each time: '"Don't worry, sooner or later I'll drive Christ out of you!"'

"Considering that the conditions of his imprisonment remained unchanged, it's easy to imagine how the pastor responded,

"One night while he was there, the pastor recounted that the devil appeared to him – he said that he was not at all ugly – and scolded him for abandoning him and going over to the Other One, that is, to Christ. The pastor refused to speak with the devil, saying only: 'Get out of my sight. You're a liar and the father of lies!'"

"In the room for the dying at Târgu-Ocna, many were gravely ill. Not one of them is alive today. During the three years he spent there, Wurmbrand saw many men die and each one died in his own way. All those who were dying asked to receive confession and Holy Communion. This was possible because there were priests among us who had the Holy Mysteries. Here the pastor had the opportunity to get to know Valeriu Gafencu, who lived and died like a saint, with the name of Jesus on his lips. The daily theological discussions he had with Valeriu were very instructive.

"Pastor Wurmbrand, having seen for himself what happened in Room #4, was so impressed that he asked to be baptized in the Orthodox faith, choosing as his baptismal name Valeriu, after Valeriu Gafencu. His wish was fulfilled by one of the priests. However, he remained Protestant after his release, telling no one that he had been baptized Orthodox. He was an unstable man. From our earliest conversations, when I would defend Orthodoxy, he was coy, he would retort, laughing,: "'You want me to be Orthodox, too? But I'm a Jew, a first-generation Christian. I can't be anything more than neo-Protestant!'

"One evening, the pastor recounted an event which took place in Bucharest in 1945 or 1946, during the first National Congress of Democratic Priests of Romania. I can no longer recall in which prestigious conference center in Bucharest these representatives all gathered; among them was the leader of Romanian Judaism in Romania, Şafran, along with other rabbis, as well as representatives of the Islamic faith, the Minister of Religion, many other notables. Many of these men were giving talks that evening.

"Pastor Wurmbrand did not figure on the list of speakers, but the stormy speech given by Rabbi Şafran persuaded him to speak. He told us that he was in the conference hall with his wife Sabina, listening to the speakers. Rabbi Şafran's turn to speak came. At a certain moment in his speech, the rabbi cried out: "'Enough of this outrageous lie that the Jews crucified Christ! It was not the Jews who crucified Him, but the Romans!'

"Şafran probably made other statements contrary to the New Testament and maintained by the Christian church. Not one of the representatives of the Orthodox or Catholic clergy got up to contradict Şafran with Biblical arguments. They were probably afraid of being accused of anti-Semitism. The pastor's wife, Sabina, said to him: "'Listen, Richard, even if it means they'll lynch you, get up and speak! Wash the cheek of Christ that has been mocked!'

"He raised his hand and asked to be allowed to speak.

"'I went up to the microphone,' the pastor recounted, 'and I spoke. I was disgusted by the statements Rabbi Şafran had made. I can no longer recall what I said. I remember only this: Let us not wonder at the fact that the Jewish people have suffered so much. Not only what they have suffered in the past, but what they will have to suffer from this point on! The curse that weighs heavily on us is that which the chief priests brought upon themselves, along with a part of the crowd that gathered at the judgment of Christ and His condemnation to death by crucifixion: '*May His blood be upon us and upon our children!*' And Pilate washed his hands before them, saying, '*I am not guilty of the blood of this just man. See to it yourselves!*' This curse follows the Jewish people and they will not escape its woeful consequences unless they accept Jesus Christ as the Messiah, as foretold by the prophets. The blood He shed on the cross has thus become the means of salvation and in no way one of condemnation.'

"As a commentary on what Wurmbrand said, I personally believe that this curse falls only upon those who themselves assumed it, while it lies upon the Jewish people as a whole only in principle. Their guilt cannot be any greater than that of Christians who disregard Christ and trample Him underfoot. There is guilt in any case, but only God, Who shed His blood on the cross for all mankind, can judge its various shades and nuances. I return to the story told by Pastor Wurmbrand:

"'After they heard what I said, all the rabbis present, including Şafran, raised their fists and began to shout and yell, to issue threats and to rush forward to where I was standing. The Orthodox priests stood up and came to my aid, forming a wall that the rabbis could not pass through. I was escorted outside, surrounded by a crowd of priests defending me. After that, I had much to endure from the Jews. For example, one day I was giving a sermon in the pulpit of our house of prayer. The hall was packed. At a certain moment, a crowd of Jews began to throw stones at the windows, then rushed into the hall, attacking those who were gathered in prayer. When I saw what was happening in the hall, I said to myself, 'A pastor does not forsake his flock, no matter what happens. The good shepherd lays down his life for the sheep!' But I was up in the pulpit, a place of shelter, while those down below were on the field of battle. At a certain moment, I noticed that the number of aggressors was gradually diminishing and I immediately discovered the reason: One of my parishioners, a woman employed as a maid, was hitting left and right with her fists, clearing a path and quickly felling the combatants.'

"At the sight of this 'spectacle,' the pastor laughed heartily and congratulated the woman for acting so effectively. I want to emphasize that the pastor was a talented storyteller, gifted with a remarkable sense of humor, although his humor was Jewish in tone.

"On many occasions, Wurmbrand admitted told to me that he loved his people very much, despite all the suffering they had caused him, and that he wished that all Jewish people would accept Jesus Christ as the Messiah. He wanted all of them to become Christians and he expressed regret that they had failed in their mission as the chosen people. He repeated the words of St. John the Evangelist: '*He came to His own and His own did not receive Him*' (John 1: 11).

"The pastor recalled jokingly that he once heard a Jew say, 'Lord, please look for another chosen people, for we have suffered enough!'

"Wurmbrand suffered much due to the lack of receptivity and hard-heartedness of Jewish people, which manifested itself in the rejection of Christian teaching. Something I recall from speaking with the pastor is an incident, recorded in Jewish written tradition, that occurred after the Resurrection of Christ. One night a rabbi, I no longer recall his name, was examining the texts of the Old Testament that refer to the coming of the Messiah. Suddenly, Jesus Christ Himself appeared in his room, in flesh and blood, and said, 'Rabbi, why do you not want to believe that I am the true Messiah, whom you are expecting? The Scriptures speak of me.' The rabbi then slapped Him across the face and right there on the spot his arm dried up from the elbow.

"Every Saturday, the Jews go to the synagogue. Each Saturday they read a selection or a chapter from the Old Testament. When they get to the 53rd chapter of the Book of Isaiah, they simply skip over it, as though it were not even there, and proceed to the next chapter. The pastor was once speaking to a rabbi, a friend of his, and said:

"'You know, Rabbi, I read Chapter 53 of the Book of Isaiah!'

"The rabbi answered, 'It's not good.'

"'Why not?'

"'Just like I said, it's not good.'

"'All right, Rabbi, now I've read it. What should I do now?'

"'I told you it's not good,' replied the rabbi.

"The pastor wasn't able to bring the discussion to any conclusion and finally gave up trying to get any kind of explanation from the rabbi.

"After I heard this, I asked the pastor what this chapter contains, this chapter that the Jews skip over and do not read. The pastor recited the entire chapter from memory. It speaks of a prophecy made 800 years before the coming of Christ on earth. Here, in this chapter, He is described exactly as He appeared during His holy Passion: his body full of wounds and covered with blood, such that He was disfigured and was named the *man of Sorrows*, who took our sins upon Himself and expiated them through His sacrifice on the cross and His death. *As a sheep is led to the slaughter and a lamb toward those who shear him, so He did not open His mouth.* In this chapter, it is very clear that Jesus Christ is the Lamb of God who takes away the sins of the world, the Messiah awaited by the Jewish people and all mankind. This is the lamb symbolized in the Old Testament when, through the blood of the lamb with which they anointed their door frames, protected the Jews from the punishment that God sent upon the Egyptians.

"I asked the pastor to explain to me why the Jews are so rebellious in the face of so much evidence. He answered with the Holy Apostle Paul's explanation: God allowed the hearts of the Jews to be hardened in order that pagans might have the opportunity to accept Jesus Christ, and through Him, God. When the numbers of pagans will be fulfilled, then the Jewish people will accept Jesus Christ as the Messiah foretold by the prophets and will convert to Christianity *en masse*. This will occur near the end of the world.[159]

---

[159]Father Mihai Lungeanu, in a notebook of memoirs as yet unpublished, made note of a few incidents recounted by Wurmbrand, about referring to his conversations with rabbis:

"Listen, Rabbi," he said to one, "don't you ever think about how much your people are suffering? Look, they're killing us everywhere. Look at what's happening to the Jewish people because they reject Christ."

"What matters, what matters," said the rabbi, "what is important is that in the end Christ be defeated."

"He won't be defeated, He is victorious. He is God."

"No, no, no," said the rabbi.

On another occasion, with a different rabbi:

"Rabbi, why don't you want to understand that Christ is the Messiah?"

"I can't."

"Why?" Wurmbrand then read to the rabbi from the New Testament, from the Sermon on the Mount. The whole time he was reading, the rabbi was weeping and saying,

"Oh, how beautiful! Oh, how beautiful!"

"All right, Rabbi, if you like the things I'm reading to you so much and are moved so deeply, why don't you accept Christ?"

"I can't."

And again the rabbi said, "Oh, how beautiful! Oh, how beautiful!"

Wurmbrand himself told me about a young Jew in Cernăuți who converted to Orthodoxy and became a novice in a monastery. It so happened that whenever Brother Vasile, as he was called, traveled by train, he would mingle with the other passengers and say to them, "Brothers, listen to what this says," and he would read to them from the New Testament. He did missionary work. One day, he was found dead in a park in Cernăuți. His sister, who at first was against the idea of conversion but then converted, believed that it was their parents, their family who had decided to assassinate Brother Vasile. Even though the murder was reported to the authorities, no measures were taken. There was no investigation, as if it had never happened. Later, after the Jews were deported, the sister arrived in a concentration camp in Poland. In this camp, she confessed Christ. An

"The pastor read from Holy Scripture every day and gave explanations. At Christmas and at Pascha he would recount events from all four Evangelists to us. I, myself, learned many Scripture texts from the pastor.

"Pastor Wurmbrand was a practical man. After his release, he emigrated to America and appeared before a Senate subcommittee. He simply stripped to the waist, revealing the scars of his wounds.

"'Look, this is what Communism means,' he told them.

"It was very convincing.

"Regarding his wounds, one day when he was at Târgu-Ocna and was being bandaged by hospital attendants, he started to yell, cry out, and wail. The attendant preparing his bandage asked him:

"'Pastor, why are you yelling and wailing like that? I have not even begun!'

"'I'm crying out like this preventively. What does it cost me?'

"We all laughed heartily."[160]

Emigrating to the West after his release from prison, Wurmbrand became coordinator of activities for sixteen Christian missions from various free countries

---

SS officer overheard her and asked if she was a Christian. She told him her story and that of her brother Vasile. The officer said to her,

"You will not die here!"

After some time, she was released and arrived home. She decided to emigrate to Israel so she could also confess Christ there. I do not know what happened to her. I heard about Brother Vasile and his sister not only from Wurmbrand, but also from Father Bartolomeu Dolhan from Iaşi, who also knew of this Jewish monk.

[160]Testimony given by Father Mihai Lungeanu to monk Moise in February 2005.

whose objective was to assist those suffering in Communist regimes. Thus, what Valeriu said when he handed over his streptomycin to Wurmbrand was proven true: The pastor, if he should survive, would use his position and connections to do much good for those who were suffering under Communism.

Wurmbrand passed from this life in the U.S., on February 17, 2002, the eve of the fiftieth anniversary of the death of Valeriu. To the great disappointment of his partners-in-suffering at Târgu-Ocna who read his books translated into Romanian, although he speaks very eloquently about the help he received from the other prisoners, nowhere does he mention the fact that Valeriu saved his life. To substantiate this, we cite a passage from his book, *In God's Underground,* in which he makes reference to Valeriu:

"Gafencu spent his entire adult life in prison, but like the other prisoners in whom the Christian faith prevailed, he did not know what other deeds to carry out so as to atone for his past mistakes. Each day he made the exemplary gesture of putting something aside from the little he had in order to help the weakest among us recover. He despised anti-Semitism, and when those who subscribed to this principle came to visit him in Room Four, he would suddenly come out with a remark that shocked them: 'I would like to see the country ruled entirely by Jews.'

"His comrades stared at him in horror.

"'Yes,' said Gafencu calmly, 'Prime Minister, legislators, civil servants—everyone. I would make only one condition. They must be men like the old Jewish rulers, like Joseph, Moses, Daniel, Peter, Paul, and Jesus Himself. Because if we have any more Jews over us like Ana Pauker, then Romania is finished.'

[…]

"He told me one day, 'My father was deported from Bessarabia by the Russians. We never had enough to eat. I was beaten in school, then jailed for running away and joining the Iron Guard. I'd never met a single good, truthful, loving person. I said to myself, "It isjust a legend about Christ. There is not anyone in the world like that today, and I do not believe there ever was." But when I had been in prison a few months I had to admit I was wrong. I met sick men who gave away their last crust. I shared a cell with a bishop who had such goodness that you felt the touch of his robe could heal.'

"Gafencu had been in Room Four a year, and in all that time he had not been able to lie on his back. It gave him too much pain. He had to propped up continually. Every day he had a little less control over his body, often fulfilling his necessities where he lay; then having to wait, sometimes at night for hours, until someone came to clean him.

Of all the many aspects of Legionnaire thought, in the end, Gafencu only retained the simplicity of Christian faith.

"Stronger patients from outside had to take over the washing for those of us who could not help ourselves, scrubbing shirts, underwear, pillowcases, sometimes twenty sheets a day, although they had to break ice in the yard to reach the water. My own things were always stiff with pus and blood, but when I tried to stop a friend from washing them he became angry.

"Gafencu never complained. He sat very still in bed, sometimes moving his head a little to nod in agreement or convey a word of thanks. When it was known that he had not long to live, his friends gathered around his bed with tears in their eyes. His last words were, 'The Spirit of God wishes us jealously for Himself.'

"When he had gone, the others knelt and prayed. I said, 'Jesus tells us that if a seed does not fall into the earth and die, it cannot bring forth fruit, and that as a seed is reborn in a beautiful flower, so man dies and his mortal body is renewed in a spiritual body. And his heart which has been nourished with Christianity's ideals will surely bear fruit.'

"After a priest had said a prayer, Gafencu was wrapped in his sheet and carried to the mortuary. During the night he was buried in a common grave by convicts, who were always given to perform this task."[161]

As can be seen, Wurmbrand never acknowledges the fact that Valeriu saved him with the price of his own life by giving him the streptomycin. He also seems to have forgotten his first name. And Wurmbrand says nothing about the theological debates he and Valeriu used to entertain, which the other prisoners remember.

In addition to these omissions, we should also make note of a few exaggerations and inaccuracies. The statement he claims Valeriu made, "I never had enough to eat," is difficult to believe considering the fact that Valeriu's family owned 100 hectares of land, as Valeriu's sisters testify. I do not see why Valeriu would lie, seeking to impress Wurmbrand with his poverty. Likewise, Valeriu never said that in his youth he considered Christ a "legend." The good deeds he did were not done in order "to atone for mistakes," but rather to fulfill Christ's commandments and cleanse his soul from passions. The statement, "I had never, in my

---

[161]Richard Wurmbrand, *In God's Underground*. Bartlesville, Living Sacrifice Book Company, 2004, p. 89-90.

life till then, met a single person who was good, faithful, loving," again, seems questionable to me, if one thinks of the atmosphere of love and the spirit of morality in which Valeriu was raised in his childhood home. Another strange detail is the "bishop full of goodness" who supposedly shared a cell with Valeriu. Virgil Maxim and Ioan Ianolide, who were with Valeriu at Aiud the entire time, recall no such person. At Pitești, there were only students, while the other prisoners at Târgu-Ocna do not recall the presence of any bishop. Likewise, if the episode had occurred at Târgu-Ocna, Wurmbrand himself would have had direct knowledge of it.

On the other hand, the pastor does not forget to state that he [Wurmbrand] gave the streptomycin sent by his wife to another sick prisoner. There are some inaccuracies with this as well. Wurmbrand recounts that he decided to give this streptomycin to Ion Sultaniuc, who was seriously ill. It is worth mentioning that, before this incident, Sultaniuc's family had sent him streptomycin, which he did not receive, because it was conditional on his willingness to become an informer, a spy.

Wurmbrand claims that Sultaniuc supposedly refused the streptomycin from him because he was Jewish, concluding that Sultaniuc was so anti-Semitic that he refused to be saved by a Jew. Based on testimonies of those who survived Târgu-Ocna, I have determined that things were not quite that way. Sultaniuc refused to accept the medication from Wurmbrand not because he was anti-Semitic but because the pastor had made some statements which he found disturbing. In discussions with the others, the pastor claimed that all the political leaders between the wars, including Corneliu Zelea Codreanu, had been "bought" by the Communists and had received money from the Communist International Party. Sultaniuc, who was very much an admirer of Codreanu, refused to speak with the pastor after this; to Sultaniuc, these absurd remarks were proof of the pastor's lack of character. Sultaniuc was not the only one. Many other prisoners, disturbed by the pastor's remarks about the Legionnaires, distanced themselves from him. Thus, the true conclusion is that Sultaniuc's refusal of Wurmbrand's help was not because of his anti-Semitism, but because of the pastor's tactless behavior[162]

---

[162]Ioan Ianolide, *op. cit.*, pp. 282-289.

Christmas at Târgu-Ocna

"It was a quiet, peaceful winter," Ianolide would later recount, "with snow, but no frost. The hills all around had turned gray. The church bells at the skete announced the monks' time of prayer to us and we joined with them and with every Christian soul in silent prayer. It is impossible that the silent prayers that were poured forth into the air by men trapped between death and torture would not be received. They were heard in heaven, they brought heaven down to earth, and I believe that God will be merciful to this world for the sake of those great and faithful souls at Târgu-Ocna.

"In Room 4 were housed, among others, Archimandrite Gherasim Iscu, beside him a Jew who had once been a Soviet agent and was now a Zionist, and finally, Ion, my friend from Piteşti, who was very ill. In a bed on the right side of the room was Valeriu, my best friend.

"Ion and Father Gherasim were in very grave conditions. Valeriu had recovered a bit and, having said his usual prayers, was now concentrating on writing some devotional testamentary poems. He also wanted to put together a special Christmas carol for Târgu-Ocna that evening.

"I gently approached Father Gherasim, who was sitting with his eyes closed. He was as thin as a rail. He had been at the Canal, where the prisoners worked sixteen hours a day followed by an additional four hours of administrative tasks. He had been assigned to a special crew for priests, with a workload meant for quick extermination. At the Canal, Father Gherasim encouraged his friends, helped many of those who were struggling with their work, and was at everyone's disposal with respect to religious services. He practiced the prayer of the heart and had tremendous spiritual resources which him strengthened him throughout his many sufferings.

"Informers had reported him many times for hearing prisoners' confessions and giving out Holy Communion; as a result, he had been beaten, isolated, starved, terrorized beyond the normal limits. Man is made of flesh and blood, and the soul cannot ignore the laws of life. The ascetic Father Gherasim contracted tuberculosis, was confined to bed and, nearing death, was brought to Târgu-Ocna to die in a 'humane' way.

"His presence in the sanatorium made itself was touching by the skillfulness with which he entered into communion with the souls of others, and encouraged them. He was sought out as a spiritual father because of these heavenly gifts. He offered himself joyfully to those who asked for him even though he exhausted himself by doing so.

"He was also a guide in the way of hesychasm[163], based not only upon his readings but also on his rich mystical experience. In Room 4, the idea of mysticism had not only been rehabilitated as an idea but and as a practical reality, but it was so vivid, thick, and intense that it was palpable. In fact, it was not necessary to hold out your hand to receive it, for God was present in that

---

[163] Hesychasm is a seclusionary tradition of prayer in the Eastern Orthodox Church, and some other Eastern Churches of the Byzantine Rite, practiced by the faithful[...]. Hesychasm in tradition has been the process of retiring inward by ceasing to register the senses, in order to achieve an experiential knowledge of God. (Parry Ken; David Melling (editors) (1999). *The Blackwell Dictionary of Eastern Christianity*. Malden, MA.: Blackwell Publishing)

room and He captivated you immediately, penetrating into your soul like an insinuating fragrance. We do not deny even for a moment the Mysteries that take place on the Holy Altars, but we testify to the fact that grace is also manifested intensely through the saints. That is what I felt around Father Gherasim.

"I approached him shyly, to get a sense of how he was. He felt my presence and opened his large, deep, dark eyes.

"'Have you come? I'm glad. I was far away, in a verdant place, full of song and fragrance, full of lights. It was wonderful there. There is peace. In fact, I can't express how it is there. There is so much happiness there that even the joy of seeing you, is suffering in comparison to that other world. I will leave soon, maybe even now, on Christmas night. And this is a gift from the Lord. I don't know how to thank Him .... I don't know how to make people live in God, in Whom is our complete joy .... I have the assurance of eternal life. I am already in it. I'm not even afraid of the Judgment, because I'm going with a humble mind and hope only in the mercy and power of God .... The spirits of darkness now rule over mankind, but do not be afraid, Christ is near, He is testing the world; but the world needs to suffer greatly .... Our enemies believe that we are defeated, but they deny the presence of God in history and do not know His ways....'

"He stopped for a moment, breathed deeply, and then continued.

"'One day there will be pilgrimages here. There are few of us here, but there is still faith in the world such that the world will be delivered. It seems impossible now, but, beyond human capacity , there is a divine plan that will renew mankind. Therefore, rejoice! I have

189

known men here before whom my mind is humbled. Tell Valeriu to pray for me …. And you pray also! I am blessed to have arrived at this hour ….'

"He spoke quietly, but with great power, such that I was profoundly impressed. He closed his eyes again and withdrew into the threshold of eternal life.

"The Jew Iacov, who occupied the next bed, had involuntarily overheard my conversation with Father Gherasim and was clearly moved. I put my hand on his forehead.

"'Do you have a fever?' I asked him.

"'No,' he answered. 'I feel well…. There is a world here that I never thought could exist; in any case, a world totally opposite to the one I come from. It's awful for me to discover myself spiritually in the Christian atmosphere that I have stubbornly resisted all my life, first through materialism, then through Zionism. Christmas night, which always stirred up a bitter fury in me, today overwhelms me with its spiritual reality. Because what happens here is not a matter of works that are human and natural, but spiritual. These are the words of a materialist, an atheist, a Jew! And my confession is not a farce. In the face of death, a man becomes sincere and has the ability to see the truth. This confession surprises you, but it has formulated itself in me slowly, quietly, beyond my own will, as a necessary recognition of reality. The true God is Christ!'

"He wept while saying these words. He was deeply moved. I tried to understand him, to take part in the profound moment he was experiencing. He was silent for a while. I sat down next to him on his bed and took his hand into my hands. I prayed for him in my heart…. what more could I have done?!

"I knew well that I could not understand his state of spiritual unrest, for I was born Christian and have lived as a Christian, while he was a Jew, had become a Communist, and was now a Zionist. Such a soul passes through terrible traumas whenever it makes a new discovery in the spiritual world, and his Christian testimony was a categorical and irreversible overturning of his entire past.

"'I thank you for listening to me,' he said after a while. 'Maybe soon we'll be brothers in Christ!'

"'May God help you,' I answered, and I got up to go to Ion.

"Ion was breathing quickly and had a fever. His face was pale and flushed. Nevertheless, there was a vital balance maintained in him. I knew that death was near. So, did he.

"'Today I confessed my sins and I prepared myself to leave,' he told me. 'But I regret the fact that I'm dying and that I won't live to see the salvation of the country.'

"He stopped talking in order to rest. He was breathing with difficulty.

"'Faith in God is the only thing I have left. Maybe only now, at this time of historical crisis, the world will realize that there is faith in God! Now it's too late for me. I'm fading out. I often have the sensation that it's getting dark, but then a blinding light bursts forth. On the threshold of death, the secrets of life are seen more clearly. It's a shame I didn't see these things all my life! My brother, that outlaw, was a man incomparably greater than I. He was a visionary!'

"'Quiet down,' I told him. 'You're exhausted.'

"'It was decided for me to die in your hands,' he continued. 'I have loved and admired you very much. May God bless you!'

"'Brother,' I answered, 'I am greatly indebted to you. You were more courageous than I. Only God can reward you for the love that you have given to others, to me and to others. I will never forget you!'

"After a longer pause, he said, 'Please tell Iacov to forgive me. I've often had arguments with him. He angered me with his Communist and Judaic statements, here, where there is no place for them.'

"I told this to Iacov, and he then got up from his bed and came over beside Ion.

"'I'm impressed that you can ask forgiveness from a man who has erred, who has lived in error all his life. Vainglory? Maybe....but rather the inability to know the truth. This truth caused me to rebel against Jesus all my life, but now I have discovered His truth. Only Satan can inspire and sustain so much falsehood and hatred toward the truth. You cannot realize the awful drama that I am living in these moments.... I opposed the truth, while you told me the truth and never behaved badly with me. I hated you, while you loved me. I was in deception, you were in the light of truth. It is I who must be forgiven by you, just as Paul needed to be forgiven by Christ. I believe that I will also become a Christian. I want to be a Christian but I am not yet the master of my soul. I ask you to be kind with me!'

"Ion wept. I stretched out my hand and comforted him.

"'May God help you! Your confession has caused rays of light to burst within me; it has infused me with trust for this world that I am leaving, a world embroiled in mercy in these sorrowful conditions. Wonderful are the ways of the Lord!'

"Iacov withdrew. Ion asked me to go to Father Gherasim in order to receive a final blessing.

"Peace was restored and I went up to Valeriu. He was sitting with his back leaning on the edge of the bed, with his head falling forward onto his chest and his eyes half-closed, but I had the impression that he was looking at me. His blue eyes opened, immense and bright, and enveloped me with their warmth.

"He smiled happily and said, 'How good that I feel you near me! I'm composing a beautiful song for Târgu-Ocna.'

"'Take it easy,' I said to him, and sat down on a chair to watch.

"He said to me, 'You'll be the first person to hear my Christmas carol. I'll tell you the verses.'

On the banks of the Trotuş[164]
The servants of the Lord are singing,
Yoked in His yoke.
But their singing is muted,
Because it comes from much suffering
And is interwoven with tears.

In the heart of a servant
The Lord makes His manger
In the night of Christmas.
Lilies from heaven rain down
Upon His new manger
And the flowers drip dew.

A little child stands in the light
And looks in wonder
At the prison window.

---

[164]Trotuş - a river in east-central Romania that flows through Târgu-Ocna. (Translator's note)

Beside the little child
Stands a little angel,
And whispers to him gently:

"Today Christmas has moved
From the palace to the prison,
Where the Lord has been jailed."
And the child [standing] in the light
Came to the prison
To celebrate the great feast.

Refrain:
Let the children come,
To bring me from the garden
White flowers for the feast,
White, white flowers!

"Valeriu looked at me a little and then added, 'I dedicate this carol to Father Gherasim. He is the little child that the last verses of the carol refer to.'

"Valeriu was calm, serene, and joyful. I thanked him for caroling me. He smiled at me and withdrew into himself.

"It was so quiet that I could hear the labored breathing of the sick, the falling of the snowflakes, the beating of my heart. In that miserable mixture of prison and tuberculosis there was an obvious spiritual vibrancy such that everything seemed unearthly, miraculous. Time passed slowly. My mind was attracted by horizons of light. Meanings unfolded themselves deeply, in a sort of static motion, a paradox that only life in the spirit could bring about.

"We were locked up, but our souls dwelt outside of prison. We were sick in body, but spiritually robust.

We were on the threshold of life and death, but death was swallowed up by life. Our prayer was interwoven with that of the angels and carolers whom we felt nearby. That evening witnessed an unusual intensity of communion with God. But I was lucid and present to this reality, therefore, I believe matter was spirit for me and spirit was matter. No contrast troubled me.

"Every so often I went up Ion and Father Gherasim, who were going out slowly, all the more alive as they approached death. Iacov was not sleeping. His eyes were open, but he was not saying anything.

"Late into the night, toward dawn, I realized that I needed the stub of a candle and a match, things that were strictly forbidden, but which I kept inside a mattress and used sparingly, only for two or three minutes, whenever someone departed from among us.

"Ion was the first to go, like a little child, he, a man of such great soul. His last look was sad, sad and full of love. Perhaps there was prayer in it, maybe also a prompting, perhaps a hope also flickered.

"I had just finished with Ion, when I was called to Father Gherasim. He opened his deep eyes once again, eyes that had been drawn back in their sockets.

"'Let me look at you one last time, my dear ones, my children, my brothers, my parents!' he said softly.

"He coughed, and then added, 'I am leaving! May God bless you!'

"He breathed deeply and quickly, contracted a bit and relinquished his soul. I closed his eyes.

"I had closed the eyes of hundreds of men and I saw, I knew better that each one died better than how he had lived. Perhaps a man can be portrayed more accurately by the moments of death than by how he lived.

"Although that night had been difficult and I hadn't rested at all, I did not feel at all tired, neither was I sad, and I had no regrets. The reality of life was penetrated by the reality of immortality. My body felt light. Time was expanded, I had no sense of it passing, neither did I want it to pass. I felt the presence of those who had departed just as much as those who were still alive. An immense peace filled my soul. In this spiritual state, I prepared the two men who had died for burial.

"Now and then, I would take a look at Valeriu. He was joyful, happy within himself, with his eyelids half-closed, his head hanging on his chest, leaning on the edge of his bed. He had not been able to rest that night either. After I had finished, he called me to him.

"'The carol is finished,' he said. 'Maybe these verses will be my testament.... Let's carry faith even farther, until we reach the end that has no end!'

"For a while, silence again filled the room. Prayer, like a heavenly ladder, brought angels down from heaven to earth. Heaven was there, heaven was everywhere."[165]

[165]Ioan Ianolide, *op. cit.*, pp. 282-289.

Passage to Eternity

Valeriu fell asleep in the Lord on February 18, 1952. Two weeks prior to his passing, on February 2, he called a partner in suffering, Nicolae Itul, to his side and confessed that the date of his departure from this life had been revealed to him: February 18. He asked Itul to prepare the necessary things: a white shirt, underwear, a match, the stub of a candle. He also asked that a small cross be placed in his mouth after he died so that, if God should so ordain, he might later be identified.

On February 18, after confessing and receiving Holy Communion in the morning, in a state of angelic calm, Valeriu rendered his soul into the hands of God. Ianolide later testified to the state of grace in which Valeriu was found on the day he passed into eternity: "It was the happiest day I have ever known, even though it was the day that the most precious man I have ever known died. But on that day, he was the one who transmitted to me the state of inner fulfillment that accompanies me to this day. I believe that I was in heaven. I also believe that I was beside Christ, because Christ was present in Valeriu."[166]

Knowing ahead of time that Valeriu would soon depart from them, his partners in suffering came one by one to bid him farewell. Although very weak, he found the strength to give each one of them a word of strength and encouragement.

"He spoke to many, and after speaking he would always rest with his head falling forward on his chest. A few of his friends sang some of his own songs to him. He

---

[166]*Ibid*, p. 251.

listened and seemed to embody the very song itself. Then he thanked the boys gratefully.

"'Give glory to God all your lives!' he told them.

"To a young man of rare purity he said, 'You are a flower! Devote all the fragrance of your soul to Him who gave you such beautiful gifts!'

"'Do not be afraid to commit yourself to Christ,' he said to another young man, 'for all your doubts and uncertainties will receive an answer and you will understand life and the world through the Holy Spirit.'

"A poet also came, and Valeriu looked at him with love. "'You have talent. Dedicate it to Christ! There is a need for Christian culture. Poets have great gifts and great responsibility. Glorify God and all His works.'

"The poet was so moved that afterward he could not remember what Valeriu had said to him. He was bewildered, and went outside and called me, asking me to repeat what Valeriu had said.

"A Protestant doctor who had looked after Valeriu during the final period of his life also came. "'Doctor, I amm grateful for the love with which you helped me,' Valeriu greeted him. 'The two of us have often had theological debates. The end of my life is a final Orthodox witness. I would be very glad to see you return to the true Church.'

"Every time he started to speak, Valeriu spread power around him; this moved me deeply. He was so full of grace and I shared in his light. Everything happened normally, simply, spontaneously, as a work of God.

"Wurmbrand also came, full of awe and reverence, unlike his usual self.

"'Thank God I made it here,' he said. 'God brought me here for my salvation. Here I have come to know

Christ purely. I thank you for everything you have done for me. The words you have said to me will not remain fruitless, nor the Orthodox truth that you have revealed to me. Forgive me for the trouble I have caused. Pray for me, for I need this prayer. My wish is that we both enter the Kingdom of God through the same gate!'

"'I am glad that we met,' Valeriu answered him. 'I understand your concern, but I ask you to come to Christ like Paul, without wavering, without detouring, without reservation. Let us pray together for the repentance and Christianization of the Jewish people. No nation in the world, especially [the Jews], has salvation apart from Christ. May the grace of God lead you to the Truth!'

"Wurmbrand was deeply moved. He went back to his bed and continued looking at Valeriu."[167]

"'Around ten o'clock the medical visit arrived,' recalls Nicolae Itul. 'Dr. Danielescu, a woman who had been like a mother to those who were sick, came in accompanied by a military policeman and by our usual medics, who were themselves prisoners. Valeriu bid farewell to all of them.'

"'I am leaving today,' he said to the doctor.

"'What are you saying?' spat out the military policeman. 'Where are you going?'

"'I am going where you, yourself, will go come one day,.' answered Valeriu.

"The doctor, visibly moved, was not able to control her tears."[168]

---

[167] *Ibid*, pp. 187-188.

[168] Testimony given to monk Moise by Nicolae Itul in September 2005.

Completely exhausted physically, supported only by the power of grace, Valeriu entrusted his final thoughts to his brother-in-suffering Ianolide.

"'In the first place, I dedicate my mind and my soul to the Lord. I am thankful that I came here. I am going to Him. I beseech you to follow Him, to glorify Him, to serve Him. I am truly blessed to die for Christ. It is to Him that I owe the gift of this day. Everything is a miracle. I am leaving, but all of you will have to bear a heavy cross and a holy mission. To the degree to which I will be allowed, I will pray for you from the place where I will be and I will be beside you. You will have many troubles. Be strong in faith, for Christ will destroy all His enemies. Be bold and pray! Preserve the Truth unchanged, but avoid fanaticism. The madness of faith is divine power, but it is exactly through this that it is balanced, lucid, and profoundly human. Love and serve mankind. People need help because there are enemies, predators who seek to deceive them. Atheism will be defeated, but be careful about what will replace it!'

"Now and then, he paused in order to regain his strength.

"'I thank you from the bottom of my heart for everything you have done for me. I ask you to forgive me…. May any man whom I have offended forgive me…. I am thinking about my mother and my sisters with much love. My wish is that they go along the paths of the Lord. I ask you to look after them…. These words are my final testament. The Christian world needs to establish a new beginning, more pure, closer to the truth. I ask Christian politicians to take Christ into account and to follow His teaching. They are charged with great responsibilities.'

"Noon had already passed. Outside, big, velvety snowflakes were falling and frolicking in the air. The ill were served their dinner. Valeriu was alive and fading away at the same time. He was breathing with difficulty. He spoke less and less. I remained deeply moved.

"'Ioan,' he said, 'carry the spirit even farther, all of you! God has done His work here!'

"A long pause followed. He turned a bit red in the face then came back serene, beautiful, blessed. He was still able to say:

"'It is finished!'

"He raised his blue eyes toward heaven and I saw how wonders ever more deeper, ever more astounding wonders were revealed in those eyes. Everything was made up of unearthly but real light, a sort of perfect reality, the very sight of which sanctifies you."[169]

"After his life had been extinguished," recalls Aristide Lefa, "a profound sadness spread throughout the sanatorium. Even those who assumed the position of the re-educated were impressed. Many men had died at Târgu-Ocna, and they had done so reconciled with God and their brothers. But never had our entire community been so deeply affected as on that sad day.

"At that time, the section chief was a policeman, namde Orban Petre, a man intrinsically evil, who felt a sadistic pleasure in causing all kinds of trouble for the prisoners. Whenever someone died, he locked us all up in our rooms, so that we could not pay our last respects to the one who had died or put a flower at his head, for we did not have candles. But this time, when he learned of Valeriu's death, he left the section and stayed at the gate for two hours, thereby giving all of us the chance to

---

[169]Ioan Ianolide, *op. cit.*, pp. 189-190.

see him for the last time and to pay him all due respects. When he came back, in a gentle voice he asked Ioan Ianolide, whom he knew had been Valeriu's closest friend, if he wanted to take anything that belonged to Valeriu. This had never happened before. Ianolide replied that he did not need anything. He was too grieved by the loss of his most beloved brother-in-suffering.

"Whenever someone died, his body was placed into a trunk used to transport cadavers to the grave. There, the bodies were thrown without a coffin, sometimes into a common, or mass, grave. When not in use, the trunk was kept outside, behind a sort of screen made out of stone. A short while after Valeriu was taken out of the room, it started to snow gently, with big flakes, so that in a short time everything was covered with an immaculate layer, as immaculate as his pure soul had been."[170]

Those who died in prison were buried on the edge of the local cemetery. In order to prevent later identification, their heads were crushed with a hoe before the bodies were dropped into the grave.

With respect to Valeriu's final passage to the Lord, Radu Constandache had a dream that seems quite impressive.

"I left Târgu-Ocna in 1951. In February 1952, while I was imprisoned at Făgăraş, I had a dream. In my dream, I was at Târgu-Ocna, in one of the interior courtyards, with a few other prisoners. Someone came from another courtyard and said, 'Valeriu Gafencu died!' We stopped our walk and went to the other side.

---

[170]Nicolae Trifoiu, *op. cit.*, pp. 109-110.

"Everyone was gathered in front of the hospital. Just then, Valeriu Gafencu was being taken out, dead, on a stretcher, and was placed in the courtyard, beside a small flower garden. Everyone was singing 'Holy God, Holy Mighty, Holy Immortal, have mercy on us.' The atmosphere was unusual, touching.

"Then the stretcher seemed to be transformed into a throne of remarkable light, such as I have never seen. Valeriu was sitting on the throne, alive, with his arms resting on the armrest of the throne, his whole being full of light. The entire throne was enveloped by a bright, rosy cloud. Valeriu was entirely illuminated. His face seemed to shine with a beaming smile. The throne and Valeriu began to rise slowly. He looked at us down below and made a gesture to us with his hands. We kept looking up until the throne, rising ever higher, could no longer be seen except for a light that also gradually disappeared. We dispersed, plunged in thought.

"Later, I found out that Valeriu had died on the very same day I had the dream."[171]

---

[171] Radu Constandache, excerpt from the televised documentary *Noaptea pătimirilor* (Night of Suffering), an episode dedicated to Valeriu Gafencu.

Valeriu's Disciples

Valeriu guided many prisoners on a spiritual path at Târgu-Ocna. Among all the examples I could bring forth, I will mention only two individuals who were of a remarkable purity, Gheorghe Niţescu and Gheorghe Jimboiu. These two must be among those exceptional people from the Communist prisons that deserve a place in the calendar [of saints].

Gheorghe Niţescu was born on April 24, 1924, in the village Brăneşti, county Dâmboviţa. He attended Gheorghe Lazăr High School in Bucharest, where he graduated with honors. He then enrolled in the Polytechnic in Bucharest. He was arrested in 1948 and sentenced to eight years in prison. He went through the prison at Piteşti and then he arrived at Târgu-Ocna. Ion Popescu, one of the supervisors at Târgu-Ocna, recalls:

"Gheorghe Niţescu was a sincere man, with an optimistic, cheerful, and unreserved nature. Sentenced to prison as a Legionnaire, he had been at Piteşti, but being sick with TB he was taken to Târgu-Ocna before re-education [at Pitesti] had begun. He arrived at Târgu-Ocna at the same time as Valeriu Gafencu.

"He had come from Piteşti seriously ill, but nevertheless, at first, he was still able to move, he was not yet immobilized in bed. Toward the end, when his illness was worsening steadily, he was moved to Room #4, the room for the dying, along with Valeriu. Under Valeriu's influence, he improved tremendously, from a spiritual point of view, and he practiced the Jesus prayer. When he arrived in prison, his spiritual level was that of a moral Christian who believes in God and goes to church, but who was not particularly interested in mysticism. He had, however, a spiritual purity that made him very receptive to spiritual work. He knew that his illness was serious, that he had no chance of surviving, but he was not sad, he was not afraid. With serenity he entrusted himself to the will of God. This was his position when streptomycin arrived for the very ill. He was called by the political officer, who said to him:

"'If you want to live, you have to sign an agreement to give us information.'

"He indignantly refused. Now, if you definitely wanted to live but did not want to be a traitor, you could sign such an agreement but not abide by it. In other words, you could try to get around it. You could bargain with yourself, saying, 'I will sign, take the medication, and then give them inoffensive information. Maybe things will change and I will survive.' But Nițescu did not think that way. For him, with his spiritual purity, the very act of signing, even without giving information, was itself already a compromise, a sin. He considered this a great sin. Therefore, he refused, taking a Christian stance rather than taking the stance of so-called philosophical ethics.

"After he spoke to the political officer, he came back very indignant.

"'How can I write down that I will give information? That is a compromise, a sin, I cannot do such a thing! How could he consider me a traitor?'

"In the depths of his heart, he could not accept such a thing.

"'I cannot be a traitor, and even if I die, maybe God will forgive me for this.'

"He died with this serenity, he had no regrets or doubts regarding what he had done. I was near him until the end. He died at night; I spoke to him the day before.

"The sickness was progressing and his strength was gradually diminishing. He went out serenely, like a candle that has run out of wax. Spiritually speaking, Niţescu was under the influence of Valeriu, he was a kind of disciple."[172]

"Gheorghe was another young man who seemed rather superficial," recounts Ianolide about Niţescu. "Many thought that he was incapable of deep spiritual endeavors; they were amazed when he attended spiritual discussions. He often sought out Valeriu and asked his advice about prayer of the heart, which he practiced in secret. Since he was quite sick and spent most of his time in bed, we did not realize the efforts he was making until Valeriu brought this to our attention.

"Gheorghe had ascended to the higher levels of prayer. He was quiet and joyful. He had received spiritual gifts, including the gift of clear sight. He was pure, gentle, wise, and happy. He had also been called by the agent to receive streptomycin in return for becoming an informer, but his refusal had been so abrupt and categorical that the officer cursed him and sent him back to his bed. He was like a child. He died with a smile on his face."[173]

Father Mihai Lungeanu recalls a conversation with Niţescu not long before his death.

"'Do not be angry, Gheorghe, but if it so happens that I am freed (although I did not believe I would be), what do you want me to say to your family on your behalf?'

"'But Mihai, what can I say…. That our suffering was for the sake of a higher cause And especially for God.

---

[172]Testimony given to monk Moise by Ion Popescu in April 2005.

[173]Ioan Ianolide, *op. cit.*, pg.p. 150.

206

Justice is on our side. We are right. But, God forgive me, it seems to me that it was a bit beyond our strength. But I do not blame God. That is how it should be. But it seems to me it was a bit too much. Too much, that's all. I am dying peacefully, though. I have no regrets.'"

In other words, a man resigned to his fate, full of dignity. He died on August 25, 1952.

"Another young man of exceptional purity," continues Father Mihai Lungeanu, "was Gheorghe Jimboiu. When, at the request of Valeriu Gafencu, I began a week of prayer so that Traian Maniu might return to God, I took a 'spiritual bath.' In other words, since we had no priests among us at that time – they came shortly thereafter – we confessed our sins and errors to each other, in turn. I realized then how much inner purity Jimboiu had. He was one of the purest. From him I learned that, after six months of striving, he had received the gift of prayer of the heart. He prayed continuously. If you woke up at night, you would find him sitting with his head on his chest; he was saying the prayer. He was of a rare purity. He told me about what he felt during prayer. Later on, from the books I read, I realized that he had attained the states of prayer that the Holy Fathers speak of."[174]

Gheorghe Jimboiu was born on October 18, 1921, in the village Vela, near Craiova. His father died when he was a small child, and he was raised by his mother, who decided not to remarry. In 1949, while a student at the Academy for Commerce, [a technical school], in Braşov, he was arrested for Legionnaire activities. He contracted tuberculosis as a result of harsh prison conditions, but so

---

[174]Testimony given to monk Moise by Father Lungeanu in February 2005.

managed to avoid re-education at Piteşti and was sent to the sanatorium at Târgu-Ocna, along with Gafencu.

He died in 1963 at Aiud. Although suffering from a serious liver ailment as well as tuberculosis, he received no medical attention because he refused the re-education program proposed by Commander Crăciun.

Dumitru Bordeianu, who met Jimboiu during Great Lent at Gherla in 1954, considered him "Gafencu's brightest pupil." Before meeting Gheorghe Jimboiu, Bordeianu had gone through re-education, from which, according to his own testimony, he emerged demonically possessed. With the help of Jimboiu, he managed to free himself from the unclean spirit that had tormented him for four years.

"A few days later I got there, while I was moving about the room, a young man who seemed different from all the others caught my attention. He had the look of an eastern ascetic and radiated goodness.

"I noticed that the young man was also gazing at me. At a certain moment, he caught me looking at him. I had to lean against the wall in order not to lose my balance. Something inexplicable had seized me, and it seemed to me that a force apart from my own will was opposing itself to that look. I shuddered when I realized that a spirit other than the one that possessed me was ravishing my soul.

"Exhausted, I stretched out on my bunk. My face was like that of a corpse. The blood had drained from my face. Noticing my pallor, my cellmates asked me what the matter was. I said that I did not feel well. I will never forget the night that followed. The satanic spirit that had taken control of me tortured and frightened me, probably because it could not bear the look that Jimboiu – that was the young man's name – had given me.

"The next morning, he walked up to me and invited me over to his bunk to talk. The spirit that controlled me tried to stop me from going, but Jimboiu had taken me by the hand and this made me follow him.

"'Brother, you are sick,' were the first words he said to me. 'Do not be afraid and put your trust in me. Open your soul and tell me what is in your heart. Maybe I can help you somehow.'

"In a few words, I told him everything that was on my conscience. At my disclosure, he answered:

"'You have sinned greatly against God. Why did you not try nevertheless to continue praying even at Piteşti?'

"I responded that someone unknown had prevented me. He asked me if I was still praying now.

"'I pray, but I do not feel anything,' I answered. 'My heart is made of stone.'

"'When you pray, do you ask forgiveness from God?'

"At my negative response, he continued, 'Have you wept?'

"Again, no.

"'I would like to know how you pray.'

"After I recited to him the prayer that I used, he told me that I prayed well.

"'But I feel as though God has abandoned me.'

"'Don't offend God! He did not abandon you, you offended Him!' he asserted.

"After this exchange of words, I believed that I had spoken with an angel, because the power that emanated from him had reduced the spirits that tormented me to silence.

"After that, he invited me to come and talk with him every day. Realizing what kind of man he was and how great his spiritual power was, I implored him to also pray for me.

"'I will pray for you,' he answered, 'but you must make a personal effort. The offense that you brought against God cannot be wiped clean except by the tears of repentance. Only when you pray to God with tears and repent will God hear your voice and forgive you.'

"The days leading up to Pascha 1954 were so horrible for me that I cannot find the words to express the state I experienced. I have no way of making anyone understand.

"As I increased my discussions with Jimboiu, so did my torment become all the more unbearable. Every day I expected to wake up crazy from lack of sleep. Paradoxically, my thinking and my powers of judgment were functioning normally and I was aware of the state I was in; this did me a lot of harm."[175]

The description of the moment when God freed Bordeianu on the night of Pascha is impressive:

"It was Holy Saturday. The day before, I had prayed more deeply than I ever have in my life. At the same time, I also felt despair at the thought that my prayer might not be heard.

"Saturday evening, however, at ten o'clock, when the bell rang for lights-out, I stretched out on my bunk. For the past several nights I had not been able to sleep. Toward midnight, something urged me to get out of bed and walk around the room. I walked up to the window and at that moment I heard the church bells in Gherla ring, announcing the service of the Resurrection. The sound of the bells was so harmonious, that it seemed to come from another world.

_____

[175]Dumitru Bordeianu, *op. cit.*, pp. 376-379.

"I fell on my knees before the window, and, with my hands crossed in prayer, I cried out from the depths of my soul, 'Lord Jesus Christ, Son of God, I confess that I have offended Thee, but Thou knowest, O Lord, that I have reached my limit of suffering and patience. I can endure no longer. Do with me whatever Thou will! I had fled from Thee, O Lord, but I ask Thee with all my heart, if it be possible, forgive me and resurrect my soul, because I have boundless faith in Thy Resurrection!'

"At that moment, as I stood on my knees with my hands clasped and my eyes fixed on the iron grating on the window, my entire being trembled and streams of tears began to flow from my eyes.

"In the midst of my tears, I was only able to say, 'Lord, be merciful unto me!' Before I was even able to finish these words, my whole body was seized with trembling and a writhing like that of the possessed, and I felt that a foreign power left my body and soul. It was the spirit of Satan that had tortured and possessed me for four whole years.

"I liken my healing, for a healing it truly was, to the atonement done by a man who carries a great burden on his back, until he falls beneath its weight and can no longer get up. Then someone else lifts the burden from him and he feels so light as though he can fly. That is how I felt when that satanic force left me.

"I fell down with my head on the concrete, faint, with my shirt wet from sweat and my tears continuing to flow in streams. I felt my forehead wet from tears that had fallen on the cold concrete that I was kissing. They were the tears of repentance that God had deigned to receive, forgiving the offense I had brought to Him. During my four years of torment, I had not shed a single tear, but now my soul was immersed in a bath of repentance and the wonder of God.

"I got up late, no longer knowing where I was. I felt like a different person, I felt so light that I seemed to float in other spheres. At the Resurrection, God had healed me and had also resurrected me.

"I knelt down once again and stretched out with my face to the earth, I cried out with all my soul, 'Lord, Thou art so good and merciful to sinners that I do not know how to thank Thee.' And then, the words of Jesus when He healed the possessed man came to me: *Behold, you have been healed. Go and sin no more.*' And I felt a joy in my heart that only those who have experienced it could understand. If until then I had been in hell, at that moment I felt that the joy of heaven was not far from my soul.

"I got up from the concrete floor. Before me stood Jimboiu, like a specter from the world of dreams. I embraced him, saying with all my heart, 'Christ is risen!' 'Truly he is risen!' he responded, full of gentleness and affection. We both wept for a while. In my entire life, I have never felt so close to anyone as I did then to Jimboiu. Together we lived the joy of my resurrection. I wanted to thank him for his guidance, but he was content to say, 'Your tears are accepted by God and His mercy healed you. I saw everything that happened after you got down from your bunk. I was not sleeping either. I rejoice with all my heart for you.'

"Dawn broke and the others in the room got up. The light of the Resurrection was bathing me in its rays. I was another person, because 'I was lost and now I am found, I was dead and now I am brought back to life.'"[176]

---

[176]*Ibid*, pp. 381-384.

Behold, a page from a possible *Paterikon* of Romanian prisons.

Also, Bordeianu tells us of other things that shed even more light on this young man, Jimboiu: "A young man, both physically and spiritually pure, endowed with much gentleness and goodness. He was the only person I met who never complained of hunger. He loved everyone no matter who they were, friends or enemies, even to the point of self-sacrifice. He had such understanding for his enemies and for tormentors that it cannot be explained rationally. He was so convinced of his earthly mission to do good that he seemed to come from another world. If I had not known this young man, I would be doubtful about many pure things or would simply not believe them.

"Jimboiu, as the saints understood, identified himself with the calling of the Son of God: 'Come to Me, all ye who are tired and heavy laden, and I will grant thee rest.'

"From the moment I met Jimboiu, I no longer read the *Lives of the Saints* in the same way. After knowing him, every doubt, every suspicion regarding whether or not saints have existed or still exist on this earth was forever dispelled from my soul. This martyr, who looked like a Byzantine saint, was for me the ultimate model of what man has to be and what he has to do become for the sake of his own salvation and that of the nation that gave rise to him.

The Mystical-Legionnaire Group at Târgu-Ocna

In the archives of *the Consiliul National de Studiu al Activitatii Securiste* (CNSAS; Archives of the National Council for the Study of Securitate), at index #P237, there is a file, in 21 volumes, on the "mystical-Legionnaire group of Târgu-Ocna." Under this designation, a trial was held in 1959 involving some of those who were imprisoned with Valeriu Gafencu at Târgu-Ocna during the fifties.

Following this farce sham of a trial, a typical example of the fanciful frame-ups contrived by Securitate in order to prosecute innocent people, twenty-nine men were sentenced to prison: nine were sentenced to hard labor, three were sentenced to 25 years in prison, while the others – with the exception of two persons who received lighter punishments – received sentences between 15 and 22 years.

The first accusation concerned the Christian support they had given to the more seriously ill at Târgu-Ocna. The fact that they gave their food to the weakest among the sick, that they sacrificed themselves in taking care of them, cleaning their wounds, their bandages and clothes stained by pus, that they prayed, sang carols, confessed their sins, learned prayers, akathists and texts from Holy Scripture, all of these were construed by the demonic minds of the Securitate as "Legionnaire assistance" and "subversive Legionnaire activity" disguised under the guise of "mysticism."

In addition, the fact that they maintained the spiritual line adopted by Valeriu Gafencu and other confessors from Târgu-Ocna after their release from prison, as well as their attempt to maintain connections with one another, seeking each other out, supporting each other in time of need, coming together in times of joy and sorrow, meeting each other at church or going on pilgrimages to monasteries, all of these actions represented for the Securitate nothing other than the formation of a "subversive organization" that continued Legionnaire activity under the mask of religion.

For Communists, the only thing necessary for a person to be considered more dangerous than dynamite was for that person to be a Legionnaire. It was no great matter if Voicescu had a meeting with Cazacu, but it was an altogether different matter if the Legionnaire Voicescu had a meeting with the Legionnaire Cazacu. Even the most natural behavior and, the most banal of events had, in the minds of Securitate agents, a subversive and dangerous character if it involved Legionnaires.

Thus, from reading a verbal process of interrogation, we discover how the baptism of the son of a former prisoner at Târgu-Ocna was deemed and act of "Legionnairism." Despite the torture under which it was obtained, the following juvenile declaration, proves the paranoia the Securitate had of Legionnairism and their capability to transform the most ordinary of events into "Legionnaire activity."

"What gave this baptism a Legionnaire character was the fact that, just as at the wedding, all the former Legionnaires sat at one table. We sang *Many Years*, [a traditional song at special events such as birthdays, wedding, and baptisms]. [177] The way in which we

---

[177] This is a traditional song at special events such as birthdays, wedding, and baptisms.

congratulated Ion Cazacu also had a Legionnaire character, because each one of us said to him, 'May he [your child] live long and may you make him a good Romanian," that is, a good Legionnaire.[178]

In the spiritual family of Târgu-Ocna in 1954, Father Constantin Voicescu, then a student of theology, enjoyed a certain authority. What follows is taken from the CNSAS archives mentioned above. It describes a meeting among friends, location unknown, where the discussion turned to the possibility of assisting those in various difficulties. The story, however, extracted by the Securitate through torture, is recorded in Securitate language and designated a "Legionnaire meeting."

"During the meetings held at the home of Voicescu, we usually discussed political events, both domestic and international, and we spent a few minutes discussing job situations, family, each other's health. At the end of these discussions, usually I, but sometimes Constantin Voicescu, brought to the attention of those Legionnaires present the situation of various Legionnaires who were sick or newly released from prison. We then asked everyone's opinion as to what measures could be taken to help them. After we all gave our opinions, we agreed to a specific method to assist the Legionnaires in question, which usually meant that each of us was to give different sums of money, as well as food, according to the agreed-upon objective.

"Likewise, after we drew the discussion to a close and decided what we had to do, we all said a prayer, the *Our Father*. The prayer was said aloud by Constantin Voicescu, while the rest of us listened and made the sign of the cross. After prayer, dinner was served, and when

---

[178]Archive CNSAS, Penal Account, File 327, vol. 1, pg.p. 213.

we were finished, we again said a prayer to thank God for the nourishment He had given us.

"During other Legionnaire meetings held at the home of Constantin Voicescu and other places, we appointed two different Legionnaires for every Sunday to go to the sanatorium at Baloteşti, to see Ion Sultaniuc and to bring him food. Among various Legionnaire problems discussed at the meetings, we also discussed problems of a religious nature; Constantin Voicescu occupied himself primarily with our mystical-hostile education."[179]

The stroller given to the Voicescu family by those closest to them on the occasion of the birth of their son Mihai was designated "Legionnaire assistance." The gift was accompanied by a note written by Aurora Sultaniuc, the sister of Ion Sultaniuc, and signed by all those who contributed toward the gift. The note itself was attached to the file, as obvious proof of "Legionnaire assistance." Also attached to the file were the conclusions of a handwriting expert who had analyzed the writing of Aurora Sultaniuc and verified that she was the author of the note, whose contents were both dangerous and clearly Legionnaire:

"Welcome, little Mihai, both small and dear!

"We ask the good God to give you full health, much luck and wisdom, that you may be the joy of your parents and of all those who love you and will love you."[180]

Another "Legionnaire manifestation" according to the Securitate was the recitation of poems written by Valeriu Gafencu, or "the poems of Radu Gyr, which had

---

[179]Archive CNSAS, Penal Account, File 327, vol. 1, pg.p. 215.

[180]Archive CNSAS, Penal Account, File 327, vol. 6, Pg.P. 1.

a Legionnaire tone to them, as for example, the poem *Iisus în Celulă* (Jesus in Prison).

Only the sick mind of a Securitate agent who extorts such absurd declarations by means of torture, could possibly find a "Legionnaire tone" in the poem *Iisus în Celulă*.

Related to poetry, an interesting dialogue is also included in the CNSAS file: the interrogation of Gheorghe Penciu. A notebook of poems written a long time ago had been confiscated from him; according to the interrogator, the poetry had a "Legionnaire tone." What follows is a part of the interrogation.

"Question: Declare the names of all persons to whom you made these Legionnaire verses known after the year 1946.

"Answer: I have not made these verses known to anyone and I maintain the no one knows that I keep this notebook of poems.

"Question: You are trying to mislead the interrogation. The truth is that the other Legionnaires know about your Legionnaire verses. What have you got to say?

"Answer: I affirm what I declared before, in the sense that no one knows about my Legionnaire verses since I have not spoken to anyone about them.

"Question: Then why did you write them?

"Answer: I wrote them with the intention of keeping them for myself; I did not plan to give them to other Legionnaires.

"Question: In what way did you use these verses?

"Answer: I didn't write them with the intention of using them for anything.

"Question: Then why did you bother writing them?

"Answer: I wrote these verses in order to acquire skill in writing poetry.

"Question: I want to make you aware that you're trying to minimize the Legionnaire spirit in which you wrote. Could you not have acquired this skill with verses that were favorable to the present regime?

"Answer: Both in prison and in freedom, I wrote these verses with the intention of making known to others the lives of Legionnaires sentenced to prison for subversive activity, as well as of other prisoners. This was the reason for writing the verses about which I am questioned."[181]

As it is recorded in the file, we could consider this dialogue to be civilized, even amusing, if we were to put aside the last response. We can certainly deduce that between the last question and the last answer there was a pause in which, with methods characteristic of the Securitate, he who was interrogated was "convinced" to declare what was expected of him.[182]

According to the frame of mind of the Securitate, a baptism performed at the "Legionnaire church" St. Ilie Gorgani in Bucharest also had a dangerous and

---

[181] Archive CNSAS, Penal Account, File 327, vol. 3, pg.p. 135.

[182] That the interrogation was not at all civilized is also seen in the testimony of Father Voicescu: "But if I were to tell you that one can rejoice when one is told that he will be sentenced to life in prison at hard labor, that one can really feel such a joy?! I myself felt this joy…. When, after a period of interrogation, which was something extraordinarily difficult, both physically and spiritually, especially spiritually, the interrogator informed me – I believed it to be the last meeting with him - that the interrogation ended and that I would be sentenced to hard labor for life, I rejoiced greatly! I went back to my cell with an extraordinary joy, with a sense of relief, relief that I was done with the interrogation." – *Părintele Voicescu - un duhovnic al cetății*, pg.p. 140.

obviously Legionnaire character, in that the newborn was baptized Corneliu, and this was the first name of [Legionnaire] Captain Corneliu Zelea Codreanu. It is clear that the figure of Codreanu and the church of St. Ilie Gorgani were dear to those in Father Voicescu's group, but this can hardly represent grounds for sentencing someone to long, hard years of imprisonment. In addition, the trial that sentenced Voicescu at hard labor for life, in addition to other "serious" offenses also cited the following: "The defendant gave priests in the churches and monasteries he visited *pomelnice* [183] which included the names of deceased Legionnaire commanders Corneliu Zelea Codreanu, Moță-Mărin, Valeriu Gafencu, and others."[184]

A majority of those [re]sentenced to prison in the summer of '58 had been at Târgu-Ocna while Gafencu was still alive and were released during the following years. And yet some of those who were sentenced, such as Ioan Ianolide and Constantin Dragodan, had remained in prison, never having been released. If Gafencu had survived, he certainly would have been [re]sentenced as well.

Valeriu and Ianolide were considered by the Securitate to be the principal ringleaders. They had indoctrinated the others along the "mystical-hostile" line, had encouraged them to lead a Christian life, to study theology after release from prison, even to be ordained priests, if possible. To the Securitate, it was quite clear that this was nothing more than a mask

---

[183]Very common Romanian custom when visiting a church or monastery, to leave a *pomelnic*, a list of friends and relatives to be prayed for.

[184]Archive CNSAS, Penal Account, File 327, vol. 7, pg.p. 432.

behind which they could continue their hostile Legionnaire activity. Furthermore, Valeriu had compiled a list of Christian principles, found written on a book that had been confiscated from Father Voicescu. Of course, these principles, which Father Voicescu had learned from Ianolide, were Legionnaire in the opinion of the Securitate. Since Gafencu was dead, all responsibility was placed with Ianolide, the scapegoat considered the spiritual mentor for the others.[185]

Under interrogation, speaking of the Christian principles compiled by Valeriu, Ianolide said, "The principles Valeriu Gafencu listed have only minimal similarity with the doctrine of Corneliu Zelea Codreanu and the writings of other Legionnaire leaders. The Legionnaire Valeriu Gafencu arrived at the conclusion that Codreanu, in his doctrine, deviated from true Christianity, subordinating it to nationalistic and political ideas. In his principles, the Legionnaire Valeriu Gafencu set down a spiritual plan that included all peoples."[186]

---

[185] Also in the same file 327, vol. 12, page 173, we find a characterization of Ioan Ianolide [while a prisoner at Aiud], authored by the commander of the prison, Colonel Crăciun, dated July 10, 1963, in which he states, "In general, he is a recalcitrant and fanatical element. In 1962, he received special training in cultural and educational work. He took a combative stance from the very beginning. At present, he maintains the same position of reserve and insubordination, exerting a negative influence in the ranks of the prisoners. He is not used for work." The "cultural and educational work" that Crăciun refers to actually means the project of re-education at Aiud – a Pitești more refined than Pitești, as someone defined it. As a good Christian, Ianolide could not but have had a "clearly oppositional stance" toward this attempt at spiritual mutilation.

[186] Archive CNSAS, Penal Account, File 327, vol. 11, pg.p. 331

Similarly, Ianolide declared at one of his trials, "I know that Valeriu Gafencu renounced the political line and dedicated himself to the religious one. He wrote down these principles and these poems. I deny that there might be any similarity between the principles of Gafencu and Legionnaire principles. The principles of Gafencu embody the Christian Church. I discussed Christian problems with all the prisoners. There is not one single prisoner who has not taken part in discussions of Christian problems, especially Christian principles. I believe that I also would have become a priest if I had remained free. Valeriu Gafencu said that he would have liked to have been tonsured a monk. Discussing these issues, it is possible that both Gafencu and I were overheard by others. Among his poems, there is a hymn written in 1942 which had a Legionnaire character, but nonetheless, he later changed in favor of a spiritual life."[187]

Even if it may have been that the agents of the Securitate suspected those interrogated of Legionnaire activity, it is not absurd to admit that in the beginning of the rounding up of Legionnaires and in subsequent interrogations, Securitate agents had doubts. It is impossible, however, for them not to have been ultimately convinced of their prisoners' innocence. The fact that they still doled out harsh prison sentences shows very clearly what really bothered the Securitate: Their faith in God. Legionnairism was only a pretext. The animosity of the Communists toward the Legionnaires was fundamentally nothing other than the hatred of the devil for the servants of Christ.

---

[187]Archive CNSAS, Penal Account, File 327, vol. 7, pg.p. 156.

Dialogues with Valeriu[188]

About Monasticism

I discovered Christ, and my wish was to follow Him on the narrowest of paths, out of an inner need to offer myself completely, along with the conviction that only through Christ can the world be redeemed. I did not depart from the world, but for the sake of the world I parted with what was worldly within me. By wanting to become a monk, I did not renounce life, but I wanted to serve life in a higher form.

Neither virginity nor ascetic hardship are the most exalted attributes of monasticism, but a spirit enlightened by grace put in the service of life. The monk prays for all mankind. The aversion a monk has for the world must be understood as an ascetic method, because monasticism is an exceptional life, a life given in exchange for life. Monks are crazy fools who defy even nature itself in order to be united with Christ and serve mankind. Their virginity is an expression of chastity, and this world burdened by passions has need of it. The physiological effect of chastity becomes a spring of spiritual power, but not with any personal aim, as some think, but with a communal aim, as the Lord teaches. Monasticism is a superior path of preparation for the world, for the world needs the madness of the saints in order to be sanctified.

We are now living in an age in which Christians have found another path of confession: the folly of the

---

[188]Ioan Ianolide, *op. cit.*, pp. 482-507.

cross, of sacrifice for the Truth. The enemies of Christ have unleashed the greatest and cruelest persecution of Christians. Today, anyone who believes must be prepared to die. This path is a spiritual privilege of great beauty, in which monasticism appears with new values and significance.

I have, therefore, considered it necessary to take the monastic vow, even though we find ourselves on the path of martyrdom. When you are put in a situation in which your very life is required of you, the harsh vows of a monk seem distant, but their value lies in that they manifest zeal for holy things. When one witnesses to one's faith through humiliation and torture, all ascetic endeavors seem easy, but accepting them reveals the spiritual meaning of sacrifice. So then, now that I am put in a situation in which I must give my life for my faith, my monastic vow, although it was not done formally, is a great comfort to my soul.

Monasticism appeared in the history of Christianity when the Church became official, and zealous believers, dissatisfied with the lifestyle of Christian society at that time, withdrew in order to live the Gospel authentically. The monasteries constituted true centers of high Christian spirituality and had a great influence on the medieval Christian world and even on the modern world. It is a known fact that monasteries played a major cultural role, a brilliant educational role, as well as a social role of charity and the role of propagating Christianity. Through men who were bearers of the Spirit, monasteries frequently influenced politics and history, although they did not always succeed in raising them to the level of Christian consciousness.

Today, however, Satan is afraid of losing power over the world, and so is waging war against Christians, both monks and laymen. Monasticism is discredited through false slogans created with evil intent. The devil tempts Christians today, as he tempted the Lord on the mountain, to be like him. But when they refuse, he resorts to methods of extermination through any possible means. Some come with gold in order to buy us, while others come with a sword to cut us. We, however, immerse ourselves in the spirit of the Gospel.

We have need of those who live and witness to the Christian faith, both monks and laymen. We do not withdraw from the battle of history, but we shape ourselves and steel ourselves in its fierce tension. All power in heaven and on earth was entrusted to Christ. The tortures to which we are subjected are the doors through which Christ renews and raises up the Church and the world.

About the Priesthood

Q: Valeriu, do you believe that it is good to have a celibate priesthood?

A: From the point of view of self-sacrifice, it is good, for celibacy facilitates detachment from any human interest or connection. But celibacy is very difficult to maintain, and from this perspective it is a great temptation. The Orthodox solution seems to me very wise: Monastic bishops and married priests.

Q: But does not the practice of having married priests also have its drawbacks?

A: Ideally a priest, even if he has a family, must stand ready to tear himself from its bosom for Christ; if he has material things, he must live as if he did not have them. In order to be alive for Christ, a priest must be dead to the world, and this precisely in order to serve the world. Before all else, he must be an example of Christian living. Priests should let the world of sin bury its own dead, and they must forsake it in order to build a Christian world. It would be well for the material problems of the families of priests to be integrated and assumed by the community. The bourgeois theory of the rich, well-to-do priest must be rejected.

Q: Should priests and hierarchs get involved in politics?

A: A priest is the spiritual guide of Christian people, but he is also interested in the problems of the whole of mankind. Therefore, he is engaged in all human problems, and so much the more in those concerning the world's orientation. Therefore, if politics means orientation, a priest can preoccupy himself with politics. Bearing in mind the imperfection of the human condition in which forms are continually subject to change, priests do not govern, but watch over governments. They place themselves on a moral-spiritual and idealistic level. The clergy must maintain freedom and independence in relation to the political sector exactly so as to be able to influence it or even renew it. But to allow the world to be governed by chance means losing the priest's clerical mission. The ideal is a society led by the cooperation between divinity and humankind, clergy and laity, church and state. The clergy has the difficult mission of shaping the spirituality upon which history will unfold.

Q: What are the domains in which the clergy can work directly?

A: First, the domain of the sacred is reserved to it. All Christians have grace, but only the clergy

226

administers it. Second, the clergy has the word, in all its forms of expression: speech, sound, movement, color, image. Therefore, the clergy can get involved in education, learning, philosophy, poetry, art, music, journalism, science, sociology, and economy. Likewise, priests are called to think politically and to voice their opinion regarding political problems, but this depends on the context of historical circumstances. Sometimes Christians have rejected certain governments, at other times they have recognized them without appropriating them, and when they were able, they formulated their own governments. Often these governments are Christian *pro forma*, but without Christian content, because political forces succeeded in stifling the Christian point of view. In this sense, we recall the struggle carried out by St. John Chrysostom with the emperor Arcadius and the slavery that was practiced in the Christian world.

Q: If Christianity propagates the idea of equality among men, why then is there a church hierarchy?

A: All people are equal in the sight of God, as unique creatures. We are also equal in regard to the law, the right to life, freedom of speech, but it is exactly in our self-assertion that we manifest our diversity. Through creation – therefore ontologically, naturally – we are different. Equality among men does not lead to uniformity, but to hierarchy. The problem is not to abolish the hierarchy of values, but to establish a healthy criterion for hierarchies. The world itself is created hierarchically. The angels are also positioned hierarchically. Therefore people, in accordance with their worthiness and aptitudes, occupy hierarchical ranks as well. Spiritual life itself passes through hierarchical stages on the road to perfection. But even

Satan in hell has his own hierarchy, and evil men arrange themselves in a hierarchy in their own wickedness. In contrast to the hierarchy of evil - vainglory, passions, and egotism - Christians form a hierarchy of goodness, virtues, humility, and love. The church hierarchy has three levels of ordination, but they must also be levels of living, otherwise we risk introducing the hierarchical model of evil into the hierarchy of good under the mask of Christianity. Therefore, in principle, there is no conflict between the idea of equality and that of hierarchy.

About Mysticism

Q: Valeriu, nowadays the notion of mysticism is often disparaged. Nevertheless, people believe in God and have need of communion with Him. You yourself have had a profound spiritual life. What has to be done?

A: First, we have to acknowledge the bad faith of those who have succeeded, here and in other places, in discrediting the idea of mysticism. Mysticism will remain the center of the Christian rebirth that is to come, for it is the means by which a Christian enters into communion with Christ through a gradual spiritual process of purification and perfection. Its starting point is when a man turns within himself in order to seek Christ and to attain to union with God through love. The inner experience transforms nature, fills the mind with knowledge, strengthens the will, purifies the heart, and makes man a bearer of Christ. In contrast to morality, which enforces the strictness of commandments, mysticism is a living, intimate act of life in the Holy Spirit. Being an "art," it presupposes a guide, a counselor. This is an "avva," a spiritual father, who in addition to administering grace, has himself a deep inner spiritual life and hesychastic experience.

Q: What is the beginning of inner life in Christ?

A: Faith in God. There are people who have come to believe because of their makeup and the environment in which they have been raised. There are those who arrive at faith through their own efforts, after much searching and wandering. There are those who corrupt their faith through practices that are strange, degrading, or even Satanic. Faith is a latent component of our spiritual structure, but it requires an attentive and orderly process of learning. The church has the role of teaching us the true faith.

Q: If the beginning of inner spiritual life is faith, what is its end, its culmination?

A: Faith is a small seed that grows continuously in this life and in the future life, leading ultimately to the perfection of man and his union with God through love. Therefore, love is the greatest virtue. It does not replace faith, but rather strengthens it.

About the "Medieval" Character of Christianity

A politician of liberal[189] convictions once said to Valeriu:

"For me, faith is an institution that must be encouraged as a corrective to selfishness and various human abuses. It holds no interest for me other than its

---

[189] In Romania, the liberals were members of the Liberal National Party. Their views followed classical liberalism, with emphasis on freedom and the right of property. As in the case of all other historical parties, the prominent figures were imprisoned by the Communists. (O.G.).

socio-political role. The political man has no need of God. Faith must be politically restrained in order to avoid another period like the Dark Ages."

"For someone like you," Valeriu responded, "suffering is redeeming. Through suffering you will attain to the light of faith. You will understand then that you are small and imperfect, that your light is darkness, that only through God can you be a true man, that only through faith do the horizons of knowledge open and, in the end, that the world can only be saved through faith. You have a preconceived idea about the Middle Ages and false ideas about the concept of Christianity. More than anyone else, a politician should be believer because by determining the direction the world must go in, he fulfills the will of God and so he has great responsibility. Regarding the Church and its role as an institution, it does not correct, but integrates the world into Christ. It is not concerned with only a part of life but all of life. In as much as you have not been willing to accept faith because of materialist egotism, look how suffering and death are coming upon you through materialistic atheism. Bourgeois selfishness is now being crushed by its more awful offspring, atheist-materialist pride. I deeply hope that you will arrive at faith before you die, but this will mean following Christ."

That man later arrived at faith.

About Peace

Q: Valeriu, what is peace?

A: Peace is a mystery and is only found in Christ, through by Christ, and for Christ.

Q: Is peace present in souls or in the world, in history or in eternity?

230

A: Being found in Christ, it is in all and through all.

Q: Can there be a false inner peace?

A: The passions lead to an impassioned state that can become permanent but is not peace. Mistakes can lead to a state of delusion that considers itself all-knowing, but a moment of truth can come that proves such a state to be a false peace. The spirit of evil can possess someone to the point of blindness, but this is not peace, but slavery. The ego, pride, vainglory, or the desire for domination tend to deceive us through personal peace, devoid of God, but man will find that he is but a creation and cannot find peace apart from God.

Q: Can inner peace possibly co-exist with unseen warfare?

A: He who does not struggle, and does not defeat the passions and ignorance, does not know peace.

Q: What actually is the unseen war?

A: Turn within yourself and you will see!

Q: Can one have inner peace without being at peace with others?

A: As long as you stand guilty in relation to others, voluntarily or involuntarily, knowingly or unknowingly, through omission or through acts, you cannot be reconciled with God or with yourself.

Q: What is inner peace in Christ?

A: It is life in the Spirit of Truth, the kingdom of the Holy Spirit in man. It requires discernment of the spirits and the ability to remain steadfast in the Truth.

Q: To me it seems difficult to distinguish between good and evil.

A: That's why man is man, free man, emperor, king, in order to distinguish the spirits. If we do not have discernment, we are not worthy to be called men. Men must be saints.

Q: Peace lies in the Law or in Grace?

A: In Grace!

Q: Peace, both in the hearts of men and in the world, seems to be totally unstable!

A: Peace among men depends upon the measure in which they are found in the Spirit of Truth, and is therefore a spiritual problem, even though it manifests itself on the political, social, economic, cultural, educational and moral planes [of life levels]. All problems of mankind are problems of conscience, while the conscience does not find peace except in the religious domain. The religious realm is fundamental in history.

Q: Valeriu, is peace determined by conscience or by power?

A: It is a mistake to accept the peace of power without truth. The peace of slavery is not acceptable! The peace of evil is not acceptable! Satan offers you his power if you worship him, but all power in heaven and earth was given to Christ. Therefore, Christians cannot accept the alluring, tempting peace of Satan.

Q: Valeriu, is peace a struggle?

A: Peace derives from the victory of good over evil, both at the level of conscience and at the level of history. Here we see the sense of the unseen warfare of ascetics, and the apocalyptic sense of history.

Q: Therefore, peace must be unceasingly on the offensive?

A: Peace must be on the offensive and always vigilant. The peace of God came down through the "offensive" of the incarnation of the Lord Christ and through the "offensive" of the Holy Spirit, Who will work in the world until His second coming. Christianity means bearing witness, searching, boldness, perseverance, work, struggle, self-sacrifice. Christians cannot accept anything other than the peace of Christ, no matter how many sacrifices are required of them.

Q: Must peace be defended?

A: Some defend the peace of God; others defend the peace of Satan. But the power of the apocalyptic beast will be annihilated by the power of the Lamb.

Q: What are the Christian methods of struggle?

A: In its struggle for assertion, Christianity is spiritual and therefore free. In their own defense, Christians are often obliged to respond to an aggressor with his own arms: David had to kill Goliath, St. Nestor killed Lius Lyaeus with a spear and received martyrdom.

Q: Are we in favor of peace or in favor of war?

A: There is a peace that is more destructive than any war and there is a war that brings peace. Examine the spirit that gave birth to events and the final goal to which it aspires and thus you will know what you should do.

Q: We always hear talk about peace!

A: Every power promotes its own peace, but all of them are hypocrites, concealing under the vague notion of peace their own domination.

Q: What is missing in the Christian world of today: faith, truth, or power?

A: First of all, there is a crisis of faith. As a result, the world has situated itself apart from truth, and for this reason God has taken power from the hands of Christians.

Q: How should we interpret the satanic power of our age?

233

A: Apart from historical explanations, there are structural and, ultimately, spiritual explanations. The structures of this world are materialistic-atheistic. The forces in the East are inclined toward the destruction of the planet. People are so possessed by [notions of] power, wealth, and pleasure, that they live as though they are hallucinating. Disaster is imminent, be it by the path of peace, be it by the path of war, because of the evil spirit that controls the modern way of life. The world needs suffering in order to be spiritually re-oriented. God has His own ways of intervening in history. We did not participate in this disaster, but we were crushed under its destructive steamroller, because we bear witness to the Truth. But people nowadays do not accept it, because once again they are sons of Satan.

About Freedom

Q: Is freedom a product of evil?

A: By no means. Evil does not exist ontologically. In God there is no evil. Evil is a distortion of the freedom that the Creator bestowed upon mankind and the angels, His creatures to whom he gave freedom of choice. Evil began with the pride of Satan and the disobedience of man.

Q: Does God respect man's freedom?

A: Through His omniscience, God has ontologically respected the freedom of man, for at the time of creation he foresaw the birth of His Son, while through His great goodness, God was made man and suffers together with us until the world will be saved. Man is free by nature. But absolute freedom is not in creation, but in the Creator.

Q: Does Satan respect man's freedom?

A: Satan does not know man inwardly, but makes use of every means to enslave man, for he himself is a useless servant. There is no freedom in evil.

Q: Does man respect man's freedom?

A: Through egotism and the desire for domination, man is a wolf to [other] men. Through virtue and the enlightenment of grace, man is like Christ to other men. Man's respect for his fellow man is a question of the deification of man.

Q: What is the liberation of man?

A: Man must liberate himself from the tyranny of sin, from the tyranny of nature, from the tyranny of his fellow man, from the tyranny of ignorance, and finally, to defeat death. All these things can be accomplished only through Christ.

Q: But what is slavery?

A: It is the opposite of liberation, in other words slavery to passions, to the laws of nature, to man, the slavery of ignorance, and in the final analysis, slavery to death.

Q: Can freedom be an attribute of evil?

A: Evil does have a certain freedom, but people have to defend their own freedom, their own dignity, their own integrity, their own values, their own faith. The freedom of evil does not entitle it to govern. It must be confronted and eliminated from the world.

Q: Is it possible for a false freedom to exist?

A: If there can be a false christ, then it is natural that there be also a false freedom. It can be spiritual, political, or social. All the expressions of freedom find their value only in Truth.

Q: What is the relationship between freedom and authority?

A: In our world, freedom cannot exist without authority and neither can authority exist without freedom. Here they exist in an unstable balance; only in God are they absolute.

Q: What are the essential criteria of a free conscience?

A: First of all, the commandments of God, then natural and vital necessities, and afterward values sanctioned by human experience and laws established by men – but all these things must be redefined and understood in context.

Q: What is the authority that gives weight to freedom?

A: It is obvious that man is not the creator and master of the world and of life, that man in and of himself does not have the right to be the master of other men. Only man in communion with God, man deified, has dominion over the world and enters into universal communion.

Q: Given the fact that man is free and imperfect, how do you see the problem of the infallibility of Man?

A: On the level of personal conscience, man is infallible through his personal assurance of the truth, but with exactly the reservation of his lack of infallibility. Therefore, man alone cannot be infallible. Only Christ was an infallible man.

Q: What is then the freedom of man?

A: It is the environment in which human personality develops. It is the condition of human responsibility and also the justification of man as King.

Q: What is the difference between freedom and liberties?

A: Freedom is a condition, liberties are rights. Liberties define and at the same time limit freedom. Freedom lies in spirit, liberties lie in the letter of the law.

Q: What is the status of the universe in relation to man?

A: The universe and nature were created in order to correspond to the freedom of man. There is an amazing equilibrium between multiple forces. Man's material universe functions the same way as man's spiritual universe and both of them steer man toward God.

Q: Can man on his own determine his own destiny?

A: Atheistic materialists, obsessed with pleasure, the desire for domination, and egotism, have created modern civilization, which culminates in technology. They have isolated human nature and have abandoned the commandments of God. Their attempt to create an earthly and sensual paradise has failed. Nature has been exhausted and polluted, it and has become unsuitable for life. Technology, in turn, has a much greater capacity for destruction than construction. On top of all this is the worst evil of all: man's alienation. In these conditions, the advocates of anthropocentrism no longer feel that they are in control of the fate of the world that they themselves have created. And thus, the world, alienated from God, bears the punishment for its own evil deeds.

Q: What is freedom according to atheistic materialism?

A: It is a farce, a manifestation of the false christ. Materialistic determinism culminates in the conditioning of the conscience as a complex of conditioned reflexes, through which man is erased as man, as personality, for he no longer has freedom and no longer has holiness within himself.

Q: But atheistic materialism uses the force of powerful ideas such as freedom, communism, equality, justice, matter, people, science, etc.

A: The spirit and vision of atheistic materialism pervert all values, for they put them in the service of egotism and tyranny. This proves that human values are not absolute in and of themselves, but have value in accordance with the spirit, sense, and measure in which they are used. Only in Christ is everything true, good, and useful. Apart from Him, everything is disaster.

Q: How can man be fulfilled?

A: The fulfillment of man is to be found in communion with the Holy Spirit. The Holy Spirit is called to bring unity into diversity, to bring order into history, to bring holiness into life. Holiness is not something seraphic, unearthly, or esoteric, but is an opening that Christ makes toward a world steeped in the Holy Spirit.

Q: Will the Christian world of the twentieth century accept the vision of creative and messianic freedom?

A: The tragic events through which the modern world is passing will create conditions that favor returning to faith. We must come back to the Holy Spirit, to the Gospel, to apostolic force. We have the duty of crying out with all our strength the Truth, repentance, and the world's return to God. Christianity is being reborn in the ovens of fire and torture of materialistic atheism. It is exactly through his own methods of operation that Satan will lose the world that he thinks he will gain. Christ appears clearly as Savior, as Messiah, and mankind will follow Him with faith.

About Community

"I have the impression, Valeriu," a friend once said to him, "that you concentrate on spiritual problems, on your own personal inner life, and neglect the social aspect of Christianity."

"The solution that I present to Christian people is Christian spirituality," Valeriu answered, "which is an integral conception of life. It is not permissible for us to confine ourselves to our own inner spiritual lives while neglecting our fellow man, but neither is it possible to construct a world without having a spiritual life. Christian spirituality means the reign of the Holy Spirit. Our inner spiritual efforts serve as a preparation for a spiritual life in society. To omit these efforts means to head for disaster, for then we abandon Christ. If Christianity did not include inner spiritual life, it would not show respect for man and would not recognize his freedom. Inner spiritual life is combined with social order. Nowadays, however, things are very much hanging in the balance. Let us prepare ourselves for death, in order to gain life.

Q: What is the difference between a Christian community and other societies?

A: A Christian community is based upon the Holy Spirit and love. It is free. It ensures the perfection of man, as well as brotherly love. A Christian community is neither collectivist fiction, nor individualistic tyranny, but truth and love, freedom and work.

Q: What is the idea of Christian property?

A: That of communal property.

Q: Is a Christian an owner?

A: He is an administrator, a steward.

Q: Is it good to live on the charity of others?

A: Mercy will never cease, but it is not good for society to be divided into those who bestow charity and those who receive it, for those who receive can feel humiliated, they can feel that their human dignity has been violated. Charity is an individual act. Mutual assistance is characteristic of the community. Justice lies in the domain of politics. But even in the most perfect humanity, mercy will continue to characterize human relations.

Q: What have you got to say about man's exploitation of man?

A: Man's exploitation of man is cruel and terrible. It presupposes a materialistic and egocentric individualistic-bourgeois society that has no point of contact with Christianity. But man can be exploited even more terribly by the state; this presupposes a society that is tyrannical, deterministic, materialistic, and anti-Christian.

Q: It has been proved, however, that productivity and creativity are superior in individualistic societies exactly because of material instincts and self-interest. What do you say about this?

A: Only when forced by circumstances have capitalists taken the social meaning of profits into consideration; otherwise, they would exploit workers without mercy. Individualism can be corrective, an alternative to collectivism, just as collectivism can be a correction and an alternative to individualism. The social game of freedom must be moral. The social game of authority, likewise, must be moral. Only a community that is free, conscientious, and dominated by holy values can reconcile the conflict between individualism and collectivism.

Q: Is a community a problem of interests or of generosity?

A: It is a problem of conscience, of knowledge, of lucidity, for it is the only formula that gives both spiritual satisfaction and also resolves the material aspects of life. Through the community, life and society develop in a way that is united and harmoniously and in solidarity.

Q: Does the individual in a community have freedom, initiative, and vitality?

A: On the one hand, an individual offer everything to the community, and on the other hand the community offers him the freedom to work and create. A community cannot be lively and productive except through the vitality of the strengths of all its members who comprise it.

Q: Who makes the decisions in a community?

A: I believe decisions have to be communal. The community stands in the service of the people and the people must be the ones who decide. Leaders and elites, therefore, have to have the support of the people.

Q: Does the universal community have to be centralized?

A: Communities have to develop naturally. However, there is also a need for awareness of the universal community and for a way of participating in it, but not through centralized direction and planning, for in that way one arrives at tyranny.

Q: What are the spiritual enemies of the Christian community?

A: Evil, sin, passions, selfishness, gluttony, greed, pride, envy, the desire for domination, laziness, indifference, ignorance, anxiety, disobedience, lack of correctness, disbelief.

Q: What are the material enemies of the Christian community?

A: The enemy is not material, but rather a false or mistaken understanding and use of matter itself. The enemy is not life's necessities, but the distortion of necessities. Laws and forms are not bad, but turning them into absolutes is bad. Neither are ideas bad, for ideas are good, but in their own place and time. The enemy is not life, because life is the goal of our existence, but an egocentric and wrongly understood life.

Q: Who are the enemies from outside the Christian community?

A: There are individual interests that oppose the community through egotism and pride, there are interests that organize themselves collectively in order to defend egotism and pride and, finally, there is the pride and egotism that are organized politically and that undermine the Christian community.

Q: In the face of so many enemies, what must Christians do?

A: They must struggle, they must be bold, they must confront all those who oppose goodness and truth, responding equally to individuals, organizations, and all forms of anti-Christian politics.

Q: Must Christians, therefore, acquire political power?

A: They must make use of political power in order to impose respect and freedom on the political power. A people with a lively Christian conscience will have a government based upon Christian principles. The community, however, must not be confused with the state, as this may lead to tyranny and abuses.

Q: Therefore, what must be done?

A: We must cultivate and develop the Christian consciousness of mankind.

Q: But there are too many Christians who do not understand the meaning and purpose of the Christian community.

A: Unfortunately, this is true. Christians baptized today do not even have the spiritual preparation that the catechumens and penitents of olden days had.

Q: Did in fact the new wine of the Gospels once have wineskins that were worthy of it?

A: There were once those who lived lives of holiness, there were societies that strove for justice, but there is still much to do. Christianity cannot declare itself satisfied with a certain number of saints, or a certain number of monasteries, but rather with a Christian way of life and a Christian society.

Q: Do you have confidence in man?

A: Yes, but there must also be responsibility.

Q: In attempting to change the world, is there not the risk of falling into historicity and humanism?

A: Man cannot be saved without God. History cannot be perfected without transcendental aspirations, and that is why faith is the basis of the entire Christian world. We need grace. We thank God that He has given us grace, and, in turn, we seek to fulfill ourselves as men. We were saved through Christ. It remains to us now to save ourselves through our deeds.

About Marxism

Q: Valeriu, what is Marxism?

A: A false Christianity, a counterfeit Christianity, the materialization of the spirit, the anthropomorphism

243

of God, the overturning of all values, the incarnation imprisonment of the world, both philosophically and politically. Marxism is prison. In the Marxist spirit, all values, all reasoning, all things, all actions become a prison for man. Marx refused any transcendence.

Q: And socialism?

A: Socialism is a bizarre mixture of Communism and bourgeois materialism.

Q: And national-socialism?

A: A confused and vague response to Marxism.

Q: Is Christian socialism possible?

A: Christianity is, before all else, a spirituality, but it also has its own historical expression. It is found in the service of mankind, and therefore we can speak of a Christian socialism, but I would prefer to call it *communitarism*, simply in order to distinguish it from Marxist-atheist socialism. The very essence of these two concepts is in opposition to each other, as are the historical forms that they give rise to, as well as their results.

Q: What do you think of Western social Christianity?

A: It has no chance of success because it is not strong enough. The world needs the water of life in order to awaken it from the dead water of materialism. It is waiting, therefore, for a definition and affirmation of an integral Christian socialism.

Q: Can Marxism possibly be confused with Communism or Sovietism?

A: Atheism, scientism, the legitimacy of historical dialectics, class hatred and the dictatorship of the proletariat, all these Marxist principles stand at the basis of Communism and Sovietism. Nothing happens in the international Communist movement outside of Marx.

Q: Has Stalin brought anything new?

A: Stalin is a faithful embodiment of Marxism-Leninism. Just like Stalin there are also Mao, Trotsky, Ana Pauker, Gheorghiu-Dej and all those who are like them. It is a big mistake to confuse Communism with a person; apart from Marx and Lenin, all Communists are made of the same stuff. The struggle should not be with its leaders, against people, but with the very concept of Communism – that is the poison!

Q: Is t a conflict between Communists possible?

A: If Christian love has not succeeded in ridding the world of hatred, how then will things be in the Communist world, which believes in hatred?! Conflicts between Communists are inherent (and violent), but they don't resolve problems, but only aggravate them. Mankind can only be saved by returning to Christ.

Q: Was the Soviet Revolution Russian?

A: The Russians and all the Soviet peoples are the material matter with by which the architects of Communism have constructed the Soviet empire. It is certainly true that the material has its role and its importance in a construction, but what is important is the concept that stands at the base of for the construction. Russians are the first victims of Marxism. Lenin himself is no longer a Russian, for his thinking is westernized.

Q: How do you explain Marx's hatred for religion?

A: Marx denies Christ and also Moses, and every founder of religion. Marx denies the priority of spirit over matter. He justifies his hatred of religion by pointing out its historical inability to resolve the social problems of oppressed and exploited peoples. As a result, he declares religion "the opium of the people," he replaces love with hatred, and replaces freedom with tyranny and the dictatorship of the proletariat dictatorship. He rejects spirituality and thereby makes nihilism the absolute of the world. Marx becomes the world's god – he, poor Marx, who was in fact a spiritual amputee, with a narrow and obscure outlook, putting venom in everything he did, a man who was embittered, possessed, fanatical, limited, and unrealistic.

Q: If Marxism is so obtuse, how can we explain its explosion in the world, which has astonished the 20th century with its dominant role?

A: Marx made use of major ideas that can mobilize people but which acquired a degraded sense in the context of Marxism. Marx played upon all the weaknesses of the bourgeois world, which was indeed a cruel reality, and mobilized the world in revolution. He led many astray through the complexity of the concept of historical dialectic materialism. Anyone who does not look at Marx or Marxism or Communism from a spiritual perspective risks being lured away by Marxism.

Q: What is the most repulsive aspect of Communism?

A: Its poverty is hard to endure, its imprisonment of man within a system is indeed serious, but nothing is more dreadful than the subjugation of conscience, which transforms man into a controlled tool.

Q: But doesn't Communism have its weaknesses, its cracks, its fissures?

A: It has many ideological "fissures," but they are kept concealed, for Communist power cannot accept any freedom outside of it, it cannot give anyone the right to criticize or deny Communism. Communist tyranny is formidable. Communism was created to be an institutionalized system that holds on to power relentlessly and which seeks at any and all cost to extend itself. The prospects of a triumphant Communist empire in this century are opening up with a degree of darkness never before imagined. The "re-education" at Piteşti is but a symbol of the new Communist world order.

Q: Therefore, what future do you then see for humankind?

A: God works in the world. Mankind will be delivered through many sufferings and Communism will be defeated, but the world has even more serious problems to solve. The world must change its style of life and its orientation. Therefore, Communism will perish, but what it is important is what will replace it.

About the Present

Q: Valeriu, you often speak about the current state of Christianity.

A: Christ is present always and everywhere in history, in a mystical way, a secret way, through and by the conscience and actions of the faithful.

Q: What are the means by which the faith can be actualized, can be realized?

A: There are spiritual means, such as inner life, spiritual striving, morality, virtue, the struggle with sin, inner renewal, spiritual atmosphere, to which may be added learning, speech, creation, study, science, the arts, work and others. There are also means of organization that result from those things mentioned above.

Q: Are there still saints in our world?

A: This century has given us a multitude of saints and martyrs, but we simply haven't heard of them. Christ is present and active in today's world through saints, martyrs, confessors, and heroes. But the Christian world of today is not united with its saints because it doesn't follow their example. If the modern saints had lived in the early centuries of Christianity, every Christian soul would have lived with them, through them, for them. We are not Christians and therefore we don't know the saints.

Q: How do you understand the terms *saint* and *sainthood*?

A: All of mankind can be holy. We have saints who prayed in the wilderness, we have confessor saints from the Roman arenas, we have saints from the catacombs and the prisons, we have holy emperors and heroes, we have holy priests and laymen. All people, in every domain of life, are called to sainthood, that is, to "life lived in the light of the Holy Spirit." And a specification: Those who are sanctified are not necessarily saints, but only invested with the economy of divine grace. The world needs both the saints and the sanctified.

Q: Do you believe that there are hidden hypocrisies in Christianity?

A: Looking at things from a human point of view, Christians unfortunately have often explained their own inadequacies and cowardice through all sorts of philosophies and principles. It is not acceptable to say, "I am praying, so you can die of hunger," or, "I am contemplating God; the world can stay in its misery." Faith without deeds is dead.

Q: Then how must we understand the words "Give to Caesar what is Caesar's and give to God what is God's?"

A: As long as "Caesar" is pagan and un-Christian, Christianity co-exists with him peacefully, respecting his domain, but keeping intact the authenticity of faith. For example, in the Roman Empire, the faith was in no way compromised before an oppressive Caesar, even though this led to crucifixion and arenas full of wild beasts. Therefore, those who throughout history made compromises with political powers, justifying and concealing themselves by citing various the previous statement you mention, in fact betray both God and Christian people. The identity of Christianity must be preserved and affirmed with wisdom.

Q: Will the world succeed in understanding and accepting authentic Christianity?

A: It will succeed, but with difficulty, for this is a united effort of God and man, but with great difficulty.

About Crises

Q: Valeriu, what is the essence of today's crisis?

A: Atheism.

Q: What do you see in today's world?

A: I see internal chaos, a decomposition that is leading toward nihilism, because people are obsessed with the nothingness of matter, with the fiction of forms, with sensual exhaustion, with historicism without transcendence, with ceremonialism without God, with consumerism without spirituality, by the falseness that conceals itself within the self-deification of man. Disaster is unfolding on all planes of fortitude of human life. Much suffering will be necessary in order to re-orient the world spiritually and to change its way of life.

Q: Why did God allow the world to sink into this present crisis, after some 2000 years of Christianity?

A: This crisis is not from God, nor is it from faith, but rather from the freedom of the human conscience. In the past few centuries, man has profaned the world, devastated souls, encouraged sensuality, and has fallen prey to the pride of materialism and atheism. At the same time, satanic forces are more refined and better organized in the 20th century than in the first Christian age. The way in which saints are killed by the beast and perish in the 20th century is much more diabolical, more perverse, more complete, better studied, more horrible than the way in which martyrs were killed during the age of the catacombs. Millions of Christians today are not at the spiritual level of the catacombs, but in this century, sainthood and martyrdom are greater than ever in intensity and manifestation. The enemies of Christianity, those who brought about this martyrdom, want to conceal it and make the world forget about Christ, but they are deceiving themselves and provE to be powerless. They have succeeded in ruling the world, but in doing so have created saints and martyrs. They have succeeded in closing the mouths of men, but they have not been able to conceal the light of the saints. God works in the world even through those who do not believe. This seems to be the reason for the crisis that the 20th century has experienced: the purification necessary for a higher level of spirituality and existence.

Q: What methods might there be to escape from this crisis?

A: Returning to Christ. A Christian elite is necessary, one that will not abandon the people but will struggle boldly against all forms of oppression and slavery. The people cannot be defended only through prayers and almsgiving, through dry formalism, but also through struggle, boldness, and power. The world is under the dominion of Christ and Christians do not have the right to abandon it. There is no accusation graver than to say that the Church has abandoned the people, because then it has abandoned Christ, no matter how many dogmas it might establish and observe.

Q: Why is faith necessary in the world?

A: Because of the wisdom with which God made the world. The world is imperfect; so imperfect, in fact, that nothing perfect exists within it. Neither its social-political-social and economic order, nor culture, the arts, the sciences, the philosophies, or the religions. People, who are created free and conscious, no matter how dominion they may have over the world, cannot achieve perfection except through union with God. If this connection with the divine is taken from him, man declines into bestiality and non-being. Belief is therefore a necessity.

Q: Christianity is often discredited by materialists as backward, obscure, medieval, inquisitional, Jesuit, deceptive. How can we respond?

A: The materialism that denigrates Christianity today has science as its theoretical basis. It is exactly science that is anti-materialist and reveals that materialism as tyrannical, limited, mechanistic, nihilistic, and disastrous. The light of materialism is darkness; the orientation of progressivism is contrary to nature; the sensuality of materialism has dissolved nature; the humanism of materialism has bestialized the world. The laws of materialism are fictitious, and therefore for a time they imprisoned human thought. Science has reached the limits of material knowledge and it too anchors the world in the transcendental.

Q: How is it possible to escape from the crisis of materialism?

A: Through Christ, but He is not accepted by today's world. No one nowadays is willing to modify his outlook and lifestyle, even though it is leads him to disaster. Events have taken their own course and can no longer be stopped even by Christians. Nevertheless, we have the duty of crying out to mankind, "Put an end to debauchery, renounce tyranny, put your lives in order, set limits to your greed, return to nature, give up pride, destroy atomic weapons. If you are rationalistic, give up rationalism. If you are realistic, see spiritual reality. If you have knowledge, anchor yourself in the transcendent! Give your soul holiness from on high, for only in this way will you be saved. Repent! Call upon God to put order in you and in your world, on your earth and in your heaven!" But may all of this be not only abstract, moralizing advice. Christians are called upon to be vigilant. The world needs Christ, faith, and genuine Christianity.

About the Role of Charity

Q: Valeriu, what are the Christian aspirations of today's world?

A: Now and in the future, two Christian processes are necessary: one is the re-Christianization of Christians and the other is the Christianization of non-Christians. By re-Christianization, we understand the strengthening of the Christian faith, the effort toward authentic Christian living, the steps toward spiritual perfection, a Christian community that is active, united, brotherly, and the determination to live a Christian life. But Christendom has lost its messianic role and no longer has the historical force necessary to motivate and deify the world. In this way, it leaves the door open to pagans, atheists, and zionism. Anyone who believes but is not a missionary has not yet known the beauty of faith.

Q: Do you believe, Valeriu, that traditionalism, and therefore also Christianity, means living in the past?

A: By no means. Christianity is of the present. Christ exists in the present. If life is unique and always new, how can I live in the past? And if life has achieved its present forms, how can it deny its past? We do not live in the past because we observe tradition, but through this tradition we give continuity to the Holy Spirit, now and unto the ages of ages. With discernment, with care, with wisdom we will learn from tradition what is necessary in the present and in the future.

Q: Do you believe, Valeriu, that we can live from an eschatological perspective, cut off from the world, from history, from the present?

A: Such a theory is just as absurd as it is hypocritical. Eternity begins now. Only if we live eternity now will we have it eschatologically, otherwise we lose it. Therefore, Christians make history, but they are not confused with history, for only by striving ceaselessly toward eternity will we have the light and the power to fashion from history steps that are always new, always higher, leading to the Kingdom of God.

Q: What is necessary in order to build the Christian world?

A: It is good to model ourselves after the classic example of the apostolic community: to know Christian teaching well in order to see how it can be applied in the present; to unite ourselves in common effort, guided by the light of the Holy Spirit; to live in a community of love according to the will of God; to pray, to liturgize, to unite ourselves with Christ, in order that we may be in His Kingdom through His grace and power.

Q: Valeriu, what are the various factors that can save the world?

253

A: We could say that there is only one: God. We would not be mistaken, for everything is from Him, and it is through Him that the world will be perfected. But if we were to say this, we would be barred from having a good understanding of man, life, and nature. Therefore, there are two factors that determine the fate of the world: God and man, the condescension of God and human striving toward heaven, divine grace and the human will. The cooperation of God and man is the key to the salvation of the world.

Q: Is it be possible to present to the world a concrete Christian plan for life and governance?

A: Christians propose to the world a spirituality, while the world must find ways of living which correspond to its current situation. The establishment of the world on a foundation of faith means a ceaseless renewal of the Gospel. The apostolic and martyric spirit must remain always alive. The world must vibrate unceasingly with aspirations toward holiness. We strive toward a Christian world, burning in the flame of faith and love, struggling against the passions, glorifying the Resurrection, the Transfiguration, and the Ascension.

Thoughts Regarding a Common Spiritual Effort

Although Valeriu was the heart of the spiritual family at Târgu-Ocna, it would nonetheless be quite a mistake to think that the atmosphere there was exclusively due to him. God arranged it so that many particular souls were gathered around him, without whom this spiritual effort would not have succeeded.

Beyond exceptional characters who could be evoked individually, the beauty and distinctiveness of what happened at Târgu-Ocna consisted of this aspect of communion, of common effort to which each member contributed with his sacrifice according to his ability, and very often beyond his ability! For a world that is so absurdly divided, Târgu-Ocna is, more than anything else, a lesson in the experience of Christian life as communion.

The idea of Christian community – possibly set in motion by the community experience at Târgu-Ocna – dogged Valeriu during the last period of his life. As we have seen especially in the last chapter, the awareness of sin and the work of repentance did not cause him to sink down sullenly into himself, forgetting about others, but, through the grace that dwelt in his soul, he arrived at an integral Christian worldview, one capable of arriving at a very detailed understanding of the role of Christianity in today's world.

Thus, based on certain principles, he tried to define the foundation and aspirations of a spiritual community after the model of Târgu-Ocna. These principles, written down by Father Voicescu after his release in a book that was confiscated upon his arrest in 1959, have come down to us thanks to the Securitate. [190] They synthesize Valeriu's thinking, representing not only the genuine foundation of his own personal spiritual advancement, but also that of any common spiritual effort.

Principles of Christian Living

The principle of love: We subject our love in all things to the love of God, in which we love each other.

The principle of spiritual honor: We acknowledge the Truth and our position relative to it. We are impartial, allotting to each one what is his. Being aware of all the contrivances of the evil one, with wisdom we choose the honest fight, in which even those who fall are victorious.

The principle of education: From day to day, I disavow ever more the old man so that I can perfect myself in the new. Not I, but Christ lives in me.

The principle of prayer: Our entire life is accompanied by prayer, individual and common. Prayer is the first spiritual weapon.

The principle of unity: Wherever there are three or however many, we remain one. Through Christ and through the holy Christian martyrs, victorious against the gates of hell, we carry on as fighters for the chosen

---

[190] Archive CNSAS, Penal Fund, File 327, vol. 5, pg.p. 4, titled "Copy of Legionnaire activity" - (The reader should expect that the Securitate could not have named these principles anything else!) – "as developed by the convict Ioan Ianolide, diffused among the ranks of Legionnaires and reconstructed in 1954 by the convicts Constantin Voicescu and Vasile Petrescu on the pages of the book *Trilogii* by Simeon Mehedinți." In fact, these principles were put together by Valeriu Gafencu together with Ioan Ianolide.

people for the fulfillment of the Kingdom of God on earth. An enemy who is within our ranks is more dangerous than a thousand from outside. The love that unites is us is stronger than anything that could separate us.

The principle of obedience: In every way we submit our will to that of our superiors, being obedient unto death. Where two are found, one is obedient. Obedience leads the Church to victory.

The principle of liberty: In Christ we know spiritual freedom and exemplary activity, full of wisdom and boldness. Freedom in truth is mindful of obedience, adorns unity, enhances the sense of responsibility.

The principle of ecumenical advice: Each of us strives to decipher the truth, but all of us abide by a single decision made within an ecumenical council, in which we have one who is *primus inter pares* (first among equals). In this way we reconcile freedom with authority, equality with hierarchy, and innovation with tradition, all under the protection of the Holy Spirit.

The principle of community: One man completes what is lacking in the other, such that no one has in excess and no one stands in need. Those who make a total offering of themselves in humility achieve the ideal form of this principle. By incorporating the interests of the individual into the interests of the community, we proceed toward universal harmony.

The principle of spiritual bath: In a spirit of brotherly love, we confess our mistakes to each other and oversee the execution of decisions we have taken. We purify ourselves through the holy sacraments and through this spiritual bath.

The principle of permanent sacrifice: We work and sacrifice until death, having before our eyes the joy of salvation, Resurrection.

The principle of knowledge: We learn everything that can be learned and master everything that can be mastered for the use, advancement, and salvation of man. We examine everything in order to select what is good.

The Bases of Christian Unity

We are one in the body of Christ: through affiliation with God, by being born again in God, by partaking of the Holy Spirit, by the connection that we have with the saints and the Church triumphant, through Christian tradition, through our awareness of being the chosen people, through the awareness of struggle, through the love that exists between us, which is stronger than anything that could separate us. We are one by the authority of God, by the freedom with which we submit to one another, to serve the fulfillment of the same ideal. Our unity is accomplished through our faith in the prayer of Gethsemane. World history shows us that well-being and goodwill can be achieved only through unity.

A Christian Elite

To be a Christian elite means to destroy all evil within yourself and to hate all evil outside of yourself for the sake of love for God, and for the love of one's neighbor to bear the cross of Christ day by day and to lay down your life for the salvation of the world.

To be a Christian elite means to steer the boat of the world toward Christ and to follow Him. May the world, seeing the example of your life, consent to follow Christ.

Through a grace-filled elite, the world will be reconciled to God and will find peace and a happy resolution to all the problems that trouble it.

A grace-filled elite is formed by setting a good example of Christian living and by the consent of the people. Setting a bad example in life removes one from a state of grace and from the consent of the people.

Loving Christ

While loving Christ:

You must hate, you must not tolerate, and you must be numb toward worldly riches, and you will be the bearer of spiritual riches for others.

You must hate, you must not tolerate, and you must be numb toward the power of authority or domination, and as a faithful servant you will be put in authority over much.

You must hate, you must not tolerate, and you must be numb toward any thought that does not come from the Father of light, and you will be a light toward others.

You must hate, you must not tolerate, and you must be numb toward any feeling that does not spring from a pure heart, and you will be clothed in divine love.

You must hate, you must not tolerate, and you must be numb toward the root of evil within you, the material and the immaterial world, and you will be a free man.

Love Christ and you will be blessed!

We Aspire Toward the Resurrection

We want to lead our people to the Church that we might all be reconciled with God.

We want to create a school of Christian education and culture where man could reach perfection, which would gather together all human creative energies.

We want to form the new man, reborn from God and from his personal efforts.

We want to bring about the Kingdom of God on earth with the help of the Holy Spirit, fighting against satanic forces.

We want to live in a Christian community that will give unity to the diversity of forms of life and that will deliver man from physical and moral suffering. Through the new man, we want to apply a Christian understanding, in form and content, to all the problems of mankind.

Two Testimonies

We will now draw our series of testimonies about the "saint of prisons" to a close with a letter dated January 29, 1946 that Valeriu sent to his family, followed by a speech given by Father Constantin Voicescu in 1991 at a memorial service for the martyrs of Târgu-Ocna. In his letter, Valeriu speaks of the moment in which he became fully aware of his state of sinfulness – the state in which we all find ourselves. This awareness of sin, ever vigilant, stood at the base of his repentance, as those closest to him testify: "On that day," says Valeriu in his letter, "I began a conscientious struggle with sin." Purifying himself from sin through the grace of God, he attained a state of peace and light that was also perceived by others. In his speech, Father Voicescu speaks about this influence, in fact about the fruit of this influence, and about the spiritual atmosphere full of love at Târgu-Ocna – a kind of summary of everything we have said so far. These two testimonies, Valeriu's letter and Father Voicescu's speech, complement each other harmoniously.

Aiud, 29 January 1946

Life is something other than what people imagine. Man himself is something other than what he imagines himself to be. The Truth is something other than what the human mind imagines.

I want to be sincere and open, down to the deepest fibers of my soul. From the very moment in which I first set foot in prison, I wondered why I was locked up. In the realm of social life, regarding my relations with the world in which I lived, I was always considered to be a very good person, an example of moral conduct. If I entered into conflict with anyone, it was only for the sake of Truth. After much struggle and unrest, after much pain, when the cup of suffering had filled up, there came a holy day, in June 1943, when I fell to the ground on my knees, my forehead to the floor, my heart crushed, in an outburst of tears. I asked God to grant me light. By then, I had lost all confidence in man. I realized perfectly well that I was in truth, so why then was I suffering? In my entire soul, so full of longing, there remained only love. No one understood me.

In my prolonged weeping I started to do prostrations. And suddenly – O, Lord! How great art Thou, O Lord! – I saw my entire soul filled with sins. I found within myself the root of all human sins. Oh, there were so many sins, and the eyes of my soul hardened by pride had been completely blind to them! How great is God!

Seeing all my sins, I felt the need to shout them out loud, to cast them away from me. And a deep peace, a deep wave of light and love poured into my heart. As soon as the door opened, I left my cell and I went to those whom I knew loved me the most and to those who hated me and had sinned the most against me and I confessed to them openly and plainly, "I am the most sinful man. I do not deserve the trust of even the lowliest of men. I am filled with joy!"

Everyone was dumbfounded. Some of them looked at me with contempt, others with indifference, and some looked at me with a love that they themselves would have never been able to explain. Only one single person said to me, "You deserve to be kissed!" But I fled back quickly to my cell, buried my head in my pillow, and continued weeping while thanking and glorifying God.

On that day, I began a conscientious struggle with sin. If you could only know how difficult the war with sin is! I want you to know that I struggled very much with sin not only here, but also when I was free. [Here he confesses that, although he was tempted physically, he did not fall, but remained pure.]

In prison, I examined my soul and I realized that, even though I had not sinned in deed, I had sinned in word and especially in thought. After a deep examination of conscience, I went to a priest and confessed. My confession unburdened me.

And I carry on, in a continuous struggle. The struggle does not cease until death. Without repentance no one can take even one step forward. Anyone who flees from the reality of his own soul is a liar. What is life? It is a gift from God that is given to us in order to purify our souls from sin and to prepare ourselves, through Christ, to receive eternal life. What is man? A being created through the limitless love of God and to whom God gave the choice between holiness and death.

Be very careful! In social life, people regard each other and judge each other not according to what they are in essence, but according to what they seem to be in form. Have no illusions about man – anyone who does will suffer bitterly – but love him. Only one is perfect, only one is good, only one is pure: Christ-God!

And now: What is the Truth? The Truth is Christ, the Word of God. Seek to draw near to Christ sincerely and leave the world and its sins alone![191]

---

[191]Ioan Ianolide, *op. cit.*, pg.p. 231-233.

Târgu-Ocna, 21 July 1991

The service of burial underscores the pain of parting.

For those who believe in God, however, death is not a failure, it is not a final point. It is the threshold that divides the two realms, the gate through which one enters into the other plane of existence.

We Christians are not like those who have no hope. We believe in the other world, we believe in the Resurrection. Because we believe that we are something more than just flesh and blood. And it is exactly this something more – the immortal soul – that defines us as humans. Therefore, the burial service, for us and for those who are departed, is an opportunity to strengthen ourselves in the hope of the Resurrection.

The service we held today is done less frequently. After 40 years, we held a burial service for those whose lives ended as political prisoners in the penitentiary at Târgu-Ocna and were thrown here, in a common grave, without religious services, without crosses. It feels as though I can still see the *lada*[192] at the gate... many times with two of us in it; often with one or more on the lid... And after the dead bodies were dumped out, the *lada* was put back in its place to await others. It was waiting for us....

Some survived because of the mercy God showed us. We are here now, and we shed quiet tears at their grave, but we are not sad. You cannot understand the state of joy that we experienced here, as Valeriu Gafencu, the Saint of this place, put it in the verses of *Imnul Celor Cazuți* (Hymn of the Fallen). Here is a stanza from this hymn, engraved

---

[192]Lada - A large wood or metal box used to carry the dead to the cemetery. (Translator's note)

upon the troița[193] that was blessed today, and placed to mark their common grave:

> *You went, and left us in your wake*
> *The hope of meeting again in paradise.*
> *You will always be with us, and we wait*
> *To meet again with open souls.*

We are waiting to meet each other again. We are living this moment with intensity, this gathering here now, between us and also with them among us, as though it is the first step toward these heights. We can sense them looking at us from the other world. We are aware that we are treading on holy ground!

It is difficult for me to speak about Târgu-Ocna. If we speak about the "Pitești phenomenon," that satanic attempt at systematic physical and spiritual destruction of man, then I think we should speak all the more about the "Târgu-Ocna phenomenon" as the divine project for the restoration of man in the depths of Communist hell.

Someone who could tell you about Târgu-Ocna is Valeriu Gafencu, he was the pillar of fire of Christian spirituality in the Communist prisons. His big, blue eyes mirrored heaven. Looking at him, you felt so small! But his indescribable smile gave you courage and let you know that there is such a thing as the love of Christ. And no matter how great his cross of suffering was to bear, that smile never ceased to shine on his face. And so he departed to the Lord on February 18, 1952, bidding farewell to

---

[193] Troița: A cross that is especially build in a certain [public] place to commemorate a person or an event, or simply a place of prayer for passerby.

everyone…. Only a few days before, he had completed, as if a final testament, *Imnul Celor Cazuți*.

A few days before his passing, Valeriu testified to Dr. Mihai Lungeanu that the Mother of God appeared to him and said, "From now on, I will be your love!" On the very day of his death, Valeriu said to the same doctor, who had watched over him day and night, "I feel as though I am ascending steps. I breathe and I feel lighter and lighter." (During that time, according to Mihai, his breathing and his pulse were almost non-existent). His final wish was that everyone at Târgu-Ocna be given a New Testament on his behalf when it would become possible. And he left for the next world with the names of his mother and sisters on his lips.

Someone else who could tell you about Târgu-Ocna is Ioan Ianolide, Valeriu's spiritual brother and friend in Christ, who, in 23 years of prison, although relatively young, attained the philokalic wisdom of a great avva. But he also fell asleep in the Lord after being released from prison. Other men who could tell you about Târgu-Ocna include Father Gherasim Iscu, the abbot of Tismana, Father Viorel Todea, Gicu Jimboiu, Ion Plopeanu and many others who now look at us from the other world, from above, much higher than Măgura.

Others who could have spoken about Târgu-Ocna include most of the brothers in suffering, some of whom are present and some are not, who were engaged with their whole being in the life of this prison; now they stand humbly off to one side.

I was the one, however, who was chosen to speak, in my capacity as priest, about the spiritual aspect of life at Târgu-Ocna. I repeat: the others were in a better position to do so. Therefore, I have tried to make the thoughts I share with you today represent the thoughts of the others, of all of them, although I am sure you realize that it is difficult to detach yourself from a natural note of subjectivity.

As far as I am concerned, I will emphasize from the outset: It was our life at Târgu-Ocna, with its beauties and its tragedy, that convinced me to give up the study of geography that I loved dearly, in order to take up the study of theology after my release from prison in 1954 and to be ordained a priest. I was not the only one.

How can I convey the spiritual life of Târgu-Ocna in a speech? How can someone understand what happened here, from day to day, between 1950 and 1954? And words are so powerless! Nevertheless, with regret for the fact that I cannot present a full picture, I will draw up only a pale sketch.

The prison at Târgu-Ocna was an oasis in a desert of suffering. Which is not to say that there was no suffering here. On the contrary. Pain, sickness in all its hideousness, death, they were all at home here. Although it was a sanatorium, in having an appearance and living conditions a bit more humane, it was indeed still a prison.

But here I consider that God's mercy poured forth on our suffering. The cross was considered the gate of heaven. Suffering was sublimated into joy, as Valeriu Gafencu discerned in the verse: *And heaven is revealed openly / With gates in the form of a cross.*

The mercy of God was evident to us from the moment we first arrived at Târgu-Ocna, after being dumped out of the police van that brought us from Piteşti. I will never forget that late evening in May 1950. There was a full moon, the air was clean, and we greedily breathed in the scent of lime trees in bloom when the convoy of about 50 prisoners – a bunch of ghosts, most of them young

267

students – set out for the prison-sanatorium. And we could not believe our ears when we heard the kind, gentle words of the somewhat older guards who advised us, "Take it easy, son!" We were accustomed to being called "Bandit!" along with curses, fists, and blows with a stick! We were even told, "Welcome!" And the rooms where we slept the first night, with big windows and no shutters! Unimaginable for a prison! The next day we found out that we were even allowed to go outside! We could stretch out on the grass, we could see the sky and bask in the sun, we were allowed to meet and to speak with our other brothers in suffering! And then to receive a medical exam, given with care, even love, to have better and more plentiful food. And bread, even butter and milk! Forgive me, but only those who have experienced such moments can understand.

These conditions were not permanent, however. We went through periods of tight restrictions, even terror, especially when an attempt was made – unsuccessfully – to implement re-education as in Piteşti. And the activities of the Securitate officers as well as that of the informers made for continual stress. At a certain moment, the chapel in the old section of the penitentiary was shut down, and the cross on top of the steeple was taken down. The priestly vestments and the holy cloths that covered the altar were sent to the penitentiary to be used as rags to clean the floors. We were horrified by this blasphemy. We tried to gather them and hide them. I sewed an old stole in the lining of my coat, and I wore it until I was freed. I succeeded in getting it out. Might there not be a connection between this stole and the fact that I later became a priest?

Within this ambiance, what was created at Târgu-Ocna was more than just a community. It was a true spiritual family. Connections were formed here that were stronger than blood relations. Valeriu Gafencu gave his life for this family. I consider him a saint, and sooner or later the Church will canonize him.

The lives of the prisoners here were characterized by a thirst for culture and especially a thirst for Christ. A New Testament was introduced into the penitentiary, whose pages circulated around the prison. Holy texts were learned by heart. There were young men who knew almost the entire New Testament by heart. To say nothing of prayers, akathists, parakleises[194], etc. Small pieces of soap used in various ways were the *tabula cerata* which effectively replaced modern paper.

The prayer of the heart was practiced at Târgu-Ocna. Valeriu Gafencu and Ioan Ianolide brought the spiritual experience they had gained at Aiud, while those arrested after 1948 brought their hesychastic experience forged at *Rugul Aprins*[195] at Antim Monastery, where they had known great spiritual fathers such as Father Benedict, Father Sofian, Father Daniel, etc. With the blessing of the

---

[194]Paraklesis - a mass of supplication, most commonly to the Virgin Mary. (Translator's note)

[195] *Rugul Aprins*: Burning Pyre (Translator's note). Father George Calciu says that "in the Burning Pyre movement there were a lot of professors of theology and philosophy — men of science. The most important lectures were in Bucharest. They had a monk; he was a bishop from Russia who had arrived in Bucharest in 1946. [...] This man taught them about the Jesus Prayer, according to the practice they had in Russia from Elder Basil of Poiana Marului in Romania and St. Paisius Velichkovsky of Neamts. Thus, as they discovered the Jesus Prayer and the beneficial effects of this prayer upon the soul, more and more intellectuals gathered around him" (In Father George Calciu's *Interviews, Homilies, and Talks*. Saint Herman of Alaska Brotherhood, 2010, p. 30). (O.G.)

priests, the powerful name of our Lord Jesus Christ was invoked here day and night. And things took place in secret. True mystical experiences.

Fathers Gherasim Iscu, Viorel Todea, Sinesie Ioja and others assisted all of us in this "holy therapy" through all kinds of services and especially through the sacrament of confession. Even more than this: in prison we were able to partake of the Holy Body and Blood of Christ, brought here by men of God. Most of those who died were able to receive Communion beforehand.

I mentioned before that there were times in which we were not allowed to circulate from room to room, times of isolation. During one of these periods, a man who was seriously ill, a former police officer, went into a coma. He was in a coma for a week, after which he woke up and asked for a priest, but no priest was able to get to him. But then the dying man cried out, "I once killed a man!" And he gave up his spirit. This was known only to him and God. He wanted to confess to a priest. His conscience did not let him die. I am certain that his outcry, done publicly, was a true confession and that he received forgiveness.

The skete at Măgura watched over us continuously. The bells that rang on Sundays and on feast days had a distinctive echo in our hearts. They were comfort and strength. We knew that we were not alone. But the extraordinary sight of lit candles – like a chain of stars – along the winding roads of Măgura, in the holy nights of the Burial and the Resurrection!

A mysterious bell rings at midnight
And Jesus comes down to earth.
From our bloody chests
Resounds the holy hymn of Resurrection.

Come, Christians, take light,
With your souls bright and purified.
Come ye hungry, taste of the Supper:
It is the Wedding of the King's Son.
                                    -Valeriu Gafencu

On the holy days of Christmas, we sang carols both old and new, as well as those written in prison. We even sang carols passed on from other prisoners who came long before we did. This is a small piece of a carol written during our prison time:

Christmas has also come here
To comfort us in exile....
And only sorrows gather together
To lament me at the door.
                                    -Radu Gyr

We also sang the tragic carol of the Romanian prisons on the Russian steppes, composed by Ştefan Tumurug, a teacher and officer in the army reserve:

We gather at the window of memory
We sing carols to the soul of another time.
Mama, Mama, the snow drifts grow
And we are perishing....

At Târgu-Ocna, however, another type of carol blossomed, the carol of joy!

In the heart of the servant
The Lord makes His manger

271

On the night of Christmas….

Lilies rain down from heaven
Upon His new manger
And dew drops down from heaven…
                    -Valeriu Gafencu

Here, poetry was born, profundities of thought were born, music was composed, sculptures took shape, novels were conceived, much was learned. And so many other things…. Here we felt and lived holy and genuine joys. Thus, I understand my friend Sami, who, after "liberation" in 1954, confessed to me, "I miss Târgu-Ocna so much!" Because it was there that I understood what freedom in Christ means. No one would have been able to take this joy and freedom away from us!

We who are still alive by God's mercy, we were blessed to have been acquainted with young men whose lives were a ceaseless striving to live in Christ. We stand as witnesses to them.

We are not surprised by the fact that Pastor Richard Wurmbrand has testified many times that his life was saved thanks to the Christian love of these young men, who, despite accusations to the contrary, practiced no form of religious or ethnic discrimination. I recall how, after he had recovered – he had come from the Ministry of the Interior on a stretcher, with some 18 tubercular cavities in his bones and lungs –, walking about by leaning on the arm of a young man who was himself weakened by illness, the pastor, having a sense of humor, exclaimed, "Look, Judeo-Legionnaire brotherhood!" After his release, in his sermons and writings, the pastor similarly confessed that he had seen saints at the penitentiary at Târgu-Ocna. He was no doubt referring primarily to Valeriu Gafencu.

General Tobescu, former chief of the Constabulary, was also surprised that he was looked after with so much love by men whom he had sentenced to long, hard years in prison. Eduard Masikiewicz, a young student of great purity being on the verge of death, asked that a candle be lit for him. But upon awakening after a short sleep, he asked that the candle stub be blown out, because it would be needed for others. He said that he had seen the Savior, Who told him, "I am not going to take you this evening!" He called him the following night.

And very often, this Christian way living was tried and made clearer through the fire of difficult trials. When, for example, the political officer proposed to the student Goe Nițescu that he become an informer in exchange for the streptomycin that had arrived from home and that would have saved his life, he indignantly rejected the bait that the Securitate officer had offered him, preferring to die rather than sell his soul. Before him, others had done the same: Edi Masikiewicz, or Nelu Sultaniuc.

Medical care was organized under the maternal and angelic supervision of Dr. Margareta Danielescu, together with our own prisoner-doctors. Who does not remember the devotion and the sleepless nights of the doctors: Ion Ghițulescu, Constantin Banu, Nicolae Floricel (Papașa), Aristide Lefa, Mihai Lungeanu! And who could forget the young people – having tuberculosis themselves, although in somewhat better condition – who, with an impressive degree of self-sacrifice, but natural and discreet, were at the same time sisters of protection, nurses, working women who washed clothes and sheets that were sometimes full of pus, working day and night as if for Christ, when they

273

stood watch at the beds of the more seriously ill? Some of them never tasted their own ration of milk, butter, or meat. They handed them over to the sick who had acute need of them, they themselves being content to eat only beans and barley. Most of them are present here.

In the midst of these tragic realities, our youth, full of holy aspirations, bore the stamp of optimism. We were gladdened by the sight of flowers and the colors of autumn leaves. For a long time, day by day, Tinu Samargescu looked after the flowers, a joy beside the beds of those who could no longer move or the world's final smile on the chest of those who had departed.

Do you know how beautiful sparrows are? Ordinary sparrows, who boldly entered our rooms, even to the beds of the sick! The sparrows of Moş Popan, a shepherd from Maramureş, who loved them like his own sheep. And how much gentleness, delicate attention, small gifts, flowers, poems and songs were found for the occasion of name days[196] and birthdays, not only our own, but also those of our families!

And what of the technical miracles realized by Jenică Otparlic, who used cast-off pieces of iron to fashion the distillery that was absolutely necessary for a medical officer, a sterilizer for medical equipment and so many other things?

Thus lived those imprisoned at Târgu-Ocna…..

A part of those at Târgu-Ocna were released from prison in the years 1953-54. A part of us remained in prison. Those of us who got out felt an urgent need to see each other, to meet each other, in order to preserve our spiritual

---

[196]Name day – In Orthodoxy, the feast-day of one's patron saint. (Translator's note)

freedom. We came to realize that the entire country was a prison. We strove to go by the spiritual road of Târgu-Ocna. We went on pilgrimages to monasteries, we sought out great spiritual fathers, we rejoiced together on the occasion of special events in our families (weddings, baptisms, etc.)

But the "vacation" did not last long. The Securitate began to hunt us down again, considering us the "Târgu-Ocna gang," which included a few of those who had remained in prison, such as Ioan Ianolide and Constantin Dragodan. In 1959, we were sentenced [again] to long years in prison – nine of us to life in prison at hard labor – for "mystical activity" at the Târgu-Ocna penitentiary, an activity that continued even after liberation.

We were not sentenced unjustly, since the state was Communist and atheist, while we were anti-Communist and anti-atheist. The only injustice was the claim that we belonged to an organization that did not exist except in the files of the Securitate.

A very difficult period of detention followed - Jilava, Aiud. But we did not lose hope. Our faith in God was a great lever of support. We knew that if we had Christ, no one could defeat us. A poet has captured this sublimation of struggle wonderfully:

I do not hurt because of long struggles,
Nor do I hurt because of wounds in the chest
As I yearn for because of those ugly arms
That no longer wish to fight.

How much does your heart still sing,
What does a defeated arm mean,
What does it matter in the dust of a shattered sword

If you raise yourself with a holier flag?

For you are not defeated when you bleed,
Neither when your eyes are full of tears,
The most dreadful defeats
Are when you give up your dreams.

                                        -Radu Gyr

In 1964, a pardon was granted to political prisoners. We did notfeel the joy of liberation. Many found that their families had broken up. The eyes of the Securitate were always on us. We avoided meeting each other, knowing that we were being strictly supervised.

Until God gave us the miracle of the sacrifices of December 1989[197]....

Through this miracle we are here at Târgu-Ocna. Let us not forget this. We are living as though in a spell. It is hard for us to believe. Forty years ago we were behind prison walls. We could very well have been here ourselves, under the ground that we now tread upon.

We do not ask for admiration or sympathy. We reflect on the expiatory meaning of the suffering we endured. For ourselves and for others. We know that no sacrifice is done in vain. We know that nothing in the plan of divine providence happens by chance. We consider that Târgu-Ocna has a message for our Romanian community. It is the Christian message of our rebirth.

Communism destroyed a few hundred thousand people physically, but spiritually it destroyed millions. The martyrs beneath the ground we are treading on cry out to

---

[197]The Communist regime fell in Romania in December 1989, after a bloody revolt. (O.G.)

us to return to Christ, to the Church. This is the imperative of the present hour.

Valeriu, we are here to assure you that we heed your call from the other side of death:

> *You induce those of us who have remained alive:*
> *Struggle together and in the same gait,*
> *Build for God holy altars,*
> *Step forward on the path of life!*
>
> -Valeriu Gafencu

Thus may God help us![198]

*

Having arrived at the end of our testimonies about Valeriu Gafencu, I believe that we have nothing more to add except what all of those who knew him have said: "He was a saint. He is a saint."

Holy martyr Valeriu, pray to God for us!

---

[198]*Părintele Voicescu – un duhovnic al cetății*, pp. 24-35.

Afterword
The value of the book that in your hands

This book, written by father Moise, focuses primarily on the martyrdom of Valeriu Gafencu. Yet, its value goes beyond his personality and it is of utmost importance for understanding martyrdom in Christ during communist persecution as well as for comprehending the prototype of the Christian confessor nowadays, when we are living the end of history. If the ideas of this book are well understood and applied, this can become a fundamental volume for a Christian nowadays. I will expand on the value of the following lines.

1.   It speaks about a real man, who withstood the pressure of being forced to reject Christ, who did not accept re-education, and who can be an example for us to follow

Contemporary saints were people like us, to whom God offered extraordinary experiences, thus revealing their human essence. On the Judgment Day, they will be there to judge us because they lived in a similar historical context as the one we find ourselves in today. Their life was a continuous burning torch "and the light shined in darkness; and the darkness comprehended it not" (John 1: 5). Martyrs are the light, and they call us to wake up from the numbness that is our separation from God and from the things that are enslaving us.

278

2. It urges us to assume our Christianity in a responsible manner

The example of Valeriu's life, together with others from his generation who took up their cross and followed Christ, ignoring all the risks associated with such a choice, is living proof that serves as a wake-up call for us. They are an example to follow; in order to help and encourage us to refuse the offer of this faithless world,[199], searching and constantly fighting for inner change towards Christ. Otherwise, all outer manifestations (such as formal membership in the Orthodox Church, gathering of information at an intellectual level about the spiritual life, the embellishment of houses with icons, attending holy ceremonies in idiorhythmic parishes, fleeing to the mountains as a way to "fight against the system", etc.) will prove, sooner or later, worthless.

As Christians, we cannot live outside history, nor can we be isolated from the world and from contemporary life. Christianity currently plays a highly important role for humanity: "nowadays two Christian processes are needed: re-Christianizing the Christians and Christianizing the nonbelievers."[200]

Many things can be written about these two processes of Christianization, but this goes beyond the aim of this book. What is symptomatic is that a large

---

[199] "Wherefore come out from among them, and be ye separate, saith the Lord" (Corinthians 6: 17)

[200] Ioan Ianolide (2006) *Intoarcerea la Hristos*, Bucuresti: Editura Christiana, p. 505

majority of today's Christians lost the "salt" of their faith (Matthew 5: 13). They are highly "contaminated" by formalism, and their confession of faith made to nonbelievers has no influence, or even worse: "For the name of God is blasphemed among the Gentiles through you, as it is written." (Romans 2: 24).

The presence of Christians throughout the world must always be an answer, an example of the kind of attitude to be followed by those outside the Church in the face of all the problems and confusions that humanity confronts. The life of a Christian must be a light for everyone; it must be the meaning of life for those whose life seems to be meaningless. The life of a Christian must be an ideal for those outside the Church, the confession that Christ is the Way, the Truth and the Life. The Christian must "function" according to a different logic and according to different laws, the laws of the Holy Bible.

One very important lesson that can be learned from Valeriu Gafencu and his brothers is that, nowadays, our mission as Christians who form the Church can be fulfilled through **asceticism** and through liturgical life. Every Christian who wishes to confess Christ must do so through his own life, and then, eventually, through words.

3.   It urges us to become genuinely free

In accordance with the word of the Gospel, where it is written that if we seek to fulfill God's commandments, we will know the truth, and the truth will set us free (cf. John 8, 31-32), this book can be, for anyone who seeks freedom, a precious "document for a new world", a world of freedom.[201] A world of both inner and outer liberty. The endeavor to fulfill God's commands was the martyr's path to freedom, and the discovery of this freedom could not be prevented even by bars and chains.

It is crucial to have models like these, and to acquire their spiritual and moral references. Otherwise, as Ianolide says, "you can be the next re-educated!"

4. It makes us aware of the re-education to which all of us are being subjected

Why I am saying this? As I have mentioned in the introduction of the book, the ultimate goal of the communist ideology was the creation of a "new man". The communists believed that the re-education was the only way to accomplish this, as highlighted already.

However, one who studies the communist re-education in depth cannot but acknowledge the following evidence: the same principles of re-education are applied nowadays, though in a more disguised and perfidious manner. This ideology, which highly influences and governs the present society, is characterized by the same spirit of antichrist as the communist ideology. The goal is the same, only the means are different. Valeriu's dearest friend, Ioan Ianolide, already noticed in 1985: "The one who is

---

[201] As Ianolide, Valeriu's best friend, named his testimony-book project: *The Return to Christ. Document for a New World.* It is a confession of what his generation experienced in the Communist prisons. The book was published posthumously.

willing to see, can identify the re-education process all throughout the world, as well as the dialectical materialism, the atheistic, the immoral, the decadent and the repellent remolding."[202]

This was predictable for people endowed with spiritual understanding. When Communism reached its climax and nothing seemed to be able to stand in its way, Valeriu said, "Communism will perish, but what is essential is what will take its place."[203] In the 1980s Ianolide wrote: "I feel that in the foreseeable future, the powers of Communism will be annihilated, yet I remain sad and worried."[204] Sad because he can see that the same individuals responsible for unleashing Communism upon the country are now turning into the masters of the coming world; worried because he foresees the perspective of a worldwide dictatorship, without opponents and without precedent.

If we consider Ianolide's prophetic words, we can see that our own world resembles a prison more and more. He said that this is an imprisonment that is

---

[202]Ioan Ianolide (2006) *Intoarcerea la Hristos*, p.84, Bucuresti: Editura Christiana.

[203]Ioan Ianolide (2006) *Intoarcerea la Hristos(Return To Christ)*, p.94, Bucuresti: Editura Christiana.

[204]Ioan Ianolide (2009) *Detinutul profet (The Prophet Prisoner)*, p.112, Bucuresti: Editura Bonifaciu. See also father Serafim Rose: "Communism does not have the final answer because it is entirely damaging (...). However, it prepares the world for a very important event that must take place before the end of the world, that is, the unique and united world government, from which Christianity was banished - (ierom. Damaschin (2005) *Viata si lucrarile Parintelui Serafim Rose (The Life and works of Father Seraphim Rose)*, Bucuresti: Editura Sophia,p. 849).

tougher than what they had endured because now only few people are aware of the totalitarian ideology and the anti-Christian way of life, which is slowly conquering the world. Released by Christ for scrutiny, darkness reigns (Luke 22: 53). Nowadays our prison cells are guarded by our own passions, fed and cultivated by a consumerist society.

In the communist prisons, torturers used all resources available to force the prisoners to deny Christ. Nowadays, rejecting Christ is done voluntarily, as people are seduced from an early age to embrace a lifestyle which is opposite to the one to which Christ calls us. In prisons, torturers were trying to prevent every person from having any kind of privacy or moments of prayer. Nowadays, people voluntarily surrender their own privacy in favor of TV, Internet or anything which might steal their serenity and opportunity to be alone with Christ. Torturers did everything in their power to keep the prisoners away from their own families and to get them discouraged for an easier control over them. In present times, divorce has become a lifestyle.

The spirit of 're-education' is the same – both in Communism and in Capitalism – that is to say, it is characterized by a rejection of faith in God, by the giving up of traditional moral values, and by selfishness, pride, betrayal and cowardice. This is the Spirit of the Antichrist. The methods used are just slightly different: if during Communism, they wanted to obtain "the new man" through force, through demolishing and closing churches and monasteries, and through torturing or killing any opponents, in capitalism, the methods used are 'softer' and can slowly seduce even those who, under obvious Christian persecution, would have confessed and become martyrs.

In essence, re-education has two main goals. First, the removal of God from people's consciousness, the re-shaping of people's way of thinking, so that man's heart becomes insensible to God's grace, incapable of true and profound feelings. Man is thus condemned to live in a superficial manner, not only physically, but also spiritually and culturally.

Second, achieving the perfection of the "new man," modeled so that the Devil can easily take possession over him or her. Such a man would be ready to receive the Antichrist and enthrone him in "the holy place" (Matthew 24: 15) that belongs to God at the end of times.

An important clarification is needed in this context: the correct translation of the word "antichrist" is not "against Christ" but "in place of Christ/replacing Christ." In other words, the enemy no longer confronts visibly and directly Christ, but he seeks to take His place, to remove Him from people's consciousness, to neutralize people's discernment and their capacity to choose freely.

How is re-education being carried out nowadays?

The first method of re-education consists of the continuous promotion of the hedonistic message which has permeated all places: the contemporary pseudo-culture, the education systems (as in Communism, anthropology is reduced to zoology, remaining thus tributary to evolutionism, as Father Sophrony from Essex said), and the mass-media, which promote the message that the essence of life consists in enjoying oneself, feeling good, having fun, accumulating as much as possible, and being successful. Happiness in life is generally understood as the sum of moments of pleasure. Thus, people educated in this spirit constantly crave pleasure. Working like slaves, people chain themselves to monthly installments to the bank, or they steal or make compromises in order to comply with the unrealistic standards imposed by the marketing policies serving the aims of the cronies of this world.

Second, the "new man" is being molded through a horrendous instrument of mass manipulation: "political correctness." This concept aims to impose a new world order, free of all Christian principles, principles that have guided society throughout centuries, a world order where God is to become one of "nomina odiosa."

As the author of a much-acclaimed Romanian book[205] states, *"contrary to its name, it is not politics which is the essence of political correctness, but the attitude. The main demand of this philosophy is that nobody is allowed to do or say something that another group would find offensive. It also says that we should not mention our own beliefs if they might be considered by others as offensive. This attitude (…) was defined by several authors as being a 'mind police' and 'intellectual terrorism.' The term 'police' is used because researchers found that the Marxist doctrine is the origin of this phenomenon. It is indeed a <u>totalitarian mind control</u>: one can only say what political correctness ideologists decided; otherwise one could even be imprisoned."*

---

[205] *Zeul tolerantei si descrestinarea crestinismului. O perspectiva ortodoxa (The god of tolerance and the de-Christianization of Christianity)* , Bucuresti 2010, Editura Christiana, p. 45.

Another Romanian writer has the same position: *"Political correctness is a social behavior law that an enlightened minority imposes on a retarded majority.[...] They know better than anyone else what people need to live reasonably. They need political correctness. Whoever opposes or objects to this new social homogenization criterion – criterion which, let's not forget, was not established by consensus, but rather forced by the intellectual terrorism of an 'active' and 'conscious' minority – are naturally labeled as reactionary (since they oppose the 'progress' represented by the Leninist minority's ideals), enemies of human rights (human rights as understood by the activists of political correctness), briefly: public enemies."*[206]*"The classical method of social control of thoughts (by forbidding certain words or expressions) that political correctness employs differs in no way from the old fascist or communist ideal of forced ideologization of society."*[207]

Third, the same tactic that the communists so successfully applied can be noticed nowadays: the creation of a new language, where the meaning of certain classical terms is twisted. For example, "family" no longer means "the primary social entity, established by marriage, composed by husband, wife and their descendants" (according to the Etymological dictionary of Romanian, 1958), but instead "A group consisting of two parents and their children living together as a unit" (Oxford Dictionary 2014). Along the same lines, concepts that were crystal clear for the traditional society now

---

[206] Horia-Roman Patapievici (2002) *Omul recent(The recent Man)*, Bucuresti: Editura Humanitas, p. 305, 307.

[207] Horia-Roman Patapievici (2002) *Omul recent(The recent Man)*, Bucuresti: Editura Humanitas, p.312.

receive new names: baby murdering (through abortion or the so-called "contraceptives") is now innocently labeled "family planning." Similarly, affirming our belief as the Orthodox Church that "outside the Church there is no salvation" (Saint Cyprian) is equal today to being an extremist, fanatical, etc.. In the sphere of morality, every single redefinition of terms has direct consequences on man's conscience.

There is another important element proving that it is the Antichrist who is pushing to create "the new man," the "new age": both Communists and those who are striving today to control the world have one ultimate wish: to know people's thoughts. We should never forget that the Patristic Fathers of the Church firmly stress that the roughest fight with Satan takes place inside the mind, where all words, decisions, actions, are born. The devil does not know what we think; hence he resorts to all types of trickery and slyness to discover our thoughts so that he can take control of our minds and thus rule our lives.

One of the most famous and cruel prisons chiefs was colonel Craciun from the Aiud Communist prison. There, he successfully introduced different methods of re-education for the political prisoners, such as torture, starvation, solitary confinement, and forcing some of the known role model political prisoners, who already abandoned the faith, to publicly declare their atheism. This method was supposed to create chaos and insecurity among the faithful dissidents who admired those so-called role model prisoners, and urge them to do the same. Colonel Craciun said that the most dangerous dissidents are those who refuse any kind of cooperation or talks with the secret police or with the prison investigators, creating a real barrier for the investigators in their quest to know what these dissidents really think.

There are many methods used today to find out "what people think," instruments of mass surveillance such as online social networking and micro-blogging services (like Twitter, Facebook, etc.), personal blogs, forums, creating and distributing different petitions (some of them might be well intentioned; yet, some are set up only to create groups and people's profiles), surveillance of e-mails, phones, private mail and so forth. Millions of people use these mediums every day without fully realizing the implications of what they are doing.

5. It saves us from ignorance

It is important to fight the fallen man in us, the one that is tempted by ignorance and unconsciousness. By forgetting what these martyrs had to endure to keep their faith and convictions, we risk re-living the past in the present, even if in a different form. This ignorance and obliviousness will be our condemnation.

We are called to honor these martyrs as an important part of our own heritage. Through our choices we become, or rather, make ourselves into, followers of those we desire to resemble. Thus, we can follow the model of saints or heroes, whose way of living warms our hearts and whose lives we read and share. Or we can follow the model of great villains, cowards and famous and self-proclaimed scum imposed on the public consciousness, whose rhetoric and gestures (lies, corruption, thirst for power, etc.) we repeat unconsciously even as we externally might criticize and condemn these kinds of manifestations.

6. It is a courageous attitude leading to courage

Unfortunately, it has become taboo nowadays to talk about the martyrdom of those who confessed Christ in the Communist prisons (as well as to address the notion of sacrifice). This is due to the fact that people have become victims of false models in their attempt to fulfill their short lived and cheap desires. Talking about their sacrifice is against the current interpretation and representation of history which is imposed on us. One needs courage to talk about their martyrdom nowadays when the "political correctness" censorship has become much more rigorous. As C.S. Lewis said, where courage lacks, no virtue can survive.

7. It gives us hope

That which has been stated above, relating to the sacrifice of Valeriu's generation, speaks to the fact that, despite the persecution of the Christians which nearly led to their extinction during the Communist years, so many young people returned to Christ after 1989 in the former countries of the Communist bloc. Helped by the prayers of the new martyrs, their conversion was inspired by the sacrifice and the by the testimony to the Truth of those martyred for Christ during Communism. The fact that there is a plethora of books being published and read that testify to their martyrdom, and that many people are awakening to an understanding of what Christianity and patriotism meant during that generation, is proof that the sacrifice of those from the Communist prisons and those of December 1989 (when Communism actually fell) bore fruit; that their prayers were answered, that they did not die in vain. It was as if the words of those who went bare-handed to confront the arms of those defending the communists and clinging to power in December 1989, "we will die and we will be free," became true.

The spirit of those who were in political prisons, their cry, permeated those harsh December days. Their words were ever present on the lips of the next young generation, who, inspired by the sacrifice of those before them, found their courage once again – the courage to sacrifice, the courage to *be*. Because those words, which originated of one who was not "flesh and blood," speak to the very essence of Christian life. And all who went out on Romania's streets in December 1989, fighting for freedom, testify today that those days were characterized first and foremost by the gifts of grace of the Holy Spirit, and only secondarily by the courage of the Romanian people[208].

We, the Christians of the Last Days, especially those from of us living in the West, have a great opportunity. It is the opportunity about which Valeriu and the people in political prisons was speaking about: if man is sincerely looking for his salvation, soon, everything and everybody – the "old man" within him,

---

[208]The fact that today the Orthodox countries of the former Communist bloc do not have a spectacular economic growth shows once again that the prayer and the fight of the persecuted for the faith and their patriotism was not for accomplishing some socio-political development for the country, but a spiritual revival.

his family, the society, the devil – will try to annihilate his good intention. And then, if he continues on and is not tempted to turn back, the persecution will be the very thing that pushes him towards Christ's arms through the spirit of "good despondency" (when he acknowledges the fact that without Christ he is nothing and cannot accomplish anything and he starts crying incessantly after Christ), through prayer and fasting, guarding himself from the temptation of worldly comfort, refining his understanding, cleansing it. And through the quasi-general apostasy, in the middle of the amorality of the world surrounding him, the Christian has to make the right choice: Christ, and then the grace of God will help him. Because "…where sin abounded, grace abounded much more" (Romans 5: 20).

Valeriu's message was the same: "the enemies of Christianity, those who perpetrated the martyrdom, now want to hide Christ's existence in the world, they want people to forget Him, but they are mistaken and prove themselves powerless. They attained power over this world, but they made countless saints and martyrs. And while they have succeeded in silencing many voices, they were incapable of extinguishing the light of Christ's saints. God works in the world also through unfaithful people. This is the key of the crisis of the twentieth century: the cleansing of the soul that is necessary to reach a higher step of spirituality and virtue."[209].

---

[209]Ioan Ianolide (2006) *Intoarcerea la Hristos (Return to Christ)*, Bucuresti: Editura Christiana, p. 503.

8. Because it teaches us several important lessons for our days

Man's only chance to fight Evil is to fill himself with Christ (through prayer, ascetic life, and the Sacraments of the Church), as only Light can banish darkness (John, 1:4-5). Today, we should fight not against the system, the governments, the occult organizations that run the world from the shadows, nor with anti-family leagues; our fight should be, first and foremost, with ourselves, with our passions and the devil who works through them (Ephesians 6:12). In order for us to endure, we need to belong to a spiritual community: "a brother helped by his own brother is like a tall and strong fortress" (Proverbs 18:19).

As Valeriu did, as all new confessors did, we need to cultivate our inner sense of sacrifice; it is only in this way, by resembling Christ, that we can hope to receive the grace of Christ, He who sacrificed Himself for us. To sacrifice yourself for your neighbor, to do acts of mercy, to practice any type of asceticism are seen by the Orthodox Church as privileges, opportunities to become closer to God, and not as obligations or constraints on one's freedom.

We should nurture a good spiritual state of being (an important weapon against one of the greatest dangers that constantly lurks in our world – hopelessness), as well as inner peace; this kind of behavior was driving the investigators (and after all, the devil) crazy. Furthermore, once you develop such an inner state, it becomes contagious for all those around you.

Valeriu never did anything halfway. Every day, he gave Christ the best in him, being firmly convinced that he might be living his last day. How much our lives could change if we only lived in a like manner!

We must take our neighbour upon us, we must carry his burden and see beyond what drives us apart and makes us different from each other. For example, Valeriu preferred to die so that someone else could live, someone of a different religion and a different ethnicity – the protestant Jewish Pastor Wurmbrandt. "My brother is my life,", as the Fathers of the Church say.

We understand that the Love of God reveals itself through suffering, on the Cross. We can truly know Christ if we follow Him on Golgotha. In this way, we will no longer fabricate a false god for ourselves, one to fulfill our wishes and make our lives more comfortable on earth.

The study of Valeriu's life and teachings, as well as those of the new confessors, and the struggle to apply them in our lives, can help us distinguish, as they themselves learned to do, between the apparent reality (reality of our senses) and the metaphysic Truth of Christ. It can help us understand today's reality beyond the apparent. It can give us the inspiration we desperately need in the struggle for saving our souls.

Their example shows us the only Way which enables us to fight the good fight – yesterday and today, now and ever onto the ages of ages: the living Christ in His Church (Hebrews 13:8).

As I realize that, beyond all sorrow, Valeriu's life remains under the sign of victory in Christ, the Easter Paschal Homily of Saint John Chrysostom comes to my mind, which I will allow myself to paraphrase a bit:

O Death, where is your sting?
O Hell, where is your victory?
Christ has risen and you have been hollowed,
Christ has stood up and demons have fallen.
Christ has risen and angels rejoice.
Christ has risen and life reigns.
Christ has risen and tombs are emptied,
Christ has risen and **those who died for Him under the red persecution ascended from their prisons straight into the Synaxarion**.[210]

For You deserve all glory, honour and worship, now and ever and onto the ages of ages, Amen!

Father Ciprian Grădinaru

---

[210]In Orthodoxy, the Synaxarion is a compilation of all names of saints listed for each day.

Appendix
Poems and Letters from Prison[211]

> Job, resigned, yearned for
> Even deeper wounds,
> And an ever broader faith.

> –F. Strijnicu, Valeriu Gafencu

"I have had a few opportunities to engage in dramatic confrontations for my faith. I have known men who have achieved the fullness of human life, sainthood, martyrdom, but only by undergoing terrible ordeals.

"I have the strength to confess that I am a blessed man, for I have seen a man who lived, thought, smiled, and was victorious in Christ - Valeriu Gafencu.

"When he found the Lord, Valeriu renounced everything and offered himself to God completely and definitively. He carried on the great struggles – battling the passions, guarding his spoken words and all of his senses, controlling his behaviors, purifying his thoughts and even the most imperceptible internal impulses - such that the Holy Spirit gradually pervaded his body, his soul, his mind, his entire life.

"Amidst a difficult life in prison, Valeriu was a pure and steadfast rock of faith. His interior being had been perfected. His impetuosity was meek, his generosity appeared to be disguised as begging, his spiritual ascent was full of humility. He was as innocent as a child and as humble as a sinner. Although everyone obeyed him, he was humbly obedient. Although others served him

---

[211]Ioan Ianolide, *op. cit.*, pp. 221-252.

throughout his illness, he, himself, seemed to serve. Although he was exhausted by torments, secret powers made him strong. His prayer was his very life, his soul was full of grace, his mind was endowed with gifts and heavenly light. Valeriu was dead in Christ and Christ was alive in Valeriu.

"He had become a symbol and an example of life, not only in intention, but by actual living. As a bearer of Christ, he was humble, pious, lucid, ever grateful, always glorifying his Lord. In Valeriu one could feel the union of life with eternity, the union of mind with heart, the union of the body with the soul, the union of God with man, the union of man with nature, the union of all men in Christ, peace, harmony, and the unity of the world.

"Although deeply introverted, he communicated with others in a way that was lively, intelligent, and wise. He was gifted with a capacity to attract, to impress, to enlighten both friends as well as enemies. His word was full of authority, power, and authenticity. Valeriu conquered, motivated, moved, amazed, and shone.

"Lest he should seem too odd, too heavenly, too lofty, let it be said that Valeriu was a warm and modest soul who clothed everyone in his love. Relentless toward himself, he had much understanding for the world, with all its stray wanderings. He saw mankind's decadence clearly; he was saddened and prayed for the world fervently, making its deliverance [from evil] his supreme and sacrificial goal.

"He himself testified, toward the end of his life, 'I look with love at all people, although some I praise and others I bewail, and I tremble at their fate. I forgive with all my spiritual freedom those who have done me wrong. In fact, those who have struck me have pushed me all the more strongly into the Lord's arms, and for this I thank them. I pray for my friends and for Christians, and for their salvation from their enemies at the eleventh hour.'"

"The final years of Valeriu's life were full of pain: Prison, hunger, cold, persecution, humiliation, terror, isolation, sickness, the collapse of some believers and the birth of others, a death that came slowly, consciously, tormenting him. His physical suffering was immense, but he overcame it through the power given to him from on high and, in the end, he attained victory. The brilliant luster of the saints is real and Valeriu was made worthy of it at the end of his life. Although he was continuously dying, in spirit he was ever resurrecting. Death had died in Valeriu.

"His final testament to those nearest him was the Final Testament of our Lord Jesus Christ Himself, as well as these words: *I am leaving now, and even though my life was different from thatof the high priesthood, I remain a faithful soldier of the Church, for in these times Jesus had to be in prison. I am deeply moved and blessed that death for Him is offered to me. Never abandon the Church, even though that means encountering great resistance in establishing the truth! Christianity has new martyrs, and with them a new spirit is arising. I am devoid of any pride or self-satisfaction and full of fervent love for the Lord. I thank Him for everything. He must be praised and glorified now and unto the ages of ages.*

"On February 18, 1952, at the Târgu-Ocna penitentiary, Valeriu rendered his soul into the hands of Christ, but through the benevolence of Christ, he remained present in the world so that through his prayers and his love he might bear the cross of the salvation of the human race with us. Amen."

*

I will now let Valeriu speak for himself through his letters and a handful of poems composed at Târgu-Ocna. They speak about him through his words. They present the most faithful portrait of Valeriu, physically, spiritually, and devotionally.

Dated Letters

A few of Valeriu's letters written between 1942-1948 have remained. These letters, addressed to his family, evaded the penitentiary censor. They delicately capture Valeriu's inner development during his years of searching and unrest. They are his only remaining writings. We reproduce a few fragments here, to serve as a vivid expression of his manner of living.

3 July 1942
Send me my law school courses because I want to study. Also a course in the German language, since I want to learn German well. I am spiritually content and at peace with myself. I am not lying to you. It is the reality of my soul, which has found its peace in the understanding and help of the All-Powerful God. I believe that only with the truth of the Gospel can man find peace in his soul.

My dear sisters, I ask you to guard yourselves from sin, to live in purity, for that is the only way you will be successful in life!

August 1942
I have come down with jaundice. Your letters cheered me up. I miss home and freedom. I am well, spiritually. God guides me and for me His light is a beacon always lit for me. Pray much.

1 September 1942

My thoughts are directed toward beautiful Bessarabia. Draw ever nearer to God with your hearts, for only from Him comes our salvation.

14 October 1942

In the life of this accursed world, I feel alone. I spend my time continuously thinking about God. Only God fully understands me, to my great spiritual gratitude. I feel Him ever beside me, safeguarding me and lighting my path. You may never understand how happy I am when I feel the Christian spirit vibrant within me!

Those who understand Christ are so few; I do not even mention that I cannot even speak of the extremely small number of those who live in Him. In this life, faith is everything. Therefore, man without faith is dead.

1 November 1942

The fact that I have succeeded in understanding, and even living, the teaching of Christ, has made me feel grateful and as if awakened from the grave. Solitude, the life that I live, and the natural self-restraint here have never ascended to such an inner transformation.

21 June 1943

A, great day! I confessed [to a priest] and partook of Communion. I experience great moments, the greatest moments of my life! Oh, this turning point in my life! I have given myself over completely to the will of God.

10 January 1944

How many souls oriented toward You, O Lord, want to live a new life, full of peace, understanding, and

Christian love! Every day is a life of blessedness! I ask the good God to send me the ability to do the good deeds I want to do in the world. I believe that this is the goal of human life: To love all of God's creation and to do good.

10 February 1945

As long as God watches over the world, no evil will be able to shake the moral and deeply Christian foundation of souls that are pure and full of boundless love for the truth and their fellow man.

Suffering, no matter how difficult it may be, serves no other purpose than the purification of souls yearning for salvation. I want to know that you are prepared to accept even the hardest blows with the conviction that, beyond this transient life, there exists is another life, eternal and blessed, a boundless, heavenly homeland, worthy of any sacrifice, no matter how big.

I am healthy and happy, filled with joy. Nothing could possibly destroy this spiritual state. I am so happy that I would like to shout out loud so that the whole world would hear my shout, so that even Tuța[212] would hear, from wherever he might be, so that my happiness would reach even unto heaven!

20 February 1945

The Mother of God fulfills my prayers. I live on ever-pouring waves of love, waves that overwhelm my whole being, which is pervaded by the awareness of my nothingness as a man on earth. I fall on my knees before the icons, beseeching mercy, help, and love for myself and my family, parents, relations, friends, benefactors,

---

[212]Valeriu Gafencu's father.

enemies. I am as you know me. I keep completely still and I meditate for hours and days at a time. My thoughts send me far away and when I wake up to reality, I smile. I sing and I pray. My soul is joyful. Daily life is rather monotonous. My interior life is simple, vivid, full, and great, with wishes and dreams that I experience and feel deeply in my soul.

I struggle with sin. And the more deeply I look within myself, the more sins I find. But with the help of God I overcome them. I have acquired a permanent spiritual serenity and I am content with the gifts that God has given me, for they are priceless. I again confess to you the same thing: I am experiencing a state of blessedness; I taste it especially in tears and in pain. There I find it sweeter, deeper. I live with the awareness that I am a sinner. I live in God, the Source of all the joys in life. I am very thankful now that I have lived a moral and pure life. In my relationships with girls I was honorable, correct, and pure. In other words, I did not fall into sin. And I loved so much! I tell you truly, I am blessed. I understand and forgive everything. I forgive all those who have offended me.

10 April 1945

Simplify your lives more and more and as much as possible! Learn to always teach yourselves to be content with little, teach yourself to sacrifice for the good of your neighbor! Prayer is the purest expression of love for God and your neighbor. When you attain true prayer you will have peace, blessedness.

25 May 1945

I speak to you in the most serious way: make as detailed an examination of your conscience as possible.

301

Examine your life well, dive deeply into the interior of your being and know yourselves, with all the sins and mistakes you have made throughout your life. Write them down and bring them to your spiritual father for confession. It is never too late. Do not put it off even for a single day!

I speak to you as a son and a brother, with all the love that I have for you. I speak with all the conviction of my soul, not from books, but from my own experience of these past few years, the most serious and important of my life, which for me mean everything, absolutely everything. I thank the Good God with all my heart for the suffering that He has sent me. For through suffering, I have been able to enlighten my soul, and I have found the path of life.

I ask you from my heart to read the Holy Scripture. Every night before going to bed, gather together around Mama, you dear children of my heart, calmly recollect yourselves for a few moments, and each one of you read a chapter from the Gospel, a chapter from the Epistles, and a psalm. Then say the evening prayers with great reverence. It would be well to have an icon lamp in the bedroom. With a candle lit, in silence, each one should examine the deeds, thoughts, and words of the day. As soon as you find any error, confess it sincerely, and ask for forgiveness. Then, sleep well!

Love each other much, much! Always help each other! My dear ones, it would be the most beautiful thing you could achieve: a Christian family! May a troubled heart find comfort among you.

25 June 1945
I want you to know that I am not worried about your fate for one single reason: I know that your souls are pure,

that you have faith in God, and love for the whole world. These significant realities make me fully confident that you will be able to pass all the trials that may happen in the future. Look at things deeply. Do you not see that God is sending you various trials in order to strengthen your faith? In the more difficult moments, do you not taste a joy sprung forth from the inner world of your spiritual being? A new blessedness, found in tears. I would like so much to be in your midst, to enter into the depths of your souls and to open wide the gates of love that are inside of you and that await to come forth in waves; to see you bursting forth in tears of happiness, kneeling before the icon of Christ, confessing your sins and giving thanks.

Always listen to the voice of your conscience, living the truth with all the fullness of your souls. I want to see you serene and aware of the goal that you have as living beings: Salvation. I want to see you pure in heart. A maidenly purity, full of virtue. Be Christian throughout your life!

23 September 1945
Prayer is the purest expression of love for God and one's neighbor. When you attain true prayer, then you will know peace and happiness. I strive continually and the Good God watches over me and allows me to see miracles being worked at every step. I have to be sincere and recognize that I have accomplished but little. So far, I have not been able to pray with a heart purified of cares, sins, and worldly thoughts. My dear Eleonora, the only one who has tasted the deep joys of the soul can understand them. There have been moments in my life when I have wept with unrestrained tears, realizing the vanity and nothingness of my human existence and the glory of God and of His love. In these tears, springing out of the depths

of my wretched being, I found the most lofty and pure state of blessedness that I have ever experienced. How happy I would be to attain to a continual state of prayer! This life is completely transient. And everything that clings belongs to it is transient.

20 November 1945

I am greatly preoccupied with the problem of sin. Since June 1943, when I experienced my first spiritual upheaval as a result of my awareness of sin, I realized that the deeper I withdraw into myself, the more sins I discover.

In the most secret depths of my heart, I found the inexhaustible source of life: Love. I realized that I had disregarded this gift. I said then, "I have erred!" I had buried in the soil of my sins all of the precious things which God had sown within me. Because of the fact that I had disregarded this holiest gift of love, I consider myself responsible for all the sins of my fellow man, in all times and places. But I am a blessed man, the most blessed man! At every step I sense the love of God, His protection and care for me. I no longer want to live for myself, but to live for love, to contribute to the happiness of all, through the grace of God. May my own soul be saved by the salvation of my fellow men. Ah! How blessed I am! How can man, this little creature, endure so much blessedness?

Human life is a priceless gift, it is a miracle, and I strive to become childlike in spirit. After thousands of trials, I have achieved the most beautiful friendship of my life. We will live all our lives for each other, O Heavenly King!

Christmas 1945

It is night. I have just finished reading the Akathist to the Lord. Christmas was more beautiful than a fairy tale. Spiritually, I feel better prepared than I have felt in other situations. Through the weight of the suffering that I endured for the resurrection of my soul, I felt the responsibility that bore down on me for the salvation of my soul, and those of my family, relatives, friends, enemies, all people.

And the more I climbed up the ladder of ideals, the more I saw my own insignificance, my sinfulness, while I saw the ideal ever more lofty, perfect: Christ! And behold, little by little, all the false idols of my adolescence came tumbling down. My struggle with sin removed the veil that covered my eyes and what remained before me, vivid and serene, was the icon of our Lord Jesus Christ!

Thus, we succeeded in establishing peace with all our neighbors, through being trod underfoot, through recognizing our sins, through love. And I felt so much peace on Friday, when I stood before the priest! Many of us received Communion. What a great day, what a beautiful day! I experienced it fully, with all the blessings sent by the Lord!

O roaming star from the East,
With white rays of gold,
Glides toward the bright blue
Of the heavens vividly blooming.
And the star announces the Child Messiah
Born of the Virgin Mary.
A gentle lamb looks at Him and wants to kiss
The child bathed in light.
In the white and serene night of Christmas

305

A mother with her child at breast,
Pure in love, looks with wonder
At the fulfillment of the Annunciation.
A Holy Child is born in the starry night
Of the Holy Virgin and the Holy Spirit;
The true Word of the Father
Comes down today on earth
A beacon forever lit!

New Year's Day 1946

White flowers sing at the gate of my heart. He who has experienced love will understand me and rejoice at my happiness. I have prepared and continuously prepare myself to become Christian. It is not only in monasteries that men are saved. The powerlessness of human nature causes me pain, but I rejoice in love.

7 March 1946

My beloved mama, I saw you in Eleonora's heart, at the speaker.[213] You were good, gentle, and understanding regarding everything that my soul is experiencing. And I was silent and looked within myself. There I found Love. Today I am so thankful! I look quietly at my own life and that of the entire world and I see the work of the Lord in everything. I look at your lives and I see a miracle of God.

My dear mama, I feel you so much, so close to me! Tell me, mama, that you feel my love! Tell me, mama, that you feel me near you all the time! Tell me, mama, that you are happy! I want to tell you so many things, mama. At night, I awake from sleep and I pray. I send my thoughts

---

[213]The "speaker" is a window in prison where prisoners were able to speak with their visitors. Eleonora is one of Valeriu's three sisters, whom he called "Norica". (Translator's note)

to my mama, in the region of Făgăraş Country,[214] and then there is then so much peacefulness in me! And I sense Tuţa, I feel his boundless love. And I often think about the love between you and Tuţa. What a beautiful household you put together! And what beautiful love!

Mama, I remember the days of summer, when I was a student in high school and I was walking with you one day in the garden, among the fruit trees. And I remember the thoughts you shared with me regarding my future. You wanted a good daughter-in-law. But, as I recall, I was not thinking much about this. I was dreaming, however, about a wife, and I imagined her to be a beautiful girl that I would love at first sight. And that I would love with a unique love…

My essential thought during that time was to become a man of great value. By this, I meant that I should become a man who would play an overwhelming role in history, a man who would contribute much to his people. I wanted to do a lot of good in the world. But man makes plans and God decides. My life took its grand and stormy course. And so, I found myself alone at Iaşi, at the university. There I saw that truly great prospects were opening up toward the future. I was living a normal life, I was one of the most respected students, well-liked and with an unquenchable thirst for an Ideal: a new world, in which love and justice would reign, perfect harmony.

At Iaşi, even though my heart was thirsting for love, I did not tie my heart to any girl. Why not? I carried in my soul the image of a girl, my beloved, but I was never able to recognize this girl embodied in a real creature. So, I

---

[214]Tara Făgăraşului, a region of Romania at the bottom of the Făgăraş Mountains. (O.G.)

experienced love in my own way, embracing all within it, but with an emptiness in my heart that awaited fulfillment.

And look, I wound up in prison. Was I sad then? Was I joyful? I cannot say. I came to realize, however, that prison resolved a whole series of problems through suffering and being torn from the world. I had the strong conviction that I was suffering for the truth. This fact brought a deep peace into my soul. I found myself on the path of fulfilling my Ideal.

And, dear mama, I want you to know that I suffered much. During the first winter I would wake up at night and in the solitude of my cell, cold and hungry, I looked into the darkness and whispered quietly, so that only I could hear, but loud enough for God to hear, "Mama, I'm cold, I'm hungry!"

In the beginning it was terribly hard. But God was always with me. He never abandoned me even for a moment. I began by facing the sufferings of the body, and little by little I began to taste new joys. I saw that I was a sinner. I trembled at the thought of my sins, of my powerlessness. I realized then that I, who wanted an ideal world with all my heart, was myself a sinner. Therefore, first of all, I had to become a pure man, a new man. And I began to struggle with the evil within me.

Little by little, the light of truth came down on me. I began to experience joy in suffering. And the empty space within my heart that I expected would be filled by the love of my beloved, was filled by Christ, the greater Love. And I understood then that he who has great love is truly great. Truly great is he who considers himself small.

Today I am happy. Through Christ I love everyone. This is a path that is hard for people to understand and accept. But I am convinced that it is the only path that leads to happiness…..

15 May 1946

Everyone seeks happiness. Everyone wants it, everyone seeks it. To your hearts I say: seek happiness in your own souls. Do not seek it outside of yourselves. Do not expect happiness to come from anywhere else than from within yourself, from your own soul, where Christ dwells. If you expect happiness to come from somewhere outside of yourselves, you will be deceived and you will never find it. I tell you this much: seek love and live it with much humility! He who fulfills the word of Christ accomplishes everything. Everything!

15 May 1946 (another letter)

Take much care and pay attention in everything! Strive for perfect lawfulness and correctness. Have prudence in every word, spoken or written. These are very delicate moments which you may not perceive. Interact with everyone, but strictly within the context of a Christian life.

Felix! We met each other heart-to-heart on a train from Bucharest to Piatra Olt. We looked into each other's eyes, and love made us friends for life. I saw in him a huge, titanic soul that lived under the difficult burden of solitude. I do not feel worthy of his love. Even now, I cannot explain how it was that we became friends just like that. He, a mature person, with breadth and depth of knowledge, with unique possibilities and a privileged social position. I, on the other hand, having none of these things.

If he were alive today, through the love I have for him and the boundless faith he had in my honesty, he

309

would be totally transformed, he would reach the most exalted form of Christian living. He would have become, through Christian consciousness, a peerless man.

19 May 1946

I am happy, for although my physical freedom is restricted by human laws, I have been granted spiritual freedom through the mystery of love, and this spiritual freedom is the most valuable thing that I could possibly acquire in this world full of vanity. We serve our people – our nation - and we contribute to their salvation and spiritual renewal only to the degree that we serve God.

28 May 1946

There is much vanity in this earthly world, but the gifts of God sown into the human soul are so wonderful that one accepts the thought of death with joy. For death in Christ's name brings the blessedness of life eternal. We will rise from the dead and any suffering, no matter how small, accepted with love, any sacrifice made for God will carry great weight in the fearful hour of Judgment. Then, on that day of Judgment, all of our sins, all the mistakes of our lives will be brought to light. Therefore, we must confess our sins to our spiritual father and fight the good fight. For some will resurrect for life, while others for eternal punishment. Let us persevere in prayer, let us be watchful in humility and love, and let us believe in the mercy of God.

We spent this day in the usual manner. In the evening, all three of us went for a walk. We started to confess to one another, a confession of sins born of spiritual states that had been put to the test in recent days. These were great moments, moments of complete sincerity, confessions of even the finest sentiments and spiritual secrets. I feel that a life of complete purity is being asked of me, not only in words and deeds, but also in thoughts and intention.

We are going through an intense struggle with sin. In the depths of our souls, we long for the Resurrection. We are in a position that requires the greatest attention; we are on the edge of the knife. For a long time now, I have perceived and struggled with the most subtle thoughts that seek to penetrate my soul. I realize that the devil tries to penetrate the soul using paths which seem innocent.

I seek humility, for it is of great benefit in making the heart contrite. The battle with egocentricity is very difficult. I understand that the true man is he who has succeeded in vanquishing selfish-love. We have to struggle against the tendency toward solitude, and at the same time we have to struggle against personal relationships that might sustain the wall of egocentricity, meaning that we must flee from the satisfaction that the soul feels when it sees others participating in its personal life and talents.

Only one manner of living is valid: an exalted Christian life of ceaseless prayer. In other words, what one does must be pure – any deed, any thought or word, any relationship, work, rest - everything must be a state of prayer, of communion with God. Sin was defeated by Love.

Fragments of Undated Letters, also sent from Galda (1946-1948)

I find rest in the thought of total self-offering and permanent sacrifice. The Cross is dear to me. I also bear a cross. I feel the love of the Savior Christ and I run to Him when temptation comes upon this passionate body. And

311

the Lord helps me and gives me the strength to overcome evil. How good is God!

Many times I find myself struggling with the selfishness I find in me. That's why solitude is dear to me. I love to hear the rustling of leaves and the murmuring of water. I am a free man. Christ has shattered my chains of slavery!

My dear brother, never consider yourself useless. It is the will of God that you are where you are, and you have a specific goal to fulfill. With your love and humility, you will build up your brother. And you will reap much happiness. There is no sin that will remain unpunished. If, however, you sincerely repent and pray to God with contrition of heart, He will forgive you and send you His grace. And conversely, there is no good, not even a good thought, however simple, that is not rewarded. But be humble, for it is not you, but God who works through you.

I hear birds singing. How simple they are!

Just now the owner of the vineyard came. He has sunglasses. When I saw him, I reminded myself that I am a prisoner who works on his estate. This thought humbles me. But God sends me great joy. I work on God's earth. People are proud and they do not want to see that only One is the Master of all: Christ!

O, Lord! How people pass judgment and condemn their fellow men to death before God Himself judges!

I look into my soul. It is a sea of peace. And on the surface of the water, a gentle wave ripples easily and is lost in immensity, temptations that nevertheless do not succeed in destroying my peace. I do not let them penetrate deeply. I struggle with them. "And the Spirit of the Lord floats upon the waters." How great art You, O Lord!

Now, in my thoughts, I am in a monastery.

I am a small and powerless man, devoid of good deeds. In reality, this is what I am.

When I was a child, I loved doves very much, but as with most of our desires, I was not able to keep them very long. Today I understand that it was the love of God who tore me from the joys of this world in order to teach me, through renunciation, to love purely, perfectly. I still love doves, but I do not feel my soul bound to them, I love them through God. And I understand that the love of God will never abandon me. He will intervene in my life whenever I bind myself to any human joy or love. He will either help me pull myself out of it, or He will snatch me out of it Himself, in order to give me in exchange the freedom of the soul, which is the greatest good.

I am happy, serene, and confident in the destiny of my life. God has always helped me. I am prepared for anything.

Mama was a simple girl, with an elementary-school education, without any other wealth than the purity of her body and soul. Tuța was a man of integrity; he was healthy, robust, with a good upbringing, a student at the Polytechnic, and well regarded by all the men of significance in Bessarabia at the time. They loved each other. I can still see Tuța bursting into tears, trembling from love and pain: his boy, Valeriu, was leaving. And I am such a sinner!

The desire to rise up to heaven can be seen in all of nature. The mountains, the skies, the skylarks, the eagle, and the soul of man are ever thirsting to rise higher, higher, closer to the Lord, further away from this world.

I long for a quiet, distant place, for a hut or cabin hewn out of rock, for a monastic cell in the foothills, to be with the birds of the sky. With nature as a friend around me and the Lord Christ ever in my heart. To love in peace, humble and forgotten by the world. Sometimes I think about becoming a priest, but I am not worthy. I look at the soil. One day I will be earth myself and others will dig up the ground. My body will turn into dust. From my body another life will probably grow. My soul will be in heaven, where it will wait to be judged. I want to be saved.

I hear a skylark singing in the park. The nightingales are singing. They are dear to me. I struggle with sinful thoughts that try to enter my heart. In my soul there is peace.

Other Letters

31 January 1948

In all circumstances, pray to God that His will be fulfilled. I see the work of God in your souls. I see His care for you. And I am so thankful.

Love is the greatest virtue. Love is perfection itself. When, instead of bringing your love as a gift to the Source of all good, to God, and through Him to your fellow man, you give it to this earthly world, you overturn its meaning. Out of the most wonderful virtue, it then becomes the most dangerous passion.

God has endowed man with so many gifts that by striving in virtue, with the help of the Heavenly Father, he can be saved. God has granted man so many talents so that he can use them in his struggle to approach God, so that he can offer and sacrifice himself. To the degree that we do not

314

make use of the "talent" that has been entrusted to us, we are the slaves of sin.

Therefore, each one of us has to deal with the problem of how to use the talents that God has granted us. We are not permitted either to use them for evil or to bury it in the ground. "Thine own of Thine own, we offer unto Thee, on behalf of all and for all." What God has granted us, we grant unto Him. He has granted us life, therefore we live for Him. He has granted us love, so let us grant it to Him.

We atone for our sins in this life and in eternal life. In this life, atonement through suffering has two aspects, an expiatory role and a purifying role. In eternal life, atonement through suffering is eternal torment. Therefore it is fitting that we thank God when we are punished here, in this life. Let us, then, be very careful about the way in which we use the gifts of God.

7 March 1948

I watch over all and over each one of you with love and prayer. Although I am far from you in body, it is not so in spirit, for spiritually I am ever beside you.

Undated

When I see you sad, I hold your hand and say, "Hold your head up! Go forward! Courage! Any true joy is gained at the price of sacrifice. Any citadel is conquered by faith, determination, boldness, trust in our God-given mission, and especially prayer."

Walk the thorny path, endure the sufferings that a Christian endures as a lover of truth.

I want you to know that I consider this to be a time of trial and a period of atonement; my soul is serene and peaceful, filled with secret joy and with much hope. I want you to know that I am happy. These times are the confirmation of the path to which I have born witness for years. For me, this is a joy so deep that I can say that I regard death with much inner peace and with hope of future blessedness.

I wish for a long life in order to prepare myself spiritually, with the help of God. All the love of my soul.

Poems

During the last part of his life, Valeriu composed several autobiographical and confessionary poems. He had neither paper nor pencil, but composed the poems in his mind and memorized them. They were then learned and passed on by his friends.

The aesthetic exigencies can be justified, but the true value of these poems lies in the spirit that gave them life. Valeriu himself told us before he died, "*Here, at Târgu-Ocna, I wrote sixteen poems as a testament, as a real witness for those who are still to come, and I ask that they not be interpreted as mere poetry, for they have a burning and living spirit.*"

Gift

My dear brother, from the garden
I send you a gift, a lily,
To gently comfort your eyes
With its virgin vestments.

White flower, pure flower,
How much I too would give,
Clothed in your white raiment

To go forth to God.

Transplanted up there,
In the wondrous garden,
To feel my life scented
With the love of Jesus.

I weep, smothered in night,
And sigh with a withered voice:
Give me the white vestment of a Wedding,
Girded by wondrous lilies!

The profound significance of these poems is apparent even from their titles. The "gift" is more than just a flower: it is a chance to reflect upon God and to approach Him in prayer. As a result, Jesus Himself is bestowed upon the friend in the form of a lily, a gesture of great love and gentleness.

Valeriu frequently uses the symbol of a lily; here, it represents purity, perfection, and blessedness, states the author longs for, having written these words during a time of great suffering and exhaustion.

Although he conveys the feeling of relief and the joyous passage into eternity through "a wedding," he does not despise the condition in which he finds himself, but seeks only its transfiguration through spiritual renewal.

Longing

I live hungry, I live a joy
As beautiful as a lily from Paradise.
The cup of a flower is always open
And is full of tears and living water.
The cup of a flower is a kingdom.

When evil men slander and abuse me,
And in seething rage hatred also flows,
The cup of tears is poured forth
And cleanses dross from soul.
Then Jesus has much mercy on me.
I bleed from the heavy cross that weighs upon me,
With body bent from weakness.
Now and then, an angel comes down from heaven
And fills my soul with faith.
I come ever closer to victory.
Sunbeams rain secretly upon me,
Jesus refreshes me with living water,
The seeds cast into the grave come to life,
With life clothed in festival:
I live hungry, I live a joy.

Refrain:
Beneath the burning flame of love,
From early dawn until night I wait.
I call thee at night, curled up with my head on my chest:
Jesus, Jesus!
Slowly I burn up, like a candle.

The first stanza is a testimony to a state of grace, an inner joy depicted as a flower of paradise which has been tended by tears and suffering. The Holy Spirit transforms suffering into an overwhelming and unearthly joy. The poet shows us how he arrived at this state: his body and soul were harshly tormented and mocked, but he was purified through tears shed for the love of God. Nevertheless, the suffering continues, like a Calvary that ever seeks to vanquish him, but he is again saved, this time by the presence of an angel that strengthens him and builds up his faith.

And the sufferings increase step by step, but so do victory, assurance, peace, and happiness. The final stanza represents full, mystical unity with Christ. The sun is the grace that shines on him. Jesus Himself offers him the fullness of holiness and eternity. The man is prepared to be buried, with the assurance of Resurrection in glory.

The key to understanding the poem, as well as its most profound message, is contained in its first and last verse – "I live hungry, I live a joy" – which paradoxically expresses the duality of the human condition that aspires to deification.

The refrain is a realistic description of the final period of Valeriu's life, a position of watchful vigilance and a ceaseless invocation of the Name of Jesus. This is how the transfiguration that occurred in Valeriu was possible.

Poem

My eyes are sad and my forehead tired
From so much vigil and waiting.
My heart is sick, worn out
From difficult and prolonged running,
And cries like a wounded bird.

When my eyes close and I seek within myself
The power to climb Golgotha to the top,
A voice, an echo from the depths
Says to me meekly, "Life is Jesus!
The precious pearl is within you."

I look at the wondrous morning

Of the Resurrection from the grave,
With Magdalene, as before,
I kneel before You, weeping.
And I am happy and weep with You in thought.

The exhausting torment saddens his eyes and wearies his forehead. Waiting in suffering is difficult and his sick heart weeps. Exhausted, he no longer has the strength to resist, but he looks within himself and there finds Jesus, represented by the symbol of a pearl. The final stanza is a description of a state of grace at the sight of the Resurrection, which the poet contemplates with the love and the self-abandonment of Mary Magdalene', borrowing her happiness, tears, and song.

The poem ends with a hymn of praise, which bursts forth only after going through the teary, heart-rending experience of inner struggle.

The Mine

A humble and simple thought, a light,
Rises up toward You quietly, from the mine,
And the tearful soul prays:
"O, come, release me from sin!
Put your hand on my bright forehead
And call me quietly by name
As you called Your friend from the grave;
I ask you, Jesus, give me a bit of water!

Give me bread, living Water give me from the vine,
That I may feel life pulsing in the sprout,
By Your mercy, grant me a pure heart
And show Your divine face
In the hour of my happy departure

From the world of our harsh exile.

Lord Jesus, come at dawn,
Those in prison call You,
O come, illumine the mine,
And bless us!"

This is a poem dedicated to his dear friend Marin Naidim, a detainee at the lead mine at Baia-Sprie. It was learned by heart and passed on from one man to another, so the poem finally arrived at its destination.

Carol

On the banks of the Trotuş
The servants of the Lord are singing,
Yoked in His yoke.
But their singing is muted,
Because it comes from much suffering
And is interwoven with tears.

In the heart of a servant
The Lord makes His manger
In the night of Christmas.
Lilies from heaven rain down
Upon His new manger
And the flowers drip dew.

A little child stands in the light
And looks in wonder
At the prison window.
Beside the little child
Stands a little angel,
And whispers to him gently:

"Today Christmas has moved
From the palace to the prison,
Where the Lord has been jailed."
And the child in the light
Came to the prison
To celebrate the great feast.

Refrain:
Let the children come,
To bring me from the garden
White flowers for the feast,
White, white flowers!

In the first stanza, Valeriu refers to the prison at Târgu-Ocna on the banks of the Trotuş, which shelters the servants of God who "carol," mute from suffering. The poem then moves into the heart of a servant, where Christ is born as if in a new manger. From this point forward, the lilies signify the spiritual gifts that accompany man's birth in Christ.

The child who looks in amazement at the windows of the prison – for even the prison has its way of communicating with the world – is a metaphor for the unstained, faithful man in whom God has not yet been killed. An angel – an unearthly being, but perceptible to those who are pure in heart – speaks to him, revealing to him that the birth of Christ no longer takes place in a splendid, public manner, but through the persecution of faith by imprisonment. Because Christians are imprisoned, Christ Himself is also imprisoned. Renewal in Christ through suffering and persecution is a great, profound, and splendid work.

Valeriu dedicated this poem to Archimandrite Gherasim Iscu, saying that when he chose the child as symbol, Valeriu thought of him. We believe that the author himself might be the chalice in which these inner transformations actually took place and that the poem *Carol* could be considered a personal testimony.

Hymn

The Lord of Glory calls you to the light,
The martyrs call you into eternity,
Fortify the Christian Church
With living stones built into the foundation!

May there grow within your defeated hearts
A reborn, harmonious man,
May he stamp upon your faces
The seal of our Lord Jesus Christ.

A secret bell rings at midnight,
Jesus comes down to earth.
From your bloody chests
Resounds the hymn of holy Resurrection.

Tear yourself out of the midst of the evil,
Enter into the ranks of the Christian army,
Look toward the Heavenly Gates,
For the last shall be first.

Come Christians, take the Light,
With serene, purified souls,

Come ye hungry, taste of the supper,
It is the Wedding of the Emperor's Son!

Hymn is Valeriu's holy and dynamic call to the faithful Orthodox to do the work of inner renewal.

Farewell

Bleeding from deep wounds,
From sunless days,
From hidden wounds and pus,
With weak and soft bones,
I stay curled up in bed and think
That soon I will leave you,
My dear friends!

Don't weep that I am leaving from beside you,
And that I will be thrown out like garbage,
With thieves in the same cemetery;
For the faith for which I sacrificed myself
Required a hard life and the death of a martyr.

Taking Jesus as my King,
I broke through the narrow gate,
Wrestling with the devil.
For years on end I struggled
To become someone else,
A hero,
A new man.

And I wanted
To move my people
From here, down below,
To the Lord Jesus Christ.

Now, when I see how sinful I am,
How small and powerless,
That I have need of much clemency,
Of love, of mercy, of forgiveness,
For only God can do all things
And He snatches the world out of slavery,
I become an obedient child,
I am humbled
And I am happy.

From Your lofty and splendid heaven,
Father, when You take me unto Yourself,
To my friends still on earth
Restore to them, in white vestments,
A soul that loved them and understood them.
                    (The final stanza is missing.)

This is a descriptive poem in which, in addition to presenting a self-portrait, the author integrates himself in the era and the aspirations of a generation. At first, he started out wanting to "move" his people to God through a personal effort, but finding himself in the humble position of a man, he had the revelation of personal and collective transfiguration, offered by God through faith, through communion with Him.

Valeriu bids farewell to his friends in a confession that equals a testament, as well as through the prayer he raises up for his soul to remain with those whom he has loved and understood, in a continual spiritual communion of brothers, now and forever.

Valeriu also put together other poems, including a cradle song dedicated to the children of former prisoners, in which the parents are icons for their children; a long poem on the theme of the prodigal son – a young man who embodies the spiritually impoverished world of our century who, in a state of crisis, finds himself again only in relationship with the Heavenly Father. Finally, there is a carol with melody composed by him. It is a hymn to the Mother of God, for whom Valeriu had a special devotion.

There is more to be said about all of these poems. Their significance, their symbolism, the inner transformations that they describe are realities that Valeriu experienced in his own way, conscious and living.

I hope that all of his verses will be preserved, as well as other information about their author. Any attempt to locate and collect them would be a mistake, considering that any contact between former prisoners is considered suspect, interpreted with much bias, and condemned mercilessly. But I believe that Valeriu will pass through this persecution as well and will contribute to the formation of a new, Christian world.

We have striven here to present Valeriu because we see in him not only a personal experience, but also a role model, a path of deliverance from the spiritual death that is being prepared for us, a man who perfected himself through Christ.

We realize that Valeriu is not the only case of sainthood in this century. We believe that this great amount of faith and its intensity will give birth to a new Christian era, purer and more conscientious than in past times. The saintly life of Valeriu serves as a model for this new world.

Guide for Confession
Compiled by Valeriu Gafencu

Let him who is without sin be the first to cast a stone at her (John 8:7).

Most assuredly I say to you that you will weep and lament, but the world will rejoice; and you will be sorrowful, but your sorrow will be turned into joy (John 16:20).

He arose from supper and laid aside his garments, took a towel and girded Himself.

After that, he poured water into a basin and began to wash the disciples' feet, and to wipe them with the towel with which he was girded (John 13: 4-5).

Now there was leaning on Jesus' bosom one of His disciples, whom Jesus loved (John 13:23).

"A new commandment I give unto you, that you love one another; as I have loved you, that you also love one another" (John 13: 34).

"By this all will know that you are my disciples, if you have love for one another" (John 13: 35).

What sin is

Sin is treading upon the law of God, a voluntary or involuntary treading, in knowledge or in ignorance, in deed, in word, in thought.

Sin is dishonor toward God, insult, disdain, defamation, ingratitude, and wounding toward the Divine being, in an egocentric spirit.

Sin is a lack of faith and a lack of confidence in God and in His law, and too much faith and confidence in oneself, such that a man becomes a law unto himself, because whenever you break the law of God, you obey another law, your own or the devil's.

Sin is a second crucifixion of Christ, for through sin all the insults, mockery, and beatings are renewed. The nails, the spear, the thorns, Christ feels them all again when people sin. Today, however, the blows no longer come from those who defamed Him and shouted, "Crucify Him! Crucify Him!" Now they are administered by those who say they believe in Him, who say that they follow His commandments, that they love Him. Now those who are baptized spit in His face, those who call themselves Christians put the crown of thorns on His head; they slap Him, nail Him to the cross, goad Him with the spear; they are those for whom Christ suffered mockery and beating and for whom He shed His blood on Golgotha in order to make them sons of God, in order to open the gates of heaven for them, to destroy death and demolish hell.

Sin is estrangement from God and drawing near to the devil. It is estrangement from the house of the Father and life in a faraway country with the devil's pigs.

Because we are the servants of him whom we serve (John 8:34), sin means slavery to the devil.

When you sin, you no longer consider what God has done for you, you are no longer His son, and you do not think about His justice, by which He will punish those who sin against His will.

Through sin, all the creatures of God act contrary to the purpose for which they were created.

The mouth was not created by God that we might curse and swear with it, that we might slander and curse our neighbor, but that we might use it to speak things useful to the soul.

God did not give you a mind so that you can find arguments to distance yourself from Him, but that you might find arguments to draw near Him.

The eyes were not made so that we might look at things that damage the soul, but that we might look upon God's creation and give Him thanks.

Just so, the ears, hands, and feet were not made in order that we might distance ourselves from God.

Do you not want to acknowledge the goodness and long-patience of God? For you should know that time was given to you in order to gain paradise, and you waste it believing that God will no longer judge, that He will forgive us, that there are others much worse than you.

The Consequences of Sin

The evil brought about by sin:

1) Through sin, we lose the most precious gift that we have received from God. Without this gift, the soul remains deformed.

2) Through sin, the Holy Spirit is taken from us and we are no longer recognized as sons.

3) Through sin, we lose the eternal blessedness of heaven. We lose the possibility of union with God and life together with the saints. We lose eternal light and rest.

4) We descend into hell with its unquenchable fire and its eternal darkness.

5) Through sin, we lose all the good deeds that we may have done previously, for God will judge you according to the state in which He finds you.

6) Through sin, we lose the help of God (to the extent that you are found in sin).

Do you not weep at the thought that you have lost heaven?

Does the sorrow you have caused God not make you tremble?

Does the thought of hell not frighten you?

Do you not seek to acquire the state that you have lost?

Is it still possible?

Yes! But you must want it…..

From the very beginning, God has known our powerlessness and has given us the possibility of being purified from sins. He knew that man will sin as long as he lives and that no one is without sin, and therefore He said to His disciples: *Whatever you bind on earth will be bound in heaven, andwhatever you cut looseon earth will be cut loose in heaven*, words through which He instituted the sacrament of Confession.

Confession, or repentance, is a bath from which the soul emerges relieved from the weight of sin and cleansed from the filth of sin, a bath in which we are cleansed of all our defilements and errors.

Confession is a medicine that heals the soul of the wounds inflicted by demons, a medicine that renders ineffective the poison of sin.

Confession turns a sinner away from the devil and back to God and restores his connection with his Creator.

Confession leads the soul to deeds and things that are for the sake of and according to the nature of the soul itself.

Confession restores a man clean before God.

Confession prepares the soul and body to receive the body and blood of our Savior Jesus Christ.

Confess in the Church four times a year to the same spiritual father.

When you examine your conscience, consider yourself guilty, do not justify yourself; think about the following things:

1) The motive or aim with which or for which you sinned. The following day, try to avoid the same situation.

2) The intention with which you sinned.

3) The surroundings, avoid them the following day.

4) The place where you sinned.

5) Whether your sin influenced others by encouraging them to sin also.

6) The number [of times you've performed this particular sin] ….

Confession must be done with contrition of heart and a sense of regret. Contrition of heart is the grief and pain that the memory of the sin causes you.

This pain consists not only in feeling the sin, to sigh and weep for it, but consists primarily in hating the sin.

Regret is the pain that the repentant feels because he now lacks the grace of God and has earned torment.

The church has established the rule that one should fast for seven days before confession, or possibly less. The sick are excused.

Write down your sins on paper and read them alone before your spiritual father.

Make a promise before God to not repeat your sins.

The First Commandment: **I am the Lord thy God, thou shalt not have any gods before me**.

1) Do you believe in God?

2) Do you believe in the Holy Trinity?

3) Do you worship God?

4) Do you love Him?

5) Do you know Him? Have you compelled yourself to learn something about God from the books of Holy Scripture, church books, or from somewhere else?

6) Do you somehow believe in charms and magic spells?

7) Have you visited fortune tellers and astrologers?

8) Do you practice occultism?

9) Do you believe in dreams? Believe only in God.

10) Do you somehow bestow more honor upon some creature or things than to God?

11) Do you value money, food or wine, a woman or a man, more than God?

12) Have you ever grumbled against God?

13) Have you despaired because of any trouble, misfortune, or any other evil that has befallen you?

14) Have you opposed the truths of Christian teaching?

15) Have you read books that are against faith?

16) Have you given such books to someone else to read?

17) Have you attended gatherings of non-believers?

18) Have you read their books and magazines with the intention of discovering another truth other than that of the Church?

19) Have you defended lack of faith or sects or Islam?

20) Have you brought gifts to sectarians?

21) Do you believe in superstition or paganism?

22) Is God your main concern?

23) Have you always put hope in God?

24) Do you believe that heaven and hell exist?

25) Do you believe that there will be a judgment?

26) Do you put too much trust in the goodness of God and in this way not fear judgment?

27) Do you believe that God can no longer forgive you because of the multitude and gravity of your sins?

28) Have you always sought the help of God?

29) Have you prayed regularly? Evening, morning, and at noon?

30) Do you go to church regularly?

31) During prayers and at church do you think only of God?

32) At the end of the day, do you remember God?

33) Have you brought thanks to God through all your deeds?

34) Have you sought His help before doing something?

35) Do you sometimes say prayers only from habit?

36) Do you think of other things during the time of prayer?

37) Does the thought ever come to you that you cannot be saved?

38) Have you put off repentance until old age?

39) Do you deliberately go late to church?

40) Do you pay attention to the service?

41) Do you laugh or talk or look at other people when in church?

The Second Commandment: **Thou shalt make no graven image or the likeness of any thing of what is in heaven or on earth, in the sea or on the earth, nor shall you worship them or serve them**.

1) Do you believe that some men are great and have the same value that Christ had? For example philosophers or religious leaders?

2) Do you believe in the holy icons?

3) What kind of veneration do you accord them?

4) Do you believe that an icon is the saint that it depicts?

5) Do you believe in people - your wife, your husband, your child – instead of believing in God?

6) Do you worship things such as money, food, drink, or other pleasures?

7) Is your own mind your only law and do you do only that which it tells you?

The Third Commandment: **Do not take the name of the Lord Thy God in vain**.

1) Have you ever sworn by God the Father or by the Savior Jesus Christ?

2) Have you sworn by the angels, archangels?

3) Have you sworn by the Holy Virgin?

4) Have you sworn by the saints, the church, Pascha, the oil lamps, the icons, the cross, or other things?

5) Have you brought false witness to the Name of God?

6) Have you sworn other kinds of oaths, for example on your eyes, your life, the salvation of your soul? For the Savior said, „Let your speech be yes and no; for anything more than that is of the devil."

7) Have you cursed anyone? Have you sent others or yourself to the devil?

8) Do you have the habit of cursing those who do you wrong? The Savior taught us to pray for them.

9) Have you sworn a false oath?

10) Have you sworn a true oath?

11) Do you use as an oath the word "zău," which is an abbreviation for "pe Dumnezeul meu" [upon my God]?

The Fourth Commandment: **Remember to keep holy the Sabbath day**.

Sunday is the Lord's day. And all the feast days instituted by the church throughout the year have the same value.

1) Have you kept all Sundays and feast days?

2) Were you in church on each of those days?

3) Did the other members of your household keep them, did they attend church, did you prevent them for any reason?

4) Have you given others work on those days? Do you go to church late?

5) Did you keep the Lord's day in a worthy manner? Or is it for you an ordinary day or a day for parties and amusements? Do you go to church in the morning? In the afternoon do you read books that are useful and constructive for the soul?

6) Do you look after your soul more on those days than on others?

7) Have you given or participated in a *clacă*[215]?

8) Do you behave improperly in church?

9) Have you cursed the church or the servants of the Holy Altar?

10) Do you honor priests as the servants of God? Do you make fun of them or disdain them? Do you gossip about them and speak of their sins?

11) Do you pray for them? Do you obey them?

The Fifth Commandment: **Honor thy father and thy mother**.

1) Have you beaten your parents or in-laws?

2) Have you abused them or persecuted them?

3) Have you heeded their advice?

4) Have you deceived them in any way?

5) Have you taken advantage of their good faith?

6) Have you helped them when they were in difficulty?

7) Have you done church services for them after their deaths?

8) Have you helped your brothers and sisters?

9) Have you taken care of your wife and children? For St. Paul says, *If anyone does not look after his own, and especially those of his own household, such a one has abandoned the faith and is worse than a non-believer.* (1 Tim 5:8)

10) Have you beaten your wife? Have you held anything against her? Have you abused her?

11) Have you honored your husband? Have you loved your husband or wife as your own self?

12) Have you deceived your husband or wife?

---

[215] *Clacă:* An informal gathering around a campfire for conversation, music, and dancing. (Translator's note)

13) Have you made his/her life more difficult? Do you nag or criticize?

14) Have you sufficiently looked after the spiritual well-being of those in your household?

15) How have you behaved with your spiritual fathers? Godparents, teachers, priests? Have you respected them and helped them?

16) Have you been insolent or stubborn with your parents?

17) Have you upset them? Angered them?

18) Have you spoken ill of them or derided them?

19) Have you made fun of their weaknesses?

20) Have you been mindful of your religious obligations?

21) Have you been ashamed of them?

22) Have you spent money on useless things (tobacco or other pleasures), causing your family to be lacking in necessary things?

If you are a parent:

23) Have you steered your children on the path of the Church, in word and in deed?

24) Have you set a bad example with arguments, drunkenness, filthy language, lying, stealing, dishonor, gossiping, laziness?

25) Do you live with a concubine and the children see it?

26) Have you punished them for bad deeds: such as arguing, lying, fighting, stealing? Have you spared them out of mercy?

27) Have you prayed for your children, wife, husband, brothers, sisters, parents?

28) Were you too harsh or too easy on your children?

29) Have you had bad servants who taught your children things harmful for the soul?

If you are a guardian:

30) Have you fulfilled all your material and moral obligations toward the children?

If you are a master:

31) How have you behaved with your servants or apprentices?

32) Have you paid them honest wages, have you held anything back for any reason?

33) Have you encouraged them to fulfill their religious duties?

34) Have you encouraged them to commit any sin?

If you are a servant:

35) Have you obeyed your master or boss?

36) Have you diligently fulfilled all your duties?

37) Have you done your work in a careless, slipshod manner?

38) Have you stolen anything?

39) Have you told bad stories about your master's house to others?

The Sixth Commandment: **Thou shalt not kill**.

1) Have you ever killed anyone, voluntarily or involuntarily?

2) Do you want to kill anyone, or have thoughts of revenge? Have you ever praised anyone who killed?

3) Do you want anyone to die, in order to gain their wealth, or their wife, husband, etc.?

4) Have you beaten anyone?

5) Have you threatened anyone?

6) Do you hate anyone, are you reconciled with all those you know?

7) Do you wish anyone evil, death, or harm?

8) Do you rejoice when evil befalls your fellow man?

9) How do you behave with those around you?

10) If you are a man, did you permit the abortion of children?

11) If you are a woman, have you voluntarily abandoned your baby or committed abortion?

12) Have you sought to kill yourself, directly or indirectly?

13) Have you gone hunting?

The Seventh Commandment: **Thou shalt not commit adultery**.

Those unmarried commit fornication, those married adultery.

1) Have you committed fornication, or if you are married, adultery?

2) Do you live as with a concubine?

3) Do you sin against nature - masturbation or homosexuality?

4) Do you desire to sin with the husband or wife of another?

5) Do you seek opportunities to commit sexual sins?

6) Do you think about shameful things too much?

7) Do you seek to recall such scenes?

8) Do you want to see the shameful parts of the body?

9) Do you speak about shameful things?

10) Have you read books that give you sexual pleasure?

11) Have you urged anyone to commit such sins?

12) Have you caused someone else to sin through your clothing or dressing up?

The Eighth Commandment: **Thou shalt not steal.**

A priest cannot forgive the theft of something that has not been returned. Therefore, give back what you stole and then go to confession.

1) Have you stolen money or other objects from the state, society, or any man?

2) Have you done harm to others?

3) Have you helped those you have harmed to recover?

4) Have you taken adequate care of the wealth of another man that has been entrusted to you?

5) Have you given back money or other objects that you borrowed?

6) Have you received stolen things (things that were stolen)?

7) Have you given back things that you found?

8) Have you secretly changed the property line between you and your neighbor?

9) Have you urged someone else to do this?

10) Have you charged too much interest for borrowed monies?

11) Have you altered merchandise and then sold it as if it were good?

12) Have you deceived anyone by weighing or counting goods wrongly?

13) Have you taken things by force from someone smaller than you?

14) Have you accepted bribes?

15) Have you taught children to steal?

16) Do you have thoughts about making money by dishonorable means?

The Ninth Commandment: **Thou shalt not bear false witness.**

1) Have you sworn a false oath?

2) Have you lied?

3) Have you born false witness?

4) Have you behaved correctly with your neighbor?

5) Have you lied to him?

6) Have you told lies about others?

7) Have you purposefully spread false accounts about others?

The Tenth Commandment: **Thou shalt not covet thy neighbor's wife. Thou shalt not covet thy neighbor's goods.**

1) Have you desired the wife, daughter, husband, or son of your neighbors?

2) Have you desired the wealth of your neighbor?

3) Have you desired the social status of someone higher than you?

4) Have you hated your neighbor for any reason?

5) Have you desired the house, the land, the vineyard, or the work of your brother?

The Seven Deadly Sins

Pride is the source of all spiritual evil. It is a spiritual greed through which the demons fell from the grace of God.

1) Are you proud, haughty, conceited?

2) Do you put too much faith in your own beauty or your wealth, have you grown proud because of them?

3) How do you behave with those who are rich or important?

4) Do you despise anyone?

5) Are you not willing to talk to anyone?

6) Are you hypocritical (you say one thing, and do another)?

7) Have you bragged through deeds, words, or clothing?

8) Have you said something in order to be praised?

9) Have you slandered your neighbor in order to lower his honor and in order to raise up your own?

10) Have you born the offenses of him who offended you?

11) Have you forgiven those who upset you?

12) Have you prided yourself on your learning and knowledge?

Greed

Starting out as something abstract, egotism is put into effect through greed.

The Holy Apostle Paul is looking from this point of view when he says that greed is the root of all evil.

1) Are you greedy for food and drink [gluttony]?

2) Do you want to collect wealth or other things?

3) Are you greedy in accumulating money, have you deceived your neighbor for this reason?

4) Have you eaten or drunk secretly?

5) Have you eaten animal products on fast days or before the Holy Liturgy?

6) Have you eaten carrion?

Laziness is the failure to make use of the physical and spiritual powers that God has granted us to use in our lives.

1) Are you lazy?

2) Do you waste time without working?

3) Do you occupy yourself with things that are vain or pointless?

4) Do you pray regularly?

5) Do you look after your soul?

6) Do you do your duty as a clerk, worker, servant?

7) Do you force those smaller than you to do your work?

8) Have you sought a spiritual father who is more lenient?

9) Have you fulfilled your penance?

Anger is also based upon the pivot or axis of greed.

When a man cannot fulfill his desires, he becomes angry because he is prevented from achieving his evil goal.

Man is allowed to be angry only against sin.

1) Have you done evil through anger, cursing, beatings, etc.?

2) Do you get angry often? How long do you stay angry? You should know that St. Paul said, *"Do not let the sun set on your anger."* (Eph 4:26).

3) Are you presently angry with anyone?

4) Have you beaten or struck anyone with a stick, a club, or your palm?

5) Have you angered or scolded anyone without good reason, spitefully?

6) Have you wished evil on someone who trespassed against you? Or to someone who was good toward you ?

7) Have you gotten angry with a neighbor because he is somehow better than you? Have you envied him?

8) Have you shed anyone's blood (in drunkenness)?

9) Have you engaged in a duel?

10) Have you prayed, in anger, that evil come upon your enemies?

Avarice (Greed) is material and spiritual.

It is material when someone does not want to provide physical comfort to the poor, while spiritual when one does not want to steer someone away from evil.

1) Are you stingy?

2) Have you ever deprived a neighbor of necessary things out of stinginess?

3) Have you helped the poor?

4) Have you called both the rich and the poor to eat at your table? You should know that the Savior urges us to call to our table those who cannot repay us.

5) Do you sell items at too high a price?

6) Do you cheat people?

7) Do you regret any good deed that you have done?

8) Do you eat little and clothe yourself or your family poorly in order to grow rich?

9) Do you neglect the health of your children, wife, parents, brothers, in order to avoid spending money?

Envy (Quarreling or Jealousy)

When an angry man cannot prevail over the obstacles that are in his way by anger, unable to do anything else, he sweetens his heart with the passion of envy, so that he might conceal his neighbor's spiritual and physical honor and exalt himself.

1) Have you argued with anyone?

2) Do you like to argue?

3) Do you hate anyone?

4) Do you deride or disdain anyone?

5) Do you give advice maliciously?

6) Are you presently jealous of anyone?

7) Are you on speaking terms with everyone?

8) Have you given anyone a bad nickname?

9) Have you sown dissent between brothers?

10) Have you been jealous of anyone because he is somehow better than you and enjoys more honor, wealth, social standing, etc.?

Lust is also a form of greed, but not of a material or spiritual order, but of a sentimental order.

The sin of dissoluteness, unlike all other sins, is committed with the body.

The body is the temple of the Holy Spirit.

(You can commit the sin of dissoluteness by looking at or hearing things that cause you to sin. Even eating, sleeping too much, speaking, etc.)

1) Have you fallen into fornication?

2) Or adultery?

3) Do you like to see or read books that cause you to sin in your thoughts, do you like to hear or to speak vulgar or shameful words? You should know that St. Paul tells us that there should not be heard from our mouth any foul or filthy words, nor silly jokes that are improper, nor words that are imprudent.

4) Do you like enjoy speaking, sensibly or senselessly?

5) Are you mastered by any passion?

6) Do you eat or sleep too much? You should know that St. Paul also said *"All things are permitted to me, but not all things are useful."* (1 Cor 6:12).

7) Do you have in your home paintings with naked bodies? Do you look at them passionately?

8) Have you committed sexual sins with blood relatives or spiritual relatives (godchildren, godparents)?

9) Have you touched someone's body, overcome by the passion of lust?

10) Have you wanted to see the shameful parts of the body?

Outrageous Sins That Cry Out to Heaven

A. Voluntary Killing

1) Have you killed anyone?

2) Have you sought to kill?

3) Do you want to kill anyone?

4) Have you sought to gain revenge by killing someone?

5) Have you beaten anyone?

6) Have you quarreled with or threatened anyone?

B. Sodomy (coupling against nature)

1) A man with a man or any kind of animal?

2) A man with a woman against nature?

3) Masturbation. Have you masturbated?

C. Withholding the pension or the wages of orphans, widows, workers, employees, or servants.

1) Have you withheld pensions or salaries? For any reason, either as reimbursement for something broken, or for other reasons?

2) Have you withheld pay partially or unjustly?

3) Have you always compensated others for the work they have done?

D. Oppressing widows, orphans, invalids, or the helpless.

1) Have you beaten children, old people, or orphans?

2) Have you derided or made fun of them?

3) Have you oppressed anyone weaker or smaller than you?

4) Have you laughed at the cripled or the helpless?

5) Have you angered or irritated them?

6) Have you somehow been obligated to help them and failed to do so?

7) Have you helped those whom you were not required to help, or did you pass them by like the priest and the Levite in the Gospel in the story of the good Samaritan?

8) Have you deliberately caused a blind man to fall by guiding him wrong?

9) Have you made fun of anyone who is helpless, deaf, a stutterer, lame, crippled, one-eyed?

Obligations Regarding the Spiritual Life of our Neighbor

1) To protect our neighbor from sin. Have you done it or not?

2) To teach the uneducated (ignorant).

3) To give good advice to those who have need of it.

4) To pray to God for others.

5) To comfort the grieving.

6) To suffer patiently when we are treated unjustly.

7) To forgive the sins of others.

Commandments Regarding the Physical Life of Our Neighbor

1) To give food to the hungry.
2) To quench the thirst of the thirsty.
3) To clothe the naked.
4) To care for the sick.
5) To take in and show hospitality to strangers.
6) To inquire after those in prison.
7) To bury the dead.

Leading Others to Strange Sins

1) When you advise someone to sin.
2) When you order someone to sin.
3) When you permit someone to sin.
4) When you help someone to sin
5) When you praise someone who sins.
6) When you were able to but did not want to prevent someone from sinning.
7) When you know that someone is sinning but you do not tell him.

Sins against the Holy Spirit

1) Disregarding the grace of God and having excessive trust in one's own self.
2) Believing that God does not have the power to forgive you is a very great sin.
3) Believing that you are everything and that God has no power in the world.
4) Lacking of trust in God.
5) Opposition to the Truth established by the Holy Church.

6) Leaving the Orthodox Church. Guard yourself from this sin, for Christ says, "*He who blasphemes against the Holy Spirit has no forgiveness, but is guilty of eternal condemnation.*" (Mk 3:29).

The Nine Church Commandments

1) Church attendance every Sunday and every feast day.

2) Keeping the four fasting periods of the year.

3) Respect toward the Church's representatives. (priests, monks, nuns)

4) Confession of sin during the four fasts.

5) Guarding ourselves from heretics.

6) To pray for our country's leaders and the officials of the church.

7) To abstain from weddings and parties during the fast periods.

8) To protect those things belonging to the church from inappropriate use.

9) To keep the fasts and to say the prayers that the bishop ordains in times of trouble

Various Sins

1) Failure to carry out one's obligations:

a) Have you carried out all your obligations to God, to your own self, to your neighbor?

b) Have you carried out the penance given to you in confession?

2) Theft of holy things

a) Have you lied at confession?

b) Have you avoided telling everything and for what reason have you done so?

a) Go to confession at least four times a year, during the fasts.

b) Fast before confession.

c) Maintain the same spiritual father.

d) Make a serious examination of conscience before going to confession.

e) Write down all your sins, otherwise you might forget them. After confession, burn the paper at once.

f) Confess not only sins you have committed, but also those of your heart.

g) Do not conceal any sin.

h) Be reconciled with those who have offended you.

i) Avoid opportunities for sin.

j) Give up your sins – make a promise that you will no longer sin.

k) Feel contrition for your sinfulness.

l) Guard yourself from sins.

m) Receive Communion only if you feel clean. Otherwise, it will be for condemnation.

n) Fulfill in a holy manner the penance given to you by your spiritual father.

o) Judge only yourself for the sins you have committed.

Each one of us has his or her own mission to fulfill, but we must heed the advice of our spiritual father, who puts aside our own ill-informed will, making room for the will of God in each one of us. Our spiritual father reveals the will of God in us. If we don't heed him, we can wander astray and make mistakes that are even worse than the passions. I consider him to be a friend any person who sends me even one thought of love. And I wish and request that every one of my friends copy down this guide to confession.

I have written this as best as I could, in great haste, out of a genuine wish to send you this guide to confession.

With all my love, Valeriu.

The end.
And
Glory be to God!

Made in the USA
Coppell, TX
19 October 2021

64299531R00192